Classic Darksite Diving

Cave diving sites of Britain and Europe

Martyn Farr

WILD PLACES
ABERGAVENNY

WILD PLACES PUBLISHING
PO BOX 100
ABERGAVENNY NP7 9WY, UK
www.wildplaces.co.uk

First published 2013

British Library Cataloguing in Publication Data
A catalogue record for this book is available from the British Library

ISBN 978-0-9526701-8-6

Design and origination by Wild Places Publishing, Abergavenny
Printed on Amadeus Silk, a paper manufactured from sustainable sources
Printed in the United Kingdom by Cambrian Printers, Aberystwyth

CONTENTS

Preface

FROM the moment I started training divers to explore the mysterious world of flooded caves and mines, I received a constant stream of enquiries from people keen to see and experience more. It was obvious that a substantial level of interest existed in all areas of the diving community. To impart the necessary instruction to access this underground realm was relatively straightforward; structured programmes were well formulated. However, as enthusiastic newcomers progressed their cave diving skills, it was not so easy to send them off to explore new places on their own. Too often the available site information was sketchy and lacking in practicalities. No matter where divers originated, or whatever level of achievement they had attained, they still required solid, accurate details to allow them to plan their operations safely and I could perceive a real need for specific practical data relating to cave and mine diving sites.

Therefore, the objective was clear from the outset: to present divers with a range of underground sites suitable for the defined level of ability, places that are accessible, challenging and inspirational. The sites selected here are classic popular venues of relatively easy access and these are described for the benefit of people who may be wholly unfamiliar with that site or area.

It should be noted, however, that a few of the places included are clearly aspirational, at least at the outset of an individual's underground activities. In the UK sites such as Keld Head and Wookey Hole are not readily accessible to the newcomer, but they offer outstanding diving possibilities and a sufficiently motivated person may achieve such a goal in the future. Consider your experience, take a careful look at what is suitable and what is not and remember that situations change over time – a number of places appearing in this book might become accessible in the future. Other famous sites such as the Doux de Coly in France and Ojamo in Finland are blatantly tantalising; determined, dedicated practitioners could certainly find themselves probing the depths of these crystal waterways in due course.

Classic Darksite Diving will open a door to an exciting new world. Plan and execute your dive carefully and you will have a thoroughly enjoyable experience.

Key to symbols

Minimum level of training required

CAVERN   Cavern Diver
INTRO   Introductory Cave Diver
FULL   Full Cave Diver

Different parts of the site may suit more than one training level

Access and type of site

Most sites in this guide are caves: those that are not are marked with a Mine symbol   Mine

For coastal sites, access is by foot or boat: if both are possible, a boat is preferable to minimise exertion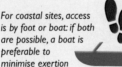

Type of dive

Through-dive   Return dive

Other Information

Warning

Specific dangers such as extreme cold, debris, poor visibility, deep water or strong currents

Abundant marine life

Cave formations

Backmount

No back-mounted cylinders
*Restrictions require that **only** side-mounted equipment is used*

Key to symbols

Symbols are used throughout this guide to indicate the nature of the dives in that section at a glance. It is important to note that the training indicated – Cavern, Intro or Full – for each site is the *minimum* required but this *may only apply to one part of the dive*

Acknowledgements

T has taken over ten years to bring *Classic Darksite Diving* to publication and during this period countless people have helped in many different ways.

First, many selfless individuals, especially in Europe, have furnished both onsite support and invaluable background information. Special mention must be made of: Klaus Berghem (Finland), Pierre-Eric Deseigne and Nadir Lasson (France), Fabio Barbieri and Luciano Tanini (Italy), Thorsten 'Toddy' Wälde (Sardinia), Javier de Miguel Domínguez, Xesús Manteca 'Teca' Fraile and Sergi Pérez (Spain), Alf Chappell (Turkey) and Fanis Nikoloudakis (Zante).

White Lady Cave, South Wales

For the donation of surveys thanks are due to Daniel Hutňan, Herbert Jantschke and the German team from Höhlenforschungsgruppe Ostalb-Kirchheim, Nadir Lasson, Rick Stanton and John Volanthen.

In the field of photography I am particularly indebted to Ric Halliwell, Chris Howes, Radoslav Husák, Gavin Newman, Gordon Ridley, Carl Ryan, Rick Stanton and Suunto for images. In this context it would be impossible not to include the hands-on photographic assistance supplied by my long-suffering caving and diving companions: Pat Cronin, Steve Marsh and Will Swift. I am especially indebted to Helen Rider, now my wife, for her unique professionalism underwater, in particular for her meticulous attention to detail, safety and versatile, invaluable support with the gruelling roles of model and photographic assistant.

For constant background support in the technical world of IT I am deeply grateful to Phil Dotchon, Jason Pepper and Will Swift. Phil has again been a star for keeping my heavily used photo equipment in reliable operational use. I thank Helen for shouldering a large part of the travel and trip organisation.

Finally, for their vision, patience, diligence and a wealth of constructive criticism relating to editing the text, redrawing surveys to a uniform appearance and working on the images, I am forever indebted to my good friends and publishers Chris Howes and Judith Calford. You are the very epitome of professionalism and I feel privileged to count you as friends.

It has, in all reality, been an absolute marathon bringing this book to fruition. But along the way it has been incredibly rewarding to meet and work with so many great and wonderful people; I sincerely express my deepest thanks to you all.

Photography

Unless otherwise stated all photographs are by the author, who is grateful to the following photographers for generously supplying additional images:

Helen Farr: p51t
Ric Halliwell: p149tr
Chris Howes: pp140, 141bl&br
Radoslav Husák: pp92, 97t, 132, 133t, 135
Gavin Newman: p145l
Gordon Ridley: pp35t&b, 37t&b, 38
Carl Ryan: back cover
Rick Stanton: p93m&b
Suunto: pp188, 189t

Introduction

Come to our rich and starry caves,
Our home amid the ocean waves;
Our coral caves are walled around
With richest gems in ocean found,
And crystal mirrors, clear and bright,
Reflecting all in magic light.
George Waldron, 1726

'**W**HERE can we go to dive?' is a question that I am asked time and time again; recreational divers have perhaps learned the requisite skills to tackle diving in an overhead environment – in flooded caves and mines – but suffer from a paucity of data for finding suitable sites to further their experience. Yes, we all know that a wealth of information on cave diving sites is available, but rarely is this sufficiently clear, balanced and reliable to permit effective planning. Achieving safe and enjoyable diving in the subterranean environment depends heavily upon your choice of site and here *Classic Darksite Diving* can help. This book is a companion volume to *Diving in Darkness*, published in 2003, and highlights some classic places that are relatively 'easy' to dive.

While *Classic Darksite Diving* is European in coverage, it has a bias towards diving in the British Isles. The scope of a book such as this cannot extend to every accessible cave or mine in Europe and, indeed, makes no attempt to do so: the inclusion or omission of a site is based largely on the practicalities of access.

An ancient support pillar in Holme Bank Chert Mine, Derbyshire

Within these pages lies a tremendous mixture of diving environments. The descriptions provide much useful information for experienced cave divers visiting somewhere for the first time, but – equally as importantly – they will prove invaluable for those making their initial tentative steps into the exciting world of cavern, cave and mine diving. Geographical location and geology both affect the nature of our dive sites, but so too do ownership and other human factors. The basic rules and general approach to diving in an overhead environment are outlined in *Diving in Darkness*, and it is the purpose of this book to provide enough specific advice about sites to enable a structured progression.

Readers will glean the essential character of a particular cave, mine or regional diving attraction from each entry. Some are harder than others to tackle and this is not an invitation to dive any or all the sites without due consideration; their inclusion here should convey an impression of what is involved and set you on your way towards that goal. While specific sites have been selected on grounds of suitability and access, it is stressed that if you visit any of these places your dive objectives must be appropriate, to both the level and type of training you have received.

Before you eagerly start thinking about undertaking a trip into (for you) unknown waters, you must develop a healthy understanding of, and respect for, the dangers of your chosen environment. *Classic Darksite Diving* should be used only after you are fully trained and have gained time underwater in the company of more experienced divers. At the risk of repetition, some warnings must be further enhanced.

Training

Proper training is imperative before embarking upon any of the dives outlined in *Classic Darksite Diving*. Remember that no verbal communication, text or video will ever replace a structured course delivered by a professional instructor. Globally, various levels of training en route to proficiency in this sphere are accepted, although the boundaries between these are somewhat blurred from country to country, among diving organisations and even due to different environments. As the specific names for such levels of training therefore differ, in order to convey an all-round impression of the sites and the degree of competence and training required to dive in them, *Classic Darksite Diving* has placed them into three broad categories. In every instance, it is presumed that good diving technique has been learned and mastered, and divers should only choose sites relevant to their ability and never exceed their level of training.

The most accessible sites, designated 'Cavern', require basic overhead environment diving experience. Divers will generally remain within the daylight zone, certainly be limited to penetrations of less than 60m and depths of less than 30m, and encounter no restrictions. Training to this level of ability is the foundation upon which all other activities in caves and mines is based.

'Introductory Cave' sites are more challenging and are appropriate for divers undertaking more specific training in the company of an instructor or mentor. Clearly defined and modest penetrations will be involved, using suitable equipment that may include side-mounted configurations.

Smooth rock sculpting and fine silt in the upstream section of Porth yr Ogof, South Wales

Decompressing in Hodge
Close Slate Quarry, Cumbria

Depths are generally less than 30m, and an emphasis upon line work, good technique and a practical awareness of possible emergency scenarios will be required.

'Full Cave' sites are for those divers who have undertaken a complete range of training and are competent and confident, with the ability to plan and undertake dives without supervision. Such practitioners will cope with and anticipate risks and potential hazards, including experience in diving solo. These sites may involve depths considerably greater than 30m, strong currents and perhaps complex navigation.

Some cave diving sites require formal certification to be presented before access is permitted; cave divers who do not hold certification indicating their training level should enquire before undertaking a trip. No formal mine diving qualification exists – the closest you will achieve is cave diving certification. Given that all mines are on private land and that landowners are becoming increasingly touchy about their legal liabilities in granting access, this is generally the only qualification that they will recognise, if they are prepared to allow entry at all.

In this age of global travel, divers should also be aware that cave and mine diving conditions vary immensely around the world. Divers must keep an open mind and be prepared to modify both their equipment and approach to a dive as and when required. Divers certified in the warm waters of Florida or Mexico, for example, should seek supplementary training before committing themselves to the challenging and colder, more restricted environments of Europe.

Safety

Divers must consider the stability of the dive environment at all times and in this regard local knowledge is of the utmost importance. Many old mine workings are inherently dangerous and should be avoided; indeed, the very air in abandoned mines is frequently unhealthy. Entering a pocket of tainted air (whether en route to the dive site or surfacing beyond it) could trigger severe repercussions for the unwary – mines must be treated with added caution and extreme respect. Never enter an unknown mine simply to find out if it possesses a dive site – again, seek local knowledge.

Visits to more distant locations clearly require more planning than a normal weekend dive nearer home. For these occasions it is strongly recommended that you liaise very closely with local divers or use the services of a dive centre in the region to avoid falling foul of local access or permit requirements. Countries around the Mediterranean have differing approaches, especially when it comes to conservation. While a site may be of great interest and offer an entertaining challenge, you must retain due reverence for the environment and never succumb to complacency. Dive centres will provide an excellent briefing and divers should be extremely wary of straying beyond the scope of that advice.

► White Reef Caverns, Zante, Greece

Contact details have been provided in each chapter for access, local dive shops and air supplies, where applicable, but these can change so always check all such information during dive preparations. All telephone numbers have been written as they would be used within each country and international telephone country codes are included in the emergency section of each chapter for calls made from outside the country, with a basic note for how to change the local number into an international one.

Green waters in Hurtle Pot,
Yorkshire Dales

Access and emergencies

Although access routes and details of permissions required
appear in this book, these do not necessarily indicate any
legal right of access. Requirements may change and divers
should research the current situation *before* visiting any
cave or mine. Dedicated websites spring up and disappear
with great regularity. These often contain detailed maps
of locations, but do not be tempted to assume that they
are reliable regarding current diving conditions or the
experience level required to tackle a particular site: make
your own assessment, taking into account the date of
posting, before using such information. Advice gained from
established dive centres is likely to be authoritative.

Third party liability insurance cover is normally
obligatory where access conditions are set by a landowner.
To ignore the wishes of the owner or any locally
negotiated access agreement is to risk closure of the
site to all. If you are in *any* doubt as to your ability to
undertake a dive, please stay away: you are not only risking
your own life, but you are almost certainly jeopardising
long-term access to what may be a unique recreational
resource. Essential access notes appear for each site listing
– such matters as paying a goodwill fee for parking or to
cross land are important and must never be disregarded.

Access to all sites in this book is relatively easy
and straightforward; this is one of the criteria used to
determine their inclusion. Though well known, some
other caves or mines are comparatively inaccessible or
have particular restrictions placed on them, making it
inappropriate to include them in this guide. However, a
few of these have been described briefly in Appendix B, in
order to explain their historical significance and provide
inspiration for the future.

As part of your dive planning, make certain you
are fully conversant with the procedures to follow in
case of emergency. Accidents can occur at any time
and being prepared is essential; it is also important to
hold appropriate insurance and documentation – see
Appendix A for useful advice and emergency contacts.

It is the personal responsibility of each
and every diver to ensure that they take
maximum care with all aspects of the dive.
Route-finding is the classic case in point and
dive lines found at any site should be treated
as suspect. Avoid 'trust me' dives where you
are taken to a complex site and blindly follow
a guide or someone you think will look after
you. Make sure that you know precisely how to
make your own way out in the event that you
have to exit unaccompanied. The surveys in
this guide are simple drawings to give a basic
impression of the site. Note that these are not
always complete and more detailed surveys for
some sites may be available locally.

Remember that water levels in caves and
mines change, often dramatically, across
the differing seasons. This will affect the
position of the dive base and also the nature
and depth of the tunnels in that system. In
the UK the water level varies between 10m
and 15m at mines such as Noxon Park in the
Forest of Dean. In dry summer weather a site
such as Joint Hole in Yorkshire will appear
as a small static pool at the back of a narrow
fissure, while at other times the water level
may be significantly higher and the cave will
be an active resurgence. Consider the weather
and water conditions carefully and make
contingency plans accordingly.

Many of the locations are remote, involve a
reasonable degree of physical fitness to reach
and may have no radio or telephone com-
munications. All divers must make adequate
and thorough preparations to cope with any
eventuality. The environment is challenging
– but it is also unforgiving.

Good buoyancy and trim are essential in cave diving, as here in the Émergence du Ressel, France

Finding locations

The latitude and longitude in degrees, minutes and seconds have been included for each site. This basic data enables sites to be located with ease on many modern navigational devices as well as on some paper maps. Google Earth software is freely available online (www.google.com/earth), where a search using these coordinates will show the site on a map or a view of the natural terrain. Depending on the version of the software in use and the settings chosen, the method of entry may need to be adjusted. As an example, the reference provided for Crab Hole in Cornwall is: 50° 27' 16.26" N, 03° 31' 01.61" W. Entering this data into Google Earth, either including the symbols for degrees, minutes and seconds or with spaces in between each number, as: 50 27 16.26 N, 03 31 01.61 W, will take you to the location.

Ordnance Survey six- or eight-figure grid references are given for all UK dive sites and some other locations, as considered necessary. Where maps are likely to be commonly available, references to the local grid are also provided for European dive sites and some other locations, together with the map name and number.

Metric distances are used throughout, although some additional measurements are given in miles for driving instructions in the UK.

Recommendations

When undertaking any dive:

▶ Complete appropriate training
▶ Choose your dives carefully and increase the level of difficulty (and your experience) in a slow and structured manner
▶ Ensure that all equipment is well maintained and suitable for the dive
▶ Always carry at least three reliable lights per diver
▶ Be aware of and regularly practise relevant emergency procedures
▶ Include emergency planning in your preparations: familiarise yourself with the advice provided in Appendix A
▶ Adhere to current access arrangements
▶ Always use a continuous guideline from the surface of the water or the entrance
▶ Avoid stirring up silt
▶ Never compromise the Rule of Thirds
▶ Avoid deep diving until suitably experienced
▶ Never become overconfident or violate recommended safety procedures

Section one

UK

Cavern Diving

WITH its temperate climate and changeable weather patterns, the UK can present challenging diving conditions. Visibility is variable and seawater temperatures range from around 5°C in winter to 18°C in summer, and often lower in Scotland.

Traditionally, caverns, caves and disused mines have attracted little attention from mainstream divers trained in open water, primarily because it is perceived that few sites are accessible and those that are have limited scope for enjoyable dives. This is, in part at least, a misconception – some are indeed suitable for recreational diving. While they hold dangers for the untrained and unwary, these may be no greater than those encountered in wrecks – which require the same sort of skills to navigate safely. In fact, a large number of caverns – where dives remain within sight of daylight – can be found in the UK and, if planning and conditions are appropriate, they can offer a great day's sport.

◄ A decompression stop in Hodge Close Slate Quarry

Beginning with a clockwise tour around the coast, in south-east Scotland, not far from the border with Northumberland, a significant cluster of short swim-throughs and caverns lies just north of St Abbs. **Tye's Tunnel**, named after David Tye of Oban Divers, is one of the better known and is situated just north of the St Abbs lighthouse, directly opposite the prominent landmark of Cleaver Rock (grid references for all locations in bold appear on p17). Accessed by boat, it is normally dived within ninety minutes of high tide. The swim-through cavern, which dissects the headland, starts as a narrow shaft but increases in size with depth. The depth varies between 6m and 20m and the 15m long dive emerges into a sheltered bay on the far side. The floor of the tunnel consists of

Diving Watcombe Caves on the Devon coast: the entrance is at 'E'

small stones and bare rock, and visibility is generally good. It takes a while to negotiate the route because it twists and turns, but it is well adorned with small red sea squirts and sponges. Other similar localities can be found between St Abbs and Berwick upon Tweed, and on southwards to the Farne Islands.

The largest cluster of cavern sites in southern Britain is on the south coast of Devon. Between Teignmouth in the north and Brixham in the south, many short but interesting places can be explored. For best visibility it is recommended that these are dived at high tide and avoiding conditions when winds are from the east. Westerly or light south-westerly winds provide optimum conditions and visits to all the sites in south Devon are best undertaken from a boat. Local advice regarding sea conditions and visibility will prove invaluable.

A short distance north of Teignmouth, just east of the small village of Holcombe, lies the promontory of Hole Head. The **Parson and Clerk** cavern is located at the end, offering a short and shallow dive popular with local divers.

Around Torquay a number of sites may be tackled as a shore dive, but be warned – in most cases this is a very arduous undertaking! An easy, relatively shallow 20m long swim-through

Watcombe Caves

Smuggler's Hole

Devil's Armchair

The coast at Oddicombe

The 20m swim through
Watcombe Caves

can be achieved beneath **London Arch**, and another 35m long, smaller but shallow tunnel – **Crab Hole** – lies about 110m to the east. For a shore dive here, enter from the coastal platform 75m west of the arch.

Some 3km north of Torquay and 300m north of Watcombe Beach are the fascinating **Watcombe Caves**, which have a well-known swim-through around 20m long and a couple of other short caverns with a maximum depth of 10m. They have been described as 'big enough to drive a double-decker bus into' and are believed to have been inhabited at a time when water levels were lower.

Just 200m south-east from Watcombe Beach a set of very prominent openings are known as **Smuggler's Hole**. This site presents an interesting opportunity as it has a considerable airspace even at high water. Be advised: Watcombe Beach has no authorised road access and the 0.4km long descent is best described as 'very steep'. From the shore, the approach swim to Smuggler's Hole is in excess of 200m; it is twice as far to Watcombe Caves.

Three short caverns may be found at the northern end of Oddicombe Beach. The first two are small and lie within the intertidal zone, but some 50m further east is an impressive tall fissure known locally as the **Devil's Armchair**. There is no car parking at the beach itself, although equipment may be dropped off before leaving the car in Babbacombe and perhaps descending on the cliff railway.

Hope's Nose headland, east of Torquay, contains some very short caves and an intricate set of fissures at its north-easterly tip. These may be approached on foot via a 500m long descent from the nearest road. About 1km offshore south-west from Hope's Nose lies a 34m high rock, the **Ore Stone**. An easy, shallow swim-through in a tall fissure at the south-western end of the island is approximately 35m long with a depth of only a few metres (boat access is essential).

Another set of diveable caves can be explored at Berry Head, near Brixham at the southern extremity of Tor Bay. As with all sites in exposed locations, the currents may be strong. Several of the short caverns can be accessed by shore entry from Berry Head Country Park, a nature reserve. Formal permission is required to gain road access to the quarry at the northern side of the headland, from which point two short fissure networks – **Garfish Cave** and **Cuttlefish Cave** – may be reached by approaching from the rocks about 40m east of Garfish Cave. Marine life in these caverns is deemed sensitive and divers are asked to exercise particular environmental care in this area. Another truly spectacular cavern, **Durl Head Cave**, lies some 350m west of Durl Head along the coast to the south of Berry Head, where a short penetration of 20m gives access to an enormous shingle-floored lake chamber with a substantial daylight opening high on the north side.

Some undersea caves have also been reported at Plymouth, but with few details.

The remote coastline of Cornwall harbours numerous caverns; many more are likely to exist than are currently recorded and dived. Two of the best known – Seal Hole at Prussia Cove and the Kynance Cove caves – are situated between Penzance and the Lizard. Considering that this area faces south and south-west, directly into the prevailing UK weather, the state of the sea is especially important when planning any activities. Optimum conditions are those when easterly or northerly winds are prevalent. More information about Seal Hole and the Kynance Cove caves appears on pp19-22.

Top: Berry Head near Brixham, and Hope's Nose with the Ore Stone in the far distance

Above and left: The dry entrance to Durl Head Cave, and low tide within its main chamber

Dorothea Quarry: enter the water at 'E'. The shallow tunnel lies in the promontary at 'S'

Partially submerged, intertidal caves are widely distributed along the rocky coast of Pembrokeshire, with those on Ramsey and Skomer islands being especially sensitive on environmental grounds. Regardless of location, all are best approached by boat. If winds are light and from the north an interesting area to explore is the headland to the east of the sandy beach at Broad Haven near Bosherton on the south coast. Some 100m east of Saddle Point a spacious 15m long shallow dive gives access to the sheer-sided and otherwise inaccessible **Lost Lagoon**, formed from a collapsed cave. Further short caverns lie west of this point and another with a 10m long swim-through is less than 100m to the north-east. In terms of visibility and reduced surge, this diving is best undertaken at high tide when depths will be about 8m. The limestone cliffs of the Castlemartin coast make for the most spectacular scenery and another 50m long shallow dive is reported beneath the gaping cleft of the **Huntsman's Leap**. In calm conditions, this coastline presents a truly fascinating day.

In north-west Wales, a shallow cavern dive lies close to Pen-y-Cil headland at the western tip of the Llŷn Peninsula. Here, beneath a cliff and looking across to Bardsey Island, is a small underwater sea cave named **Lyn Cavern** with two interconnecting tunnels at depths of between 12m and 14m. The site can only be reached by boat and, because of its situation, the waters are notoriously fickle. However, this is a straightforward cave to locate and visitors will enjoy a classic and spacious cavern dive. The main tunnel is around 25m long with natural light visible throughout

Diving the shallow tunnel route at Dorothea

Coordinates

Dive site	Region	NGR	Lat/Long
Crab Hole	Devon	SX 924627	50° 27' 16.26" N, 03° 31' 01.61" W
Cuttlefish Cave	Devon	SX 946567	50° 24' 02.07" N, 03° 29' 08.72" W
Devil's Armchair	Devon	SX 927662	50° 29' 08.19" N, 03° 30' 47.74" W
Dorothea Slate Quarry	Gwynedd	SH 499532	53° 03' 19.33" N, 04° 14' 25.82" W
Durl Head Cave	Devon	SX 936556	50° 23' 27.53" N, 03° 29' 51.66" W
Garfish Cave	Devon	SX 946567	50° 24' 01.79" N, 03° 29' 05.89" W
Hope's Nose	Devon	SX 950637	50° 27' 50.83" N, 03° 28' 52.69" W
Huntsman's Leap	Pembrokeshire	SR 962929	51° 35' 54.69" N, 04° 56' 39.78" W
London Arch	Devon	SX 923627	50° 27' 15.57" N, 03° 31' 07.39" W
Lost Lagoon	Pembrokeshire	SR 983940	51° 36' 30.58" N, 04° 54' 53.79" W
Lyn Cavern	Gwynedd	SH 156240	52° 46' 56.52" N, 04° 44' 05.04" W
Ore Stone	Devon	SX 956629	50° 27' 24.64" N, 03° 28' 17.48" W
Parson and Clerk cavern	Devon	SX 961747	50° 33' 47.33" N, 03° 28' 07.05" W
Smuggler's Hole	Devon	SX 927671	50° 29' 39.45" N, 03° 30' 48.65" W
Sugarloaf Caves	Isle of Man	SC 194662	54° 03' 36.29" N, 04° 45' 36.49" W
Tye's Tunnel	Scottish Borders	NT 914694	55° 55' 02.00" N, 02° 08' 46.00" W
Vobster Quay	Somerset	ST 705497	51° 14' 45.71" N, 02° 25' 26.17" W
Watcombe Caves	Devon	SX 928677	50° 29' 57.49" N, 03° 30' 45.74" W

its length and plenty of anemones and other marine life to examine, but the side passages and restrictions must be treated with caution. Other caverns have been reported off Anglesey.

On the Isle of Man the **Sugarloaf Caves** are fairly well known to local divers. These caverns are located near the southernmost tip of the island, 2km south-west from Port St Mary, and are accessed by boat. With a maximum depth of about 12m and an air surface in most of the passageways, the area offers a superb dive at all levels of ability. Three caves can be found in the cliffs that extend along a 300m stretch of coast, the longest penetration being in Cave of the Birds, which has multiple entrances and contains an occasional seal, while the Fairy Hall lies some 150m to the south. The narrow fissures and sheer rock faces exclude natural light and provide an unusual and exciting dive. Visibility can be 10m, but given its geographical location this is best regarded as a calm weather site.

Scotland presents any number of cavern diving opportunities. The most adventurous must surely be those at St Kilda, over 60km into the North Atlantic (see p35), but caves are also known in rocks off the shores of Sutherland and even further afield around Shetland. These remote localities offer some exceptional dives, with a visibility of 15m to 20m being the norm. The caves at the northernmost island of Unst certainly require care and planning, while those around the southern tip of Bressay contain wreckage swept into the entrances by storm action.

Cavern dives in the form of short tunnels can also be found in quarries, mines, caves and reservoirs across the interior of the UK. As for marine settings, conditions may be variable. The benign surface environment of inland sites provides significant advantages and better protection from the elements, but the water may be susceptible to a greater range of both temperature and visibility. **Vobster Quay**, based in a flooded quarry 6km west of Frome in Somerset, is a long-established dive centre with a well-known tunnel; indeed, the 18m long passage is probably one of its best attractions. It starts at 14m depth, at no great distance from the point of entry into the water, and exits at 22m depth. Oval in shape and well lined, the tunnel is about 2m high and amply wide enough for two divers to swim side by side.

More serious, owing to depth and cold water, are the passages found in **Dorothea Slate Quarry**, situated between Penygroes and Nantlle on the B4418 in north-west Wales. There is no formal permission to dive at Dorothea and requests have been made for divers to stay away as a significant number of lives have been lost there over the years. The following information relates to cavern dives in the flooded quarry; it is mentioned on the basis that dives nevertheless continue to take place and it is better to possess accurate information than rely on disparate sources.

While Dorothea's surface water temperatures vary according to the season, below 10m depth the temperature rarely changes from 5°C. Probably the three best known of the short tunnels lie at depths of 21m, 56m and 87m. The 21m tunnel is about 12m long and can generally be dived with ambient light, being a straight-line oval passage large enough, just as at Vobster, for two divers to swim side by side. The tunnel is located in a low promontory about 100m away from and directly opposite the normal point of entry to the water in the quarry. Visibility is usually superb – 10m plus – enabling divers to see right through the tunnel.

The tunnel at 56m depth is the longest of the three at some 15m long. Given the depth, a dive here will require decompression. The entrance is about 1.5m high by 3m wide, but once inside the dimensions increase to a 2m to 3m high tunnel with a clean, relatively uncluttered floor. While this offers a relatively simple dive, a bend roughly halfway through means that it is essential to carry lighting. Unlike the 21m tunnel, locating the passage may not be straightforward.

Especially considering the fatalities that have occurred at Dorothea, this location must be treated very seriously.

The shallow tunnel at Dorothea

Sea Caves of South Cornwall

WHILE the rocky shores of Cornwall contain many caves, few are dived due to their exposed locations, difficulties of access and the vagaries of the sea. The coastal scenery is magnificent: when winds are set fair and the sky is blue, this area presents the finest cavern diving opportunities in mainland Britain. Both entries in this section lie on the south Cornwall coast and are only recommended when winds are from the north or east; both may be tackled as shore dives, but be aware that the currents are notoriously strong, especially at Kynance Cove.

Prussia Cove

Objective
A single cave at Prussia Cove, Seal Hole, presents a superb introduction to cavern diving with a maximum depth of under 8m.

CAVERN

Access
No permission is required, but please adhere to the instructions on the noticeboard at the car park: no vehicles are allowed beyond this point. Some private gardens lie immediately east of the access point to the shore; please respect the landowners' signs and information.

Location
Prussia Cove is 1.5km due south of the village of Rosudgeon, roughly midway between Helston and Penzance. Access is via a gradual 500m walk down the track to the sea from the car park (SW 555281); the cave is easily located on the rocky coastal platform leading out towards The Enys rock. The distinctive triangular-shaped pool, on the western side of the small headland, is protected to a limited extent from the direct ravage of the swell and is best dived at high water.

History
The first recorded exploration of the cave, by George A. Steven, Assistant Naturalist at the Plymouth Laboratory, took place in August 1935. A comprehensive account of Steven's swim, undertaken at low water, appeared in a report to the then Ministry of Agriculture and Fisheries (September 1935). He reported the site as a seal lodge (hence the name), a rare find in southern Cornwall, and even today seals are encountered both in the cave and in the narrow clefts close by. It is not clear when the first through-dive was made, but one was recorded by Peter Glanvill in September 1982.

Prussia Cove. The cave runs from the larger entrance at 'E', following a line of weakness in the rock heading in the direction of Bessy's Cove in the distance

Diving
Seal Hole presents a superbly spacious swim-through, trending north-west towards an inconspicuous, smaller exit in the direction of Bessy's Cove. Visibility may be 10m or more in optimum conditions, but can be altogether less when conditions are rough. The sea temperature varies from about 10°C to 19°C according to the season.

Seal Hole

A 5m high, 2m wide entrance fissure soon transforms to a tunnel over 3m in diameter, floored with copious deposits of organic seaweed detritus. The walls and ceiling are covered in a colourful array of marine organisms. At 30m from the entrance a prominent band of white rock crosses the tunnel. To the left, light from the exit is clearly visible along a smaller tunnel which surfaces abruptly at a smooth-walled, well-sculpted ascent. This area of the cave is clearly affected by the swell as the rock surfaces are devoid of marine life. To the right of the white rock band a spacious side tunnel continues for approximately 10m to reach a dead end. The maximum depth throughout is about 8m.

With lots of clefts and gullies in close proximity to the cave, this is a great little site for leisurely exploration.

Further considerations

▶ An ideal dive site when winds are light from the north or east; postpone the dive if the wind is from the south or west
▶ The car park offers limited parking and may be full by lunchtime; arrive early!
▶ Use a sturdy rucksack and make two journeys each way or, better still, use a sack truck with pneumatic tyres to transport equipment
▶ Always use a line inside the cavern

Kynance Cove

Objective

Of the two sites at Kynance Cove, Sand Crater Hole offers a superb introduction to cavern diving with a maximum depth of less than 8m; it is an impressive dive passing beneath Asparagus Island. The second cavern, The Washing Machine, is of a similar length and depth, but has no safe exit at the far end.

Access

No permission is required, but a parking fee is levied by the National Trust at the car park at the end of the toll road. Vehicles are not normally

The entrance to The Washing Machine is found on the far side of Asparagus Island; the island is accessible at low tide

The Washing Machine

Sand Crater Hole

Asparagus Island

allowed beyond this point. The usual approach to the beach is via a steep footpath that is about 350m long and involves steps.

Location

Kynance Cove is 2km north-west of Lizard Point. At low water it is possible to walk at low level from the small beach in the cove westwards to a second, much larger beach known as The Bellows. This stretch of beautiful white sand separates the mainland from Asparagus Island and both Gull Rock and The Bishop, which lie to the south. If you have to swim to reach the

The Bellows

Kynance Cove at low tide: the entrance to Sand Crater Hole is marked at 'E'

further beach, beware of strong surge currents. Entry to Sand Crater Hole is at the far side of the sandy beach, following the line of an obvious rock fracture running through Asparagus Island, whereas The Washing Machine lies in a deep recess near the middle of the south side of the island.

History

The Kynance Cove sites are less well known to local divers than Seal Hole at Prussia Cove. The caves were reported briefly in a divers' guide to south Cornwall in 1983, though it appears that open water divers made the first explorations in the 1970s.

Diving

Sand Crater Hole, as the name implies, involves a descent on a sand floor into the entrance at a depth of about 8m. A broad passage, over 4m wide, leads away across miniature sand dunes. Any swell will make the traverse to the far entrance sporting and to see the sand flowing along the entire width of the floor is an interesting phenomenon.

At the midpoint the roof lowers to give a clearance of about 2m, but thereafter the proportions increase to those of a wide and lofty canyon on the seaward side of the island. This is a lovely 50m long swim-through with a maximum depth of 8m. The walls of the cave are predictably covered

Sand Crater Hole. The sand dunes on the floor clearly indicate the degree of tidal surge

Coordinates

Dive site	NGR	Lat/Long
Prussia Cove		
Seal Hole	SW 5580 2782	50° 06' 00.38" N, 05° 24' 57.95" W
Kynance Cove caves		
Sand Crater Hole, north entrance	SW 6828 1323	49° 58' 27.21" N, 05° 14' 00.20" W
Sand Crater Hole, south entrance	SW 6828 1323	49° 58' 25.82" N, 05° 14' 00.83" W
The Washing Machine, west entrance	SW 6830 1317	49° 58' 25.17" N, 05° 13' 58.59" W

in a mixture of white and yellow anemones: *Sargartia* species, beadlets, dahlia and plumose anemones are all here, not to mention a profusion of sea squirts, crabs and shrimps.

Having passed through Sand Crater Hole to the south, visitors might consider swimming onwards around Asparagus Island in an anti-clockwise direction. Between 40m and 50m from Sand Crater Hole, on this seaward side of the island, a very prominent recess heralds the entrance to The Washing Machine. This is of a similar length and depth to Sand Crater Hole, but the surge effect is more pronounced, the visibility probably less than half and instead of clean sand the floor is covered with a mass of shifting, broken kelp and seaweed. At the far end the passage suddenly narrows to a smooth-walled chimney – any surface to air will gain a very impressive blowhole in times of storm! Realistically, there is only room for one person at a time at this daylight window and, given the rise and fall of the swell, this is not a place to be under anything less than perfect conditions. Beware!

Further considerations

► The car park has ample space; a fee is payable to the National Trust on arrival
► Use a sturdy rucksack to carry kit and make two journeys each way or, better still, use a sack truck with pneumatic tyres. If using a truck, take the longer route to the beach via the track, not the direct steep descent which involves steps
► Given the exposed location and strong currents, plan and execute any dive here with caution. It is not advisable to dive in big swell or during low water spring tides
► A boat may provide the easiest means of gaining access
► The beach at Kynance Cove is very popular with tourists during the summer; give thought to the security of bags left on shore

Air supplies

Porthkerris Divers, Porthkerris Cove, St Keverne, Helston TR12 6QJ
  Tel: 01326 280620; www.porthkerris.com

Trevair Touring Park, South Treveneague, Goldsithney, Penzance TR20 9BY
  Tel: 01736 740647; www.trevairtouringpark.co.uk

Emergencies

Emergency contacts: see Appendix A
Nearest hyperbaric centre: Plymouth
Nearest hospital: West Cornwall Hospital, St Clare Street, Penzance TR18 2PF; tel: 01736 874000

Mines of the Forest of Dean

THE iron mines of the Forest of Dean present excellent opportunities for introductory and fully certified cave divers using side-mounted equipment; these are **not** cavern diving sites. Divers will find the Forest an attractive area for making progressive penetrations into its flooded mines, two of which are described here: Bream Mine and Noxon Park Iron Mines (sometimes referred to as The Crater). Other sites are not described as they are generally more difficult to enter or potentially dangerous.

The overall diving depths range from shallow to over 50m in the deep levels. However, the depth of the water in the mines fluctuates by as much as 15m according to the season, with water levels usually at their highest in April and lowest in the autumn. The water temperature is a constant year-round 8°C to 9°C. Visibility varies according to the site, but is normally at its worst (between 3m and 4m) when levels rise and the clearest (30m to 50m) as they fall.

Access

A formal access arrangement covers all the caves and mines in the area; seek appropriate advice from the Forest of Dean Cave Conservation and Access Group Permit Secretary (e-mail: permits@fodccag.co.uk). Public liability insurance cover is required.

History

Evidence exists showing that ores were extracted and worked in the Forest of Dean well over 2,000 years ago during the Iron Age, although extensive

The entrance to Bream Mine and a diver emerging from the lower levels

iron mining dates from Roman times. Where the ores outcropped on the surface, ancient workings are marked by depressions known as scowles. Today, these are obscured and secreted amid the woodland and it is in this fascinating environment that the deeper mines are located.

During the Roman period the mines were driven to about 30m depth and, while extraction continued thereafter, it was not until the early seventeenth century and, especially, the nineteenth century that extraction techniques improved the economics of mining. Most of the mines in the area closed between 1890 and 1900 because the ore thinned at depth, while there were associated problems with pumping water and competition from cheaper Spanish ore. A resurgence of iron mining occurred during the First World War, but by 1926 virtually all activity had ceased. The last operations closed in 1946.

Known to cave and mine exploration enthusiasts for many years, Noxon Park's first systematic underwater investigation was begun in the early 1970s. Local activists John Elliott and Colin

Graham reported the first dives in these mines. Martyn Farr commenced exploring and surveying Bream Mine in 2005.

Bream Mine

Objective

FULL

The north entrance to Bream Mine is a challenging site to enter and is only suitable for fully trained and experienced cave divers, but those who venture here will encounter a great variety of underwater terrain. Much of the diving is shallow (though the deep level descends to 50m), with large tunnels, shafts, roof supports to avoid and silt to contend with; this is *not* a cavern diving site.

Location

Bream Mine lies just outside the village of Bream, on Forestry Commission land some 3 miles/5km south-south-east of Coleford. The workings lie in the same stretch of woods as the Noxon Park mines, which are less than 1km to the north-west. The entrances are fenced off for safety purposes. Approach the mines from the northern outskirts of Bream. Park with due consideration for local inhabitants on the large area of open ground at the southern perimeter of the woods (SO 595059), then follow the track directly into the woods. Some 200m from the edge of the woods there is a small gate on the left; pass through this and follow the fence to the left until it is possible to descend into the large, overgrown hollow on the other side. The entrance to Bream Mine is large and impressive, the passage descending steeply below the approach track.

Sturdy footwear and overalls, together with a helmet and appropriate head-mounted lighting, are required to enter the mine. A 45m rope, used as a hand-line, will prove extremely useful on the initial descent – if it has rained recently, this slope will be muddy, with unstable and slippery rocks underfoot.

The descent to the water surface is fairly straight-forward, but beware of vertical drops in the lower reaches; a second 20m handline will be useful near the bottom. Care must be taken to not dislodge rocks or debris onto people below. While the underground journey may

BREAM MINE:
North entrance
Bream, Forest of Dean

Backmount

−41m
−44m
−40m
−15m
−22m
▲ DANGER: loose boulder restriction
↑ N
connecting shaft
−15m
airbell
−10m
−3.5m
−7m
two pillars
0   20m
−10m
−9m
−3.5m
+10m
dive base
H
+6m
continues 200m to air at Bream South entrance
→
−3m
track
gate
Water levels
Water levels shown here are relative and vary immensely. Under low water conditions it is possible to walk along the −3m tunnel heading eastwards to emerge at the Bream South entrance.
H
H: handline useful
H
Entrance

only be 100m to reach the dive base, it is advisable to check out the route and the water level in advance of carrying equipment.

Diving

The seasonal water level fluctuations need to be considered, as final diving preparations and access to the water can be very awkward when the water is high. Low water levels make access easier and leave the end of the main orange dive line visible above water.

Once free of the silt cloud near the dive base, visibility is usually very good and may reach an exceptional 50m. This is a very extensive underwater complex with various side tunnels. Many hundreds of metres of dive line have been installed here; before relying on any, inspect it for damage. The stability of the underwater passages is mostly very good, but divers must keep a careful watch for loose debris from, for example, the drystone walls that are set in the side of the tunnel. Avoid all contact with this material. The dusting of light, orange-coloured sediment is easily disturbed and may reduce the visibility to zero.

The quality of diving is excellent as the visibility only varies slightly through the year; in general, the water is clearer than in the Noxon Park mines. Repeated, progressive, diving operations can result in a traverse dive to an adjoining mine named The Jetty. Great care is required in the deeper sections.

Noxon Park Iron Mines

Objective

Noxon Park offers a superb dive at all times, but activities are again begun deep underground, so experience in both caving and diving techniques is required: this also is not a site for cavern-trained divers. On a first visit a pair of 7 litre cylinders should enable a penetration of up to 150m – divers will then certainly wish to return for additional excursions to become more familiar with the site and explore further.

Location

Noxon Park Iron Mines lie just over 2.5 miles/4km south of Coleford on land owned by the Forestry Commission and they contain a veritable labyrinth of tunnels. As well as the one described here, several other entrances exist in the vicinity, all of which are fenced off for safety purposes. If stumbled upon, these should be viewed with extreme caution as they are not easily accessible and frequently have poor visibility, large quantities of silt and a profusion of poor line.

The mines are normally approached from the village of Sling. From the crossroads at the centre of the village, follow the south-eastern road signposted to Clements End, Oakwood and Bream for just under 1 mile/1.5km to a telephone box at the entrance to Coinros garden centre and nursery (SO 592069). Park on the roadside here with due consideration for local inhabitants; there is usually ample availability.

Walk along the road to the right of the nursery for just over 100m until a large boulder blocks the route for vehicles. Continue past the boulder, then after about 200m the footpath enters the bottom of a shallow, wooded valley. Bear left for 100m and follow the rough track uphill to the

INTRO

Backmount

The iron-rich mud at the dive base in Noxon Park Iron Mines

Coordinates

Dive site	NGR	Lat/Long
Bream Mine, north entrance	SO 593060	51° 45' 03.26" N, 02° 35' 25.36" W
Noxon Park Iron Mines	SO 589064	51° 45' 16.65" N, 02° 35' 50.04" W

right. Some fenced-off openings and shafts lie on both sides, but look for a mature beech tree and a small padlocked gate on the right. At this point turn right off the track and follow the top edge of a 5m deep working for 30m, before descending into the depression where you will find the small, oval entrance to Noxon Park which is only one metre in diameter. This should take less than fifteen minutes' walking from the parking area.

The entrance is muddy and, although the underground tunnel leading to the dive base is only 200m long, the route is challenging (though easier to enter than Bream Mine). A helmet and appropriate head-mounted lighting are required as well as suitable sturdy footwear and overalls to protect against the iron-stained mud. It is strongly advisable to check the route in advance of carrying equipment – there are steep slopes, often damp and slippery, unstable rocks underfoot and some deep holes which must be avoided. A 30m long sturdy knotted handline will prove useful around 30m inside the entrance – keep your hands free to ensure good balance at all times. The main dive base is situated in a very large, boulder-strewn tunnel over 15m high and more than 10m wide.

Diving

A line junction at 15m depth in Noxon Park Iron Mines

Plenty of lighting is recommended at the dive base, given the dark nature of the surrounding rock. Underwater, the visibility is generally very good and may be an exceptional 50m; however, after heavy or prolonged rainfall

this may reduce to 3m, but even then some sections of the flooded mines remain crystal clear.

The main underwater tunnel is large and impressive. This again is a very complex site with side tunnels leading off in several directions. Well over a kilometre of dive line has been installed and this, due to its age, should be examined carefully before it is trusted. The underwater passages are generally stable, but – as with all the mines in this area – divers must avoid disturbing loose debris, especially the thin layer of light, orange-coloured silt in the smaller passages. Good technique is essential.

Despite the challenging nature of Noxon Park, the quality of diving is second to none in the UK.

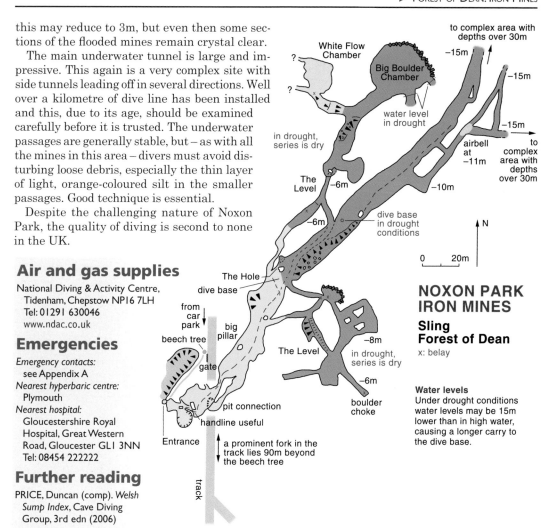

Air and gas supplies

National Diving & Activity Centre,
 Tidenham, Chepstow NP16 7LH
 Tel: 01291 630046
 www.ndac.co.uk

Emergencies

Emergency contacts:
 see Appendix A
Nearest hyperbaric centre:
 Plymouth
Nearest hospital:
 Gloucestershire Royal
 Hospital, Great Western
 Road, Gloucester GL1 3NN
 Tel: 08454 222222

Further reading

PRICE, Duncan (comp). *Welsh Sump Index*, Cave Diving Group, 3rd edn (2006)

NOXON PARK IRON MINES
Sling
Forest of Dean
x: belay

Water levels
Under drought conditions water levels may be 15m lower than in high water, causing a longer carry to the dive base.

Further considerations

▶ Make a reconnaissance to assess the approach and water conditions
▶ Wear appropriate footwear (boots or wellingtons with a deep tread) and good, helmet-mounted lighting for the journey to and from the dive base
▶ Wear a boiler suit and/or old clothes for your descent as the mud readily causes stains that are extremely difficult to remove
▶ Take large polythene bags for muddy clothing and kit on the journey home
▶ A hood and gloves for the dives are essential in all seasons
▶ Take lots of personalised clothes peg line markers (small plastic line arrows are impractical on the thick permanent lines)
▶ Use a comfortable rucksack (rather than hand-held dive bags) to transport your equipment, to keep hands free to hold the rope and ensure a good balance
▶ Protect all equipment, especially cylinder valves, in the stooping-height approach passages to the dive bases
▶ Make two carries rather than struggle with a heavy load
▶ Use 11mm diameter knotted ropes as handlines
▶ Avoid stirring up silt in the sump pools
▶ Do not add thin technical line to the existing dive lines; inspect and use current lines
▶ Conservation is as important in mines as it is in caves; ensure that the mines are left clean and tidy

Hodge Close Slate Mine

Coniston, Cumbria

INTRO

Objective
Hodge Close Slate Mine, with its associated quarry, presents opportunities for introductory and fully certified cave divers. *Cavern divers should **not** venture more than 20m from the mine entrance.* The site is diveable under all conditions, offering a return dive through a tunnel that incorporates three chambers with a maximum depth of 25m.

Access
A goodwill fee is payable for parking.

Location
Hodge Close Slate Quarry lies in a beautiful but remote site some 3 miles/4.5km north-north-east from the Lake District village of Coniston in Cumbria. To find the quarry follow the A593 Coniston to Ambleside main road, turning north at High Yewdale onto a narrow, minor lane signposted 'Hodge Close Only', which climbs slowly up the hillside and leads after about 1 mile/2.5km

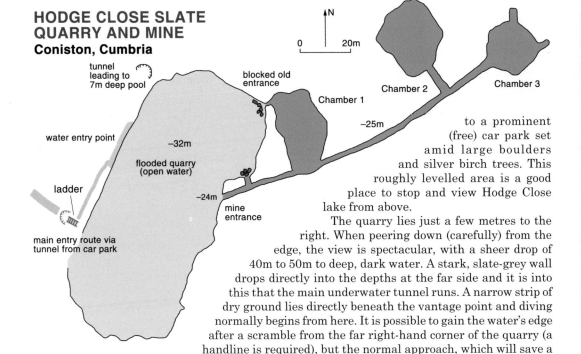

HODGE CLOSE SLATE QUARRY AND MINE
Coniston, Cumbria

tunnel leading to 7m deep pool

blocked old entrance

Chamber 1

Chamber 2

Chamber 3

0   20m

N

water entry point

−32m

−25m

flooded quarry (open water)

ladder

−24m

mine entrance

main entry route via tunnel from car park

to a prominent (free) car park set amid large boulders and silver birch trees. This roughly levelled area is a good place to stop and view Hodge Close lake from above.

The quarry lies just a few metres to the right. When peering down (carefully) from the edge, the view is spectacular, with a sheer drop of 40m to 50m to deep, dark water. A stark, slate-grey wall drops directly into the depths at the far side and it is into this that the main underwater tunnel runs. A narrow strip of dry ground lies directly beneath the vantage point and diving normally begins from here. It is possible to gain the water's edge after a scramble from the far right-hand corner of the quarry (a handline is required), but the normal approach, which will save a lot of physical effort, is via a circuitous route to the west of the quarry.

To reach the final car park, follow the narrow road further to a small group of cottages where a rough track diverges and veers off downhill to the left. Call at the right-hand cottage in the small hamlet to pay a goodwill fee for access to and parking on the land. A steel barrier post will be removed from the track: proceed down the open hillside to the parking area and the closest point to the quarry. This route is just passable with care in a car; park immediately on the far side of a small, fordable stream.

From here, walk up the watercourse for a few metres then wade through a 150m long horizontal tunnel (NY 3156 0179; 54° 24' 25" N, 03° 03' 21" W) with daylight visible at the far end. The tunnel entrance is stooping height, but thereafter the roof rises to permit walking, albeit in water a little more than knee deep. From the 'window' at the far end, a vertical 4m rigid-framed scaffold ladder leads down to the lakeside. Dive suits should be worn from the car park.

History

Slate, won primarily for roofing materials, was quarried in the Coniston area from the early 1800s and small-scale extraction still persists today, though Hodge Close Quarry itself ceased operation in the 1980s. In the early 1900s, however, Hodge Close was clearly a thriving concern with scores of people employed and, as engineering skills progressed, increasingly elaborate techniques were developed for removing the rock. Gravity inclines are an interesting feature of many slate mining regions, but the Hodge Close operation involved the fascinating and comparatively rare example of a water balance being used to raise slate blocks from the depths of the workings. The counterbalance principle enabled the slate to be brought midway up the quarry face, from where it was offloaded and taken by tram to the surface through a level. This level provides the access route to the dive base today.

The surface pool at Hodge Close Slate Quarry and one of the direction signs in the mined tunnel

Diving

Water in the quarry is about 32m deep, with the deepest point marked by a floating buoy. In recent years substantial rockfalls have occurred at the overhanging northern side of the quarry, blocking one of the flooded entrances and severely obstructing another: warning notices have been erected.

At depth in the quarry and inside the mine tunnel the water is always cold, varying between 4°C and 6°C. Visibility in the open pit is a superb

Coordinates

Dive site	NGR	Lat/Long
Hodge Close Slate Mine	NY 3169 0169	54° 24' 21.78" N, 03° 03' 14.19" W

The climb out of the quarry and a prominent underwater warning

15m plus at the outset, despite even the most adverse environmental conditions, so Hodge Close offers an interesting excursion at any time of year. Providing there have been no visitors for several days, the mine's visibility is even better, perhaps 20m or more.

The entrance to the underground complex is relatively straightforward to find, being situated in the far wall at a depth of 24m. Immediately inside, the 2m square-cut tunnel descends slightly over a debris cone then levels out and heads in a north-easterly direction at 25m depth. Some 200m of passageways may be followed by appropriately trained divers, with the furthest point lying about 150m from the initial entry.

A severely obstructed opening lies just a few metres inside the entrance on the left-hand side, beyond which the square passage runs for 20m to the substantial, 20m wide Chamber 1. Opposite the point of entry lies a conspicuous skull and crossbones warning sign – the chamber once led to an exit, off to the left-hand side, which today is completely blocked.

Continuing directly ahead, to the right of the warning sign, a swim of almost 60m gains a junction. This is a Y-fork, with both routes terminating at roughly circular chambers within a short distance. The left-hand route leads after just over 10m to an abrupt end in Chamber 2, while the right-hand tunnel extends for around 20m to Chamber 3. The passages are equipped with heavy-duty polypropylene line and some directional line markings, which is very reassuring because it is difficult to avoid stirring up the fine silt.

Given the constant depth of the mine, the cold water and the physical exertion involved, visitors should be cautious with respect to decompression. This site is best regarded as an 'altitude' dive as it lies approximately 150m above sea level, so it is sensible to make an altitude adjustment to the dive plan by adding one-quarter of the depth to the deepest point attained. The chilly water only slightly improves during summer months.

Other shallow but extremely committing tunnels exist in Hodge Close Quarry, although divers are strongly advised not to enter them due to their instability. It is also prudent to consider the level of training of all members of the party before embarking upon any penetration dive here. Other than the first few metres, Hodge Close is not generally deemed suitable as a cavern dive: three fatalities have occurred here, all inexperienced divers.

Further considerations

▶ Beware of tourists throwing stones from the top of the quarry
▶ The area has no mobile phone signal
▶ A 20m length of sturdy rope is useful as a hauling line on the ladder at the end of the approach tunnel
▶ Consider decompression carefully: the environment is cold and the return to the car is strenuous

Air supplies

Capernwray Diving Centre, Jackdaw Quarry, Capernwray Road, Capernwray, Carnforth LA6 1AD
  Tel: 01524 735132; www.dive-site.co.uk. Closed Mondays other than bank holidays

Emergencies

Emergency contacts: see Appendix A
Nearest hyperbaric centre: Wirral
Nearest hospital: Westmorland General Hospital, Burton Road, Kendal LA9 7RG; tel: 01539 732288

Holme Bank Chert Mine

Bakewell, Peak District

Objective

Holme Bank Chert Mine offers introductory divers a shallow through-dive (maximum depth 5m) with two exit points, enabling two dives of 80m and 95m long and the option of returning underwater or via a dry passage.

INTRO

Access

The entrance is gated and locked – permission will normally be given to appropriately qualified dive leaders. Contact: Oldfield Design, tel: 01629 813301.

Location

The mine is located in a small, inconspicuous quarry on the northern outskirts of Bakewell in Derbyshire. Leaving the town on the A619 heading for Baslow, cross the River Wye and after about 250m turn left into Holme Lane. From the point where Holme Lane rejoins the river, turn right up a track on the right-hand side and park after a short distance; space is available for several vehicles. The entrance lies to the right side of the track, around 20m from the parking area.

History

The mining of chert stone, which was used in the pottery industry as a whitening agent when manufacturing earthenware, has been undertaken in the area for over 200 years. Early 19th century extraction at Holme Bank was from quarries, but commercial chert mining was in place here by 1867, when the site was known as Bakewell Chert Mine. The mine closed around 1960.

A line junction near a support pillar in the flooded Holme Bank Chert Mine

Coordinates

Dive site	NGR	Lat/Long
Holme Bank Chert Mine	SK 215692	53° 13' 06.76" N, 01° 40' 46.04" W

The entrance to Holme Bank Chert Mine

Diving

The underwater sections offer straightforward dives, which normally begin only a few minutes' walk into the mine at Pump Base. The water temperature is a constant 8°C and, if you are the first to dive, the visibility will frequently be crystal clear. As the water is static, it may take some days to clear after a weekend's activity.

The water entry is easy and leads immediately to a spacious, shallow tunnel floored with a dusting of light sediment. This is a fairly popular training site, so the layout of fixed lines (all of which are 6mm) may vary, but in essence the submerged tunnel has two points where divers may leave the water following their dive and, if necessary, make their way back to the entrance through dry, walking- and stooping-height galleries. Pits Base lies some 80m from the point of water entry, while 95m further on air is once more reached just prior to Arch Base. The sump lengths may vary slightly in times of flood or drought, but the exit points remain the same. The maximum depth is 5m.

Divers should take care not to disturb any roof supports, including drystone walls. This site has no major attractions, but it offers an excellent insight to underground workings.

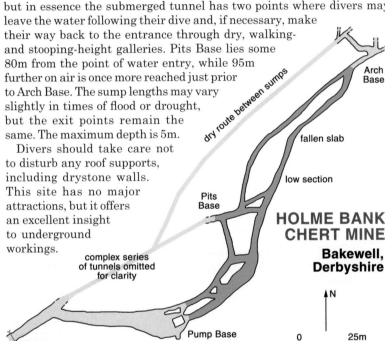

dry route between sumps

Arch Base

fallen slab

low section

Pits Base

complex series of tunnels omitted for clarity

HOLME BANK CHERT MINE

Bakewell, Derbyshire

N

Pump Base

0   25m

Entrance gate

Further considerations

▶ The tunnels are large enough to allow the use of conventional back-mounted cylinders, although, given the distances and depths involved, most experienced divers use easy-to-carry side-mounts

▶ Recce the dry route before making a through-dive and leaving the water at either Pits Base or Arch Base

Air supplies

SDS Watersports, 66-70 Station Road, Halfway, Sheffield S20 3GW
Tel: 0114 248 8688; www.sdswatersports.co.uk

Emergencies

Emergency contacts: see Appendix A
Nearest hospital: Chesterfield Royal Hospital, Calow, Chesterfield S44 5BL; tel: 01246 277271

Further reading

CARTER, Russell L. & CORDINGLEY, John N. (eds). *Peak District Sump Index*, Cave Diving Group, 5th edn (1994)

Roscobie Limestone Mine

Dunfermline, Scotland

Objective

Roscobie Limestone Mine is the best mine diving site in Scotland and offers exceptional diving for all levels of ability from cavern divers through to fully certified cave divers. The maximum depth at the 'visible entrances' is less than 10m, while the 'hidden entrances' extend to at least 18m deep.

Access

No permission is required; there are no known access difficulties.

Location

The limestone mine is located at Roscobie Quarry, a short distance south-west of Roscobie Reservoir, which lies around 4 miles/6km north of Dunfermline in Fife. From the M90 motorway, turn off at junction four and take the B914 westwards leading to Dollar, turning right after 1.9 miles/3km towards Saline. One mile/1.5km from this junction park in a layby on the right by an area of rough ground with some boulders and overgrown ruins of quarry structures, directly opposite some sheds. Space is available for three or four cars.

Take the footpath heading north from the layby; after climbing a gradual slope for 50m, this levels off for 150m then swings to the left. The final 150m to reach the flooded quarry may be overgrown. Three prominent entrances are visible at the far (north-western) side of the lake, but five deeper openings also lie hidden below the water level on the right-hand (north-eastern) side, which can be reached by swimming across the lake from this point. For diving in the visible entrances, it is possible to carry the equipment around the left-hand side of the lake and kit up on some flat ground adjacent to the openings, which avoids the need to swim across the water.

CAVERN INTRO

Poor visibility

History

During the Industrial Revolution, Fife was a prominent area for the production of iron and coal as well as the closely associated extraction of limestone. Roscobie Limestone Mine was in operation until 1957 and today the quarry is designated as a geological Site of Special Scientific Interest on the basis of its exposure of Dinantian (Lower Carboniferous) limestone containing algal mounds and overlying muddy deltaic deposits.

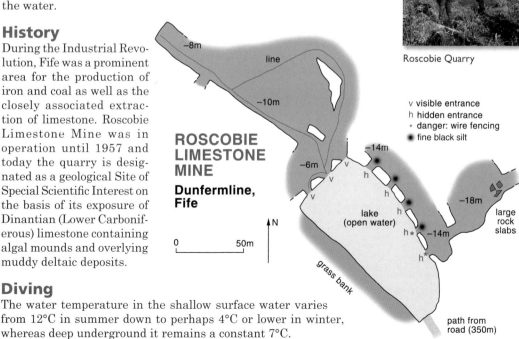

Roscobie Quarry

v visible entrance
h hidden entrance
* danger: wire fencing
● fine black silt

ROSCOBIE LIMESTONE MINE

Dunfermline, Fife

0   50m

N

line

−8m

−10m

−6m

−14m

−18m

−14m

lake (open water)

large rock slabs

grass bank

path from road (350m)

Diving

The water temperature in the shallow surface water varies from 12°C in summer down to perhaps 4°C or lower in winter, whereas deep underground it remains a constant 7°C.

Coordinates

Dive site	NGR	Lat/Long
Roscobie Limestone Mine, visible entrances	NT 091932	56° 07' 23.04" N, 03° 27' 53.27" W
Roscobie Limestone Mine, hidden entrances	NT 091932	56° 07' 22.03" N, 03° 27' 48.92" W

Entering Roscobie
Limestone Mine

Poor visibility is fairly common in the surface waters year-round – in summer, this is about 2m at the surface, impaired by a green plankton bloom. Under these conditions a noticeable thermocline occurs at around 8m depth, with a distinct wispy, cloud-like layering effect. The visibility gradually improves further into the tunnels but, given their substantial size and the copious quantities of fine silt near the entrances, very careful attention to the line is essential. Some 100m into the mine the visibility will improve to 20m or more.

The three **visible entrances** are suitable for cavern diving under the supervision of more experienced divers. They open directly to a substantial void only a few metres beneath the water surface. Starting from the first (south-westerly) entrance, a thick 6mm polypropylene line runs high in the tunnel, looping initially towards the middle entrance. From here, a separate line leads from the surface to split only a few metres inside, with both lines continuing deeper into the complex.

The more direct, shallower route is to the left and within a short distance this reaches a large and conspicuous concrete slab on the floor where the line is belayed; the tunnel then trends north-west. Beyond the slab the route becomes spacious with a passage height of between 2m and 3m. The line runs along the left-hand wall and is regularly attached to some old metal spikes some distance from the floor.

As the visibility improves, the passage becomes 5m to 6m wide and the amount of silt on the floor decreases. After a line junction about 150m from the entrance, the main line eventually terminates at a boulder some 200m from dive base. The maximum depth along this route is less than 10m with an average of between 6m and 8m.

The second line from the middle entrance connects with the 150m line junction via a deeper route through some very large chambers.

The five interconnecting and fully submerged **hidden entrances** are not suitable for cavern diving; this is terrain for more advanced practitioners. All five passages descend steeply with thick silt on the floor until at around 14m depth the slope levels off where an open space runs parallel to the surface cliff. Visitors must be extremely wary of the old fence wire that has accumulated in the vicinity of the two south-easternmost entrances. The visibility here is normally poor.

The mine drops to at least 18m depth in this undoubtedly complex area, with the likelihood that many different routes trend into deeper flooded tunnels. Mine surveys dating from 1957 indicate the existence of extensive workings behind the eastern cliff and that these interconnected with the visible entrances. Exploration continues.

Air supplies

Edinburgh Diving Centre,
1 Watson Crescent,
Edinburgh EH11 1HD
Tel: 0131 229 4838
www.edinburghdiving
.co.uk

Emergencies

Emergency contacts:
  see Appendix A
Nearest hyperbaric centre:
  Aberdeen
Nearest hospital:
  Queen Margaret Hospital,
  Whitefield Road,
  Dunfermline KY12 0SU
  Tel: 01383 623623

Further considerations

▶ A drysuit is recommended
▶ A hood and gloves are essential in all seasons
▶ Use a comfortable rucksack to transport your equipment
▶ Wear appropriate footwear – boots or wellingtons with a deep tread
▶ Do not use thin technical dive line underwater
▶ Take a number of personalised clothes peg line markers (small plastic line arrows are impractical on the thick permanent lines)

St Kilda
Outer Hebrides, Scotland

Objective
The majority of sea caves in the British Isles are short and shallow. The exception to this rule lies in the Western Isles of Scotland where St Kilda presents magnificent, challenging opportunities in a truly remote location. St Kilda offers exceptional diving to all levels of ability from cavern diver through to fully certified cave divers; depths from a few metres to 50m or more may be attained here.

Access
A live-aboard charter boat is the norm for diving in this area; landing or camping on the islands requires permission. Given the depth of the water, the vagaries of the British weather and the exposed nature of the region, a visit to St Kilda requires careful planning and execution.

Location
The St Kilda archipelago of four small islands and associated islets and sea stacks lies approximately 100 miles west of the Scottish mainland and about 40 miles beyond the main islands of the Outer Hebrides. Here, the highest sea cliffs in the UK rise sheer from the ocean and make for extremely spectacular scenery.

Topside, St Kilda is Europe's most important seabird breeding site, being home to the world's largest colony of northern gannets and the largest colonies of northern fulmars and Atlantic puffins in the British Isles. Down below, grey seals are abundant and accompany divers at many sites, while dolphins and whales are often sighted. The islands have received many significant designations: National Nature Reserve, Biosphere Reserve, National Scenic Area, Site of Special Scientific Interest, European Community Special Protection Area and in 1986 it was inscribed as Scotland's first World Heritage Site.

The view from the summit of Dùn and the island of Boreray

History
Diving here has been undertaken by adventurous open water divers since 1972, when BSAC member Reg Vallintine coordinated the first diving expedition to the area. Gordon Ridley, a legendary figure in Scottish

diving, became the leading activist on subsequent expeditions, producing an authoritative guide in 1983.

Diving

The spectacular scenery of St Kilda is reflected below water where, predictably, the steep rock walls plunge dramatically into the depths. Walls, gullies, boulders and caves abound; indeed, these are the most dramatic features. Submerged caves and arches occur throughout the islands and the following description covers only the better known sites.

Dive sites

Dùn

CAVERN

Dùn Cave lies midway along the northern side of island of Dùn at 25m depth. The flooded passage is short, closing prohibitively about 15m from the entrance at slightly shallower depth.

The finest site here is the Dùn Natural Arch near the extreme eastern end of the island. This spectacular corridor is about 20m high and 10m wide, extending for some 50m through the island at a depth of between 10m and 15m. An air surface exists over much of the route, but this can be interrupted and become confusing under a south-westerly swell. Even in good conditions this dive demands very careful boat cover.

Nearby lies the renowned and aptly named Sawcut, a deep fissure that offers one of the finest dives imaginable.

Soay

Depth and strong currents

On Soay a short conspicuous cave (cave 1) is situated in the north-western cliffs. Underwater, the passage increases in size, although it is short.

Nearby lies a superb 40m long through-tunnel running beneath the small islet of Am Plastair. The northern entrance is 24m high and 15m wide, narrowing to 8m by 4m wide on the southern face. This area is littered with 15m high boulders and narrow ravines – spectacular terrain for exploration. Am Plastair offers a superb traverse dive, but it is one

Coordinates

Dive site	NGR	Lat/Long
Boreray		
Sgarbhstac	NA 152045	57° 51′ 48.69″ N, 08° 29′ 31.33″ W
Dùn		
Dùn Cave	NF 105975	57° 47′ 50.26″ N, 08° 33′ 36.21″ W
Dùn Natural Arch	NF 108973	57° 47′ 43.09″ N, 08° 33′ 14.69″ W
Sawcut	NF 109972	57° 47′ 42.01″ N, 08° 33′ 10.06″ W
Hirta		
Geo na h-Airde and Geo Oscar	NA 088009	57° 49′ 33.16″ N, 08° 35′ 32.91″ W
Levenish		
Levenish tunnel	NF 134966	57° 47′ 32.21″ N, 08° 30′ 34.08″ W
Soay		
Am Plastair tunnel	NA 059020	57° 49′ 59.87″ N, 08° 38′ 39.42″ W
Kokelaar's Cave	NA 070017	57° 49′ 54.71″ N, 08° 37′ 30.14″ W
Soay cave 1	NA 057016	57° 49′ 47.09″ N, 08° 38′ 49.30″ W
Thompson's Cave	NA 070017	57° 49′ 55.36″ N, 08° 37′ 30.19″ W

that should only be attempted in very calm conditions.

A pair of longer caves may be found on the rocky towering eastern face of Soay. The easiest to locate is Kokelaar's Cave with a conspicuous tall entrance at the base of a prominent dyke or fissure. The opening is 5m wide with a water depth of 12m and may be entered for some 80m to 100m before the airspace ends. A large tunnel at a maximum depth of 4m has been explored for over 100m beyond this point and it is likely that the passage continues much further. The island of Soay is about 250m wide hereabouts and a complete traverse may be possible – but this is extremely committing diving!

The green of Sgarbhstac and the blue of the Am Plastair tunnel

A short distance to the north lies Thompson's Cave, which is also aligned along a prominent crack, but is far less obvious than its neighbour as the entrance is set discreetly at a depth of between 10m and 12m. Within the passage the route ascends to a depth of only 2m at the furthest point, 110m from the entrance. Here, the walls are shoulder-width and the visibility is generally poor; there are no airspaces.

Hirta

The northern coast of Hirta, the main island of St Kilda, possesses a spectacular natural arch – Geo na h-Airde – and nearby a deep cave named Geo Oscar.

Levenish

Some 2.5km east-south-east of Hirta lies the small sea stack of Levenish. A cave can be entered on the northerly facing cliffs about 30m from the easterly tip of the island, where diving in and down the line of a geological weakness reaches a depth of around 24m. Here, a narrow slot leads for 60m through the island; the cleft is about a metre wide and rises partway to within a few metres of the surface.

Even in calm conditions a significant surge runs through the tunnel. The exit on the south-east face is at 8m depth and has been described as a small cauldron – 'an ejection rather than an exit'. Maurice Davidson, who first explored this site in 1983, said that it gave 'the feeling of entering a huge, elongated letter box, glistening in all shades of jewel anemones and with seals playing all around, yet claustrophobic in 40 metre visibility.'

Further considerations

▶ Pay particular regard to diving in confined environments when conditions are challenging
▶ Remember that the nearest recompression chamber is at Fort William on the mainland
▶ Wind speeds are Force 3 or greater for over 85 per cent of the year – and Force 5 and upwards for 30 per cent of the year; the swell varies considerably
▶ Water temperatures are affected by the Gulf Stream, varying from 9°C in May to 13°C in August
▶ The visibility is magnificent; in July and August it is generally between 30m and 50m

Boreray

Just over 6km to the north-east of Hirta lies the island of Boreray. The finest, most acclaimed site here lies just off the extreme southern tip – the submarine arch of Sgarbhstac. This site was first discovered in July 1977 and, in the words of Gordon Ridley, a member of the first team to pass through the arch: 'Seeing tiny humans in 40m visibility gliding through the crystal blue waters of this vast gateway to St Kilda's underworld is an intense and quite unforgettable experience. In poor visibility and rough conditions this dive would probably be terrifying.'

▶ Head down, descending the Levenish tunnel

The top of the arch lies at a depth of 30m, beneath which the walls flare out to meet the seabed at a depth of 50m. The tunnel is about 30m long and 20m wide, with a broad geological dyke running along its base. To dive here and see seals passing through the arch and perhaps swim amid puffins is truly exhilarating. The walls are a mass of sponges, hydroids and anemones, and many divers who have been privileged to swim here have claimed this as one of the finest sites in the world.

Emergencies

Emergency contacts: see Appendix A
Nearest hyperbaric centre: Fort William
Nearest hospital: Belford Hospital, Belford Road, Fort William PH33 6BS
  Tel: 01397 702481

Further reading

RIDLEY, Gordon. *A Diver's Guide to St. Kilda*, BSAC Expeditions Scheme, Glasgow (1983)

RIDLEY, Gordon. *Dive West Scotland, The Diver Guide to Scotland Volume I*, Underwater World Publications, Teddington (1984)

RIDLEY, Gordon. *Dive North West Scotland, The Diver Guide to Scotland Volume II*, Underwater World Publications, Teddington (1985)

Cambrian Slate Mine

Glyn Ceiriog, North Wales

Objective
This short but unusual underwater traverse in Cambrian Slate Mine is appropriate for fully certified cave divers or introductory cave divers during their training in the company of an experienced instructor. All the other tunnels in the mine are only suitable for fully certified cave divers, who can undertake longer and more fascinating penetrations requiring side-mounted equipment.

Access
No formal access procedures are required.

Location
The Cambrian Slate Mine is situated near Glyn Ceiriog, not far from Llangollen in north-east Wales. Park in a small pull-in on the narrow, country lane (SJ 186381); the parking space is very limited, so please be discreet and consider the needs of farmers and other road users. Do not obstruct gates or passing places.

A public footpath heads south from the road down into the woodland and at the foot of the slope a level track curves off to the left. The main route to the entrance is on the left about 50m further on. Here, a steep, muddy and slippery vegetated incline leads for over 30m to the large, imposing entrance in what was once known as Townsend's Quarry.

At the bottom of the final slope an enormous old iron air-receiver (compressed air storage tank), the size of a small submarine, will confirm that you have found the right location. It should have taken about ten minutes to walk from the parking area to the entrance, where you can change and kit up.

History
In this quiet rural backwater, the casual visitor sees little indication of an industrial past and certainly receives no clue as to the village's important mining heritage. Slate production has been an important industry in this region for many hundreds of years, but it was not until the late 1800s that operations commenced underground at the Cambrian Mine. At the peak of the mine's fortunes in the early 1900s, some 4,000 tons of slate were produced by over 100 men.

The industry went into decline after the mid-1930s

INTRO (SUPERVISED)

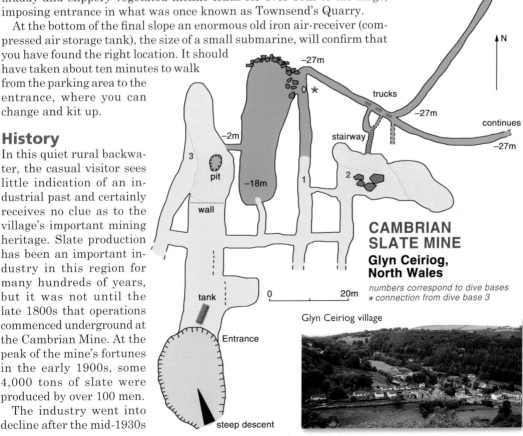

CAMBRIAN
SLATE MINE
**Glyn Ceiriog,
North Wales**
numbers correspond to dive bases
* connection from dive base 3

Glyn Ceiriog village

and the extremely severe winter of 1946/7 proved the final straw, leading to the sudden closure of the mine. In the first week of April 1947 three quarrymen made a lucky escape when snow melt caused dramatic flood-waters to inundate the mine, resulting in a number of loaded wagons being left in the depths. Today, kilometres of tunnels are still accessible both above and below water. Diving exploration commenced here in 2005.

Diving

From the level-floored area in the entrance at the air tank, head under-ground and after approximately 15m take the first stooping-height tunnel on the right. The second passage on the left leads quickly to water and this (Base 1) is the best starting point for a descent into the flooded galleries. Continuing along the dry tunnel to the T-junction and turning left, after 15m reaches a dark, dank, flooded chamber where a wooden structure protrudes just above water level. This is Base 2 and marks the beginning of an underwater stairway descent to the 27m level.

Cambrian Slate Mine: the entrance, kitting up area and dive base

Within a couple of metres from Base 1 locate a line on the right-hand side. Try to disturb the water as little as possible in the pool as any silt cloud will quickly roll down the incline and greatly reduce the visibility, which initially should be at least 10m. Diving carefully onwards, the slope continues at a steady angle until the tunnel levels off and narrows at 27m depth. Mining graffiti can be seen on the walls here.

Just prior to this point, a route can be fol-lowed from a line junction that heads vertically upwards against the right-hand side and passes through an area of pipework and debris to a huge chamber. On the far side an ascent can be made to another dive base (3), although finding this from the daylight entrance is more difficult; it lies to the left of the route to Base 1, turning off opposite the first stooping-height tunnel.

Back at the line junction, continue along the 27m tunnel to a small building on the right-hand side housing a boiler and other machinery and, just beyond, in this colourless world of black and grey, the form of a tram will suddenly take shape. Three of these small wagons are parked exactly where they were abandoned decades ago. Like wreck diving, this is a touch eerie – these subterranean corridors speak volumes from a bygone age.

The rails on the 27m level split here and diverging tunnels continue at the same depth. At the first tram a line leads vertically upwards and connects with Base 2 via the miners' stone stairway. It is strongly recommended that, prior to any attempt at a traverse dive, both routes are examined to ensure the integrity of the dive lines. A pair of 7 litre cylinders should be ample for undertaking the traverse.

The spectacular stairway has drystone walls set to either side and a roof of massive, solid

Coordinates

Dive site	NGR	Lat/Long
Cambrian Slate Mine	SJ 1865 3802	52° 56' 00.15" N, 03° 12' 42.10" W

slabs inclined at a 45 degree angle. This in itself is an amazing sight, cleaved seemingly as smooth as the huge blocks of slate so painstakingly won in the days of the industrial revolution. Air races up the roof like a turbulent freshwater stream that defies gravity, a literal channel of clear and white reflective bubbles. Occasionally, small shards of rock may be dislodged and these carve a distinct zigzag path through the water as they glide gracefully to the floor.

This tunnel, like the rest of the mine, is impregnated with so much history you can imagine scores of miners puffing and panting up the staircase after a long, arduous day toiling in the darkness, to be faced with a weary and a long walk home. Today, every surface is caked in a crumble of granular shale debris or fine silty dust, so be warned – the visibility will be poor on exit, perhaps as little as 1m.

What will also impress any first-time visitor is how incredibly dark and oppressive this mine feels – no matter how powerful your lighting, the mine will readily absorb it.

Air supplies

Frogsborn Diving Centre, Unit 2 Eastwood Court, Hawarden Industrial Park, Manor Lane, Hawarden, Deeside CH5 3QB; tel: 01244 520333; www.frogsborn.com

Emergencies

Emergency contacts: see Appendix A
Nearest hyperbaric centre: Wirral
Nearest hospital: Wrexham Maelor Hospital, Croesnewydd Road, Wrexham LL13 7TD; tel: 01978 291100

Long-forgotten miners' tally marks and an abandoned tram at –27m

The railway in the 27m level

Further considerations

▶ Slate mines can be unstable and Cambrian Slate Mine is only suited to fully certified cave divers; introductory divers should be under direct supervision

▶ Be warned: vehicles may be at risk, so leave as little as possible in them

▶ The route into the mine is strenuous and very slippery – sturdy footwear is essential

▶ The mine entrance has ample room for changing into drysuits and assembling equipment – an old groundsheet or large polythene bag is invaluable for standing on

▶ A hood and gloves are essential in all seasons

▶ Thin technical line should not be used; use nylon line of at least 4mm diameter

▶ The mine is a labyrinth of underwater tunnels, so take ample line markers to avoid confusion

▶ While backmounts can be used, side-mounted configurations are advantageous, if only for their ease of transport

▶ Use a comfortable rucksack to transport your equipment and make two carries rather than struggle with a heavy load

▶ Do not attempt any circuit or traverse from one base to another unless you are certain that a line exists throughout the route

▶ Conservation is as important in mines as it is in caves: ensure that the mine is left clean and tidy

▶ Cambrian Mine lies nearly 300m above sea level and the water temperature is about 7°C

Dinas Silica Mine

Neath Valley, South Wales

Objective
The Dinas Silica Mine is arguably the finest mine diving site in the British Isles, offering exceptional diving to all levels of ability from cavern diver through to fully cave certified with a maximum depth of 23m.

CAVERN

Access
No formal access procedures are required. The land is owned by the Forestry Commission, which has posted 'danger' signs to deter casual and inexperienced visitors from entering the mine.

Location
Dinas Silica Mine is situated near the small village of Pontneddfechan, approximately 19km north-east of Neath in South Wales. An energetic 600m walk in magnificent scenery leads to the mine entrance at 150m altitude; the effort will prove highly rewarding.

From the car park at Dinas Rock (SN 911079), take the prominent path heading in a north-easterly direction which gradually ascends to the left-hand side of the impressive main rock face. The route quickly becomes steep with smooth, bare rock surfaces and these can be slippery when wet. After a height gain of 40m the path levels off on a grassy continuation along the ridge. Around 500m from the car park, bear right and follow the obvious path down to the Sychryd valley where the brick-walled, walk-in mine entrance will be found on the left, just before reaching the river.

History
Silica rock, or quartzite – a very hard form of altered sandstone, was first extracted in the area at the start of the Industrial Revolution in the late eighteenth century. The rock was transported to the valley bottom and crushed to powder, then made into refractory (fire) bricks that were used to line the walls of iron and steel furnaces; such was their quality and reputation, that they were exported as far afield as Russia.

The techniques of extraction and transportation varied over the years and in the final stage of the mine's working life the rock was conveyed to the crushing plant by an aerial bucketway. Some of these containers may be seen just inside the main lower entrance. The mine was abandoned in 1964 and the lower levels, driven well below the adjacent River Sychryd,

The entrance to
Dinas Silica Mine

quickly filled with water and form today's diving challenge. Diving here commenced in the early 1970s and today this is the most popular underground diving site in the British Isles.

Diving

The normal dive base is approximately 80m from the main entrance and reached by easy, straightforward walking along a spacious gallery. Here you can see evidence of the type of mining undertaken, with two contrasting approaches to extraction. In the upper, dry 'Victorian' sections (to the left near the entrance) the older pillar and stall method is immediately apparent. In essence, the miners removed all the rock that they safely could, leaving roughly hewn pillars to support the roof. Below water level, in the '20th century' sector, straight and level tunnels were driven that left more rock in the supporting walls, a more structurally stable approach.

Training in the dive base pool

At the dive base the roof dips into the water at an angle of about 30 degrees – a clear indication of the local geology, where the rock strata inclines consistently to the south throughout the workings. Indeed, quite apart from having an insight to mineral extraction techniques, divers can also glean something of the fascinating geology, for example, several small faults are clearly identifiable as they intersect the mine levels.

The trend of the principal tunnels is roughly east to west. These levels run parallel to one another and become progressively deeper down the dip. Starting from dry ground at the dive base, some six interconnecting levels are

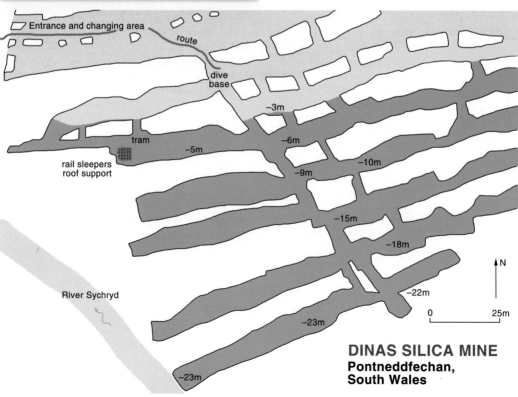

Entrance and changing area

route

dive base

−3m

tram

−5m

−6m

rail sleepers roof support

−9m

−10m

−15m

−18m

River Sychryd

−22m

N

0   25m

−23m

DINAS SILICA MINE
Pontneddfechan, South Wales

Coordinates

Dive site	NGR	Lat/Long
Dinas Silica Mine	SN 917080	51° 45' 35.87" N, 03° 34' 15.28" W

passed en route to the deepest point at –23m. Openings occur at irregular intervals along the length of each level; these windows connect one level to the next and vary in size, but are generally smaller than the tunnels which mostly have dimensions of over 2.5m high by 5m wide. The only exception is the Main Tunnel, which runs in a straight line from the dive base to the deepest point in the mine, maintaining spacious proportions along its length. This grid-like layout makes for a very stable structure, albeit a complex one.

The water surface in the mine lies at approximately 150m above sea level and has no significant fluctuation (less than a metre) at any season. The mine remains unaffected by severe weather conditions and presents an ideal venue at times when all other cave diving is washed out. Visibility is normally excellent, often 25m or more, and the temperature is fairly constant at between 7°C to 8°C year-round. As with any cave or mine environment all the flooded tunnels have a dusting of silt but, while this may be disturbed by diver activity or poor technique, it settles fairly rapidly and, given that the tunnels are large, bad visibility is rare. Several groups of divers may be accommodated at one time and visibility will nevertheless remain in excess of 10m the following day.

First-time visitors should restrict their activities to the shallow levels, where lines are generally well laid and in good condition. Diving to and along a specific level is relatively straightforward, but trying to navigate a route down through the connecting windows can be complicated. Visitors should be prudent in their dive planning and proceed according to their limits. While many of the tunnels have lines installed, it is stressed that all should be checked before they are relied upon by a diver. Using thin

The remains of an abandoned tram, now used as a line belay

technical line is strongly discouraged and any left in place will be removed by later, more experienced divers.

Relatively few industrial artefacts can be found below water, although a near-complete tram may be seen in the shallowest tunnel trending west from the normal dive base. With its exceptional visibility, this is an ideal place to take a powerful hand-held light, which will reveal a fabulous world of rich golden browns.

Diving over silica rubble

Further considerations

▶ The public car park is unsupervised and vehicles may be at risk, so leave as little as possible in them
▶ The car park is locked at the end of the afternoon, so plan to return early
▶ Mobile phone reception is normally available at the mine entrance
▶ A hood and gloves are essential in all seasons
▶ The mine is a veritable labyrinth of underwater tunnels, so take ample clothes peg line markers to avoid confusion
▶ Use a comfortable rucksack to transport your equipment and make two carries rather than struggle with a heavy load
▶ The entrance has ample room for changing into drysuits and assembling equipment
▶ Conservation is important in mines as well as caves: please ensure that the mine is left clean and tidy

Air supplies

Bristol Channel Diving, Unit 3, The Timber Yard, East Moors Road, Cardiff CF24 5EE
  Tel: 029 2046 4846; www.bristolchanneldiving.co.uk

Emergencies

Emergency contacts: see Appendix A
Nearest hyperbaric centre: Plymouth
Nearest hospital: Morriston Hospital, Heol Maes Eglwys, Morriston, Swansea SA6 6NL
  Tel: 01792 702222

Further reading

PRICE, Duncan (comp). *Welsh Sump Index*, Cave Diving Group, 3rd edn (2006)

Llygad Llwchwr

Trapp, West Wales

Objective

Llygad Llwchwr is an ideal site for introductory cave divers that also allows fully fledged cave divers to savour an extended penetration using side-mount techniques. The cave contains hundreds of metres of beautifully decorated and varied stream passages interspersed with a series of shallow sumps with, up to the fifth sump, a maximum depth of 8m. This is not a cavern diving site.

INTRO

Backmount

Access

No permission is required.

Location

Llygad Llwchwr – the Eye of the Loughor – is a discreet resurgence at the western extremity of the Brecon Beacons National Park. It is located just over 6km north-east of Ammanford and 2km south-east of the small village of Trapp. The approach road, a single-track lane, crosses some splendid countryside with a spectacular view of Carreg Cennen Castle.

It is a relatively straightforward 300m, ten-minute walk to the entrance from the parking area (SN 6716 1773; 51° 50′ 32.67″ N, 03° 55′ 46.35″ W). Cross the stile and follow the waymarked footpath pointing across the field in a north-westerly direction. Having passed an impressively large crater on the left-hand side, the route heads west and after 200m gradually descends to the cave. A low dam wall will be spotted outside the resurgence where an area of flat ground is ideal for kitting up.

The weir at Llygad Llwchwr and the entrance squeeze

History

Llygad Llwchwr was first explored by intrepid Welshman Thomas Jenkins in the early 1840s. The original small, very awkward, dry cave entrance is set a few metres above the resurgence and this is still used by groups of non-diving cavers. Some of the water emerging at the substantial resurgence originates from around 8km to the east and over 1km of complex passage has been explored above and below water.

Until 2003 all diving commenced deep inside the cave and involved a difficult portage because the upwelling resurgence was completely blocked by debris at a depth of 3m (the debris had been deliberately thrown into the hole by the local water authority in an attempt to concentrate the flow into an extraction pipe). After a lengthy project the spacious shaft was cleared and today divers can swim directly from the surface into the cave.

Diving

First-time visitors exploring the dry cave network might be forgiven for becoming confused with the orientation and hydrology in Llygad Llwchwr. It is a strange place, where twists and

turns frequently leave people perplexed with the direction of the streamway and how each part connects together though the sumps. However, from a diver's point of view, entering directly from the resurgence, it is an easy matter of following the dive lines and the flowing waterway.

A fixed dive line is normally attached to the left-hand wall of the resurgence pool about a metre below the surface. At 6m depth a low restriction – 1m wide by 50cm high – requires care to negotiate. Take a good look at this as you enter, in particular at the line position, as on exit this obstacle will be passed in greatly reduced visibility.

The small opening leads immediately into a larger tunnel with a sandy-cum-muddy silt floor. The route gradually ascends until it meets a rock wall where the passage abruptly surfaces to air in the First River Chamber. This dive, from the outside world to the inner cave, is only 30m, but it will feel longer when leaving as the formerly clear water will contain a silt cloud, reducing visibility to less than an arm's length for the entire distance.

The First River Chamber offers a welcome break, somewhere to regroup and reappraise. Above thigh-deep water, your lights will reveal a tall fissure with stark brown walls. To the right lies a scramble up and over boulders into a small, complicated dry passage

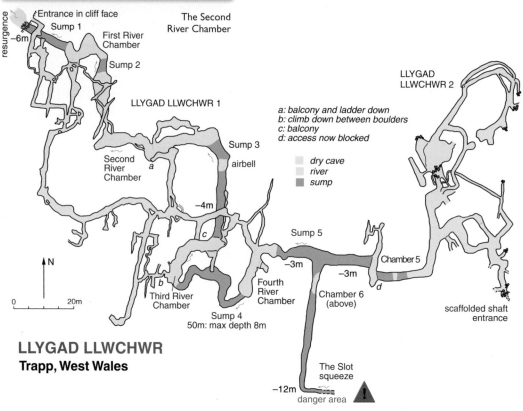

LLYGAD LLWCHWR
Trapp, West Wales

a: balcony and ladder down
b: climb down between boulders
c: balcony
d: access now blocked

dry cave
river
sump

Coordinates

Dive site	NGR	Lat/Long
Llygad Llwchwr	SN 6687 1781	51° 50′ 34.60″ N, 03° 56′ 02.08″ W

which provides a possible exit via the dry entrance in the event of an emergency.

Continue in the water to the next dive line, 10m beyond, where the tunnel turns right and a very short submersion – less than 3m – takes you to a long section of deep water canal. A heavy green line has been installed here to serve as a 'pulling line', a real aid should the flow be strong. This is an intriguing part of the cave: it is worth taking the time to appreciate the rock formations and, high overhead, some beautiful stalactites and calcite draperies.

Shortly after combating a partially submerged wall-like rib of rock, the passage rises to provide a dry, sandy floor where you leave the water. This is the Second River Chamber, and here the eagle-eyed visitor may pick out another 'dry' cavers' passage some 3m up the wall on the right. With fins in hand, walk along the obvious dry tunnel and carefully negotiate the watery ditch to, a couple of metres further on, the start of the third sump. This is an easy straightforward passage less than 50m long, with a maximum depth of 4m and an air surface one-third of the way through.

The cave is wonderfully sculpted throughout, but entering the Third River Chamber is impressive as it is very different from anything that has gone before. You emerge from Sump 3 in deep water in a mini-whirlpool with a strong flow rushing towards you. Carefully remove your fins and wade upstream into another large tunnel; the fourth dive starts in a spacious pool where an orange line is secured to the left-hand wall. This dive

An elliptical passage in Sump 4

is about 50m long and reaches a depth of 8m at a low gravel restriction three-quarters of the way through. Pass this with the line in your left hand – the slope rises uninterrupted to the lofty Fourth River Chamber, which has more stalactite decorations.

A pair of 7 litre cylinders will be more than adequate to comfortably reach this point. Given the poor visibility that will accompany the team all the way out, this is a good place to consider air reserves and the time. If you choose to see more, the sump beyond may be followed for a further 50m to Chamber 6.

Chamber 5 lies off to the left, but it is a place to avoid. This small chamber was once the site of a major underwater excavation which eventually yielded a significant extension to the cave system via a very intimidating, extremely silty restriction. Unfortunately this route is no longer passable as it is completely blocked by silt. Instead, Llygad Llwchwr 2 has its own separate dry entrance (see survey), which was dug out by local cavers in 2010.

The layout of the fixed lines may change in this sector of the cave. There is always a line to Chamber 6, but this furthermost chamber should mark the limit of any penetration as a short distance beyond it lies another major underwater excavation. Be warned: this entire section of the cave is very silty and may be unstable. The cave effectively terminates at this point.

The journey through the five sumps to Chamber 6 and a slow careful exit will require perhaps three hours inside the cave. You will emerge with a sense of exhilaration and wonder; Llygad Llwchwr epitomises all the magic of cave exploration.

Always check the weather forecast before planning a visit. Diving is possible during all seasons, but given the high rainfall in this westerly location, be prepared for disappointment if the weather is or has recently been inclement. However, unlike many caves that flood rapidly after heavy rain or snowmelt, Llygad Llwchwr does not respond dramatically. Providing that the weather, flow and visibility are good, there is little need for concern about sudden or unexpected flash flooding while inside the cave. Reassuringly, each of the chambers leading to the Fourth River Chamber has a dry exit route to the surface, although this is difficult for an inexperienced diver to navigate and virtually impossible when also carrying equipment. This upper cave never floods.

Air supplies

Bristol Channel Diving, Unit 3, The Timber Yard, East Moors Road, Cardiff CF24 5EE
Tel: 029 2046 4846
www.bristolchanneldiving.co.uk

Emergencies

Emergency contacts: see Appendix A
Nearest hyperbaric centre: Plymouth
Nearest hospital: Prince Philip Hospital, Bryngwyn Mawr, Dafen, Llanelli SA14 8QF; tel: 01554 756567

Further reading

PRICE, Duncan (comp). Welsh Sump Index, Cave Diving Group, 3rd edn (2006)

The streamway in the Fourth River Chamber

Further considerations

▶ Keep to the footpath and close gates
▶ The cave is a popular location for walkers, so consider the security of items left on the surface
▶ The area has a poor mobile phone signal
▶ Side-mounted equipment is essential
▶ A spare mask and a rudimentary tool kit are recommended
▶ Take a helmet and ample lighting for three or more hours
▶ The water temperature is around 8°C

Porth yr Ogof

Ystradfellte, South Wales

Objective
Porth yr Ogof offers several points of entry to diveable water. It is an ideal place to sample elemental cavern diving with a maximum depth of 4m, to progress from a basic introduction to cave diving that has a maximum depth of 6m, and to savour some extended penetrations as a fully fledged cave diver utilising the specialised techniques of side-mounting. In addition, visitors may wish to indulge in a brief experience of 'dry' caving, for which the site is renowned.

Access
Porth yr Ogof is leased and managed by the Brecon Beacons National Park Authority and the car park is supervised seven days a week (except Christmas Day) by an attendant; a small fee is payable. No permission is required for diving.

Location
Porth yr Ogof lies at the heart of the Brecon Beacons National Park near the small village of Ystradfellte at 250m above sea level on the course of the River Mellte, a tributary of the River Neath. It is one of the most frequented and popular caves in the British Isles, extending to over 2.25km of passages of which approximately half are only accessible to experienced cave divers.

The Tradesman's Entrance and Main Entrance to Porth yr Ogof

History
Known for many hundreds of years, Porth yr Ogof has been romantically described by many visiting travellers. While the dry cave was first systematically explored and recorded in the 1930s, it was not until the late 1960s and '70s that the lengthy underwater sections were charted.

Diving
Cavern diving takes place at two points: the Resurgence Pool and the White Horse Pool. The Resurgence Pool lies approximately 300m down-valley from the car park on a good gravel path (except for the final 20m) and the White Horse Pool is situated just inside the large Main Entrance to the cave. Line-laying practice and general scuba activities may also be undertaken a few metres further down-river from the Resurgence at the Meadow or Blue Pool. The upstream network of Porth yr Ogof, accessed at the Tradesman's Entrance (reached by turning right at the bottom of the path down to the Main Entrance), is popular with cave divers using side-mounted equipment. Additional dry entrances are used by cavers.

The riverbed is dry much of the time, however, the sheer volume of water passing down the valley and through this spectacular cave may occasionally render all access impossible. Equally important is the consideration that the water level of the River

Mellte can rise dramatically in a short space of time; it is for good reason that the river is thus named – the translation of the Welsh word *mellte* is lightning. Consulting a weather forecast and using extreme prudence are essential. Gauging the water level can be difficult and it is best to take local advice – as a rule of thumb, diving is strongly discouraged if the river is flowing more than ankle deep into the very prominent Main Entrance to the cave.

The temperature of the water can fluctuate between 3°C and 4°C in winter months, but reach 12°C or even 14°C at the height of summer. Visibility also varies considerably and, as the river sweeps in all manner of debris – silt, leaves and even whole trees – each visit must involve a careful appraisal before and during the course of the dive.

Porth yr Ogof offers opportunities for training as well as cavern and full cave dives.

Cavern diving

The Resurgence Pool has been the site of many non-diving fatalities; it is easy to become disorientated underwater so take care, even when undertaking a cavern dive.

Access to the water from the rocky ledges outside the cave must involve some thought and planning. The outfall is short and fast-flowing at this point and the boulders are smooth, slippery and strenuous to negotiate in full kit. Visitors should consider the flow conditions (and weather) very carefully; the water level may be too high to permit safe entry.

Under low flow conditions a small air surface extends back into the 'dry' cave upstream. However, this breathable airspace is of very limited extent both vertically and horizontally, whereas below water the tunnel is more spacious with a depth of slightly more than 4m. Be aware that this area contains a lot of potentially hazardous flood debris, especially in the large recess on the right-hand (eastern) side. A cautious examination in good visibility may reveal anything from lost or discarded wellington boots to tree trunks or wire netting.

The dive from the surface to the inner cave is less than 30m, though depending upon the visibility this can seem altogether longer. Surfacing in the darkness of the cave is an amazing feeling: the body's senses tune into a completely different environment where the only noise is the burbling stream running over cobbles

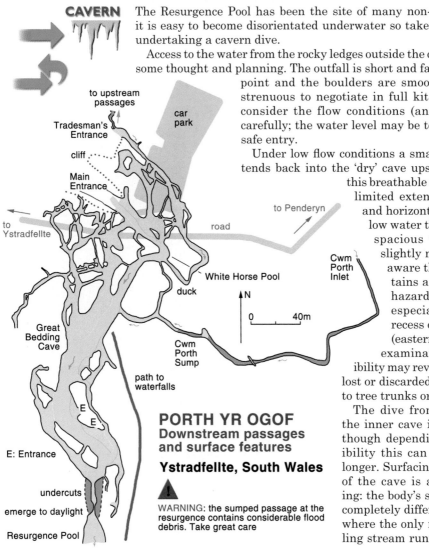

CAVERN

to upstream passages

Tradesman's Entrance

cliff

Main Entrance

to Ystradfellte

car park

road

to Penderyn

White Horse Pool

duck

N

0   40m

Cwm Porth Inlet

Great Bedding Cave

Cwm Porth Sump

path to waterfalls

E
E

E: Entrance

undercuts

emerge to daylight

Resurgence Pool

PORTH YR OGOF
Downstream passages
and surface features

Ystradfellte, South Wales

⚠

WARNING: the sumped passage at the resurgence contains considerable flood debris. Take great care and exhaled breaths fill the air with mist. Turning to view the route just traversed reveals a deep blue light filtering through the water. The dive may not be long, but this is a very atmospheric site.

Back underwater, the dark limestone walls frame the return to light. Trout, perhaps 20cm or more long, and other small bullhead fish are common and the experience provides a unique insight to the nature of British caves.

The White Horse Pool is situated in the twilight zone just inside the Main Entrance, where the main passage turns right. The pool is aptly named after the conspicuous shape of a white horse (or, some say, a giraffe) fashioned by the water in a band of pure white calcite rock facing you on the wall. Care must be exercised on the 30m approach to the pool as the floor consists of unconsolidated stream-washed cobbles: watch your step. Divers opting for a splash here may find that they have an audience of schoolchildren standing close by, as the poolside is part of a 'wild', educational tour of the cave.

Underwater, the pool descends to 2.5m in a very spacious, well-sculpted tunnel with varying visibility. Owing to caver traffic upstream or after rainfall, visibility will reduce to 2m or less, but under quiet, drought conditions or in the depths of a winter freeze, visibility can exceed 5m. It is rare to find hazardous or, indeed, any flood debris here and, as a substantial air surface lies overhead throughout the section, there is little risk of anything other than momentary disorientation due to silt disturbance. It is a great place for elementary line-laying practice and, if you rise to the water surface, you will be pleasantly surprised to see a sparkling array of flowstone or dripstone calcite deposits above you.

This downstream tunnel extends in a westerly direction for the best part of 50m, before shallowing to less than 30cm – so you cannot become lost and a swim back on the surface is always possible.

Porth yr Ogof Resurgence

In summer sunshine the tranquil Resurgence Pool appears compellingly attractive for swimming. However, many people have drowned here, so do not be deceived: the notice boards indicate the maximum flood level, which is revealing.

The Resurgence

Cave diving

FULL

Backmount

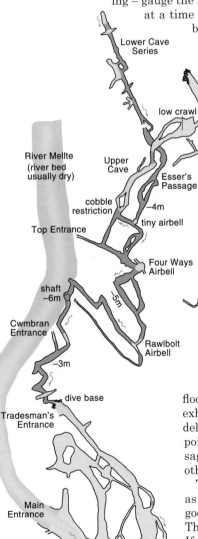

While conventional open water configurations may be appropriate for cavern diving at the Resurgence and the White Horse Pool, all other sections of the cave require specialised side-mounted equipment and appropriate training. The extensive underwater tunnel leading upstream from the Tradesman's Entrance is not a suitable environment for the inexperienced; only fully certified cave divers should enter this area. Apart from those named here, all the other entrances and submerged sections in this cave system are extremely restricted and should not be attempted.

UK-trained cave divers will find that Porth yr Ogof's upstream tunnels offer one of the finest dives in the British Isles. However, while reasonable-sized groups may operate at the cavern diving sites, activities conducted from the Tradesman's Entrance should be undertaken in pairs or solo.

At first sight, entering the boulder-obstructed rising will appear challenging: the area is restricted and the outflowing current can be unnerving – gauge the flow very carefully. Entry must be made cautiously, one at a time – it is important not to drop any equipment, as it will be swept into a restricted plughole of tumultuous, white foaming water that means it is both lost to view and difficult, if not impossible, to recover.

A stout and robust permanent line starts just inside the entrance in a metre or so depth. Beyond, the passage becomes a lovely phreatic tunnel slightly less than 2m in diameter, which wends its way up-valley at a shallow depth. A number of airbells are situated along the route, but only the more observant will spot these.

At a junction some 40m from base, adjacent to a bank of leaf debris, a line ascends steeply to the left. This is the route to the Cwmbran Entrance, a passage restricted in size and frequently blocked with flood debris. Continue along the main line, where the cave exhibits some superb oval sections. At approximately 80m a delightful, short circular shaft drops to 6m and is the deepest point in this sump; thereafter, a section of hobbit-sized passages heads on and at 150m from base leads steeply up another shaft to a small air surface known as Rawlbolt Airbell.

The original explorers' metal bolt that was inserted here as a line belay has long since corroded and gone, but it is a good place to stand, neck deep, and reassess air reserves. This is frequently the turning point for first-time visitors. If any water is flowing down the valley outside the cave, the

PORTH YR OGOF
Upstream passages

Ystradfellte,
South Wales

Coordinates

Entrance	NGR	Lat/Long
Main Entrance	SN 9281 1241	51° 48' 00.91" N, 03° 33' 20.99" W
Resurgence Pool	SN 9272 1221	51° 47' 53.62" N, 03° 33' 25.49" W
Tradesman's Entrance	SN 9284 1245	51° 48' 02.29" N, 03° 33' 19.72" W

Further considerations

► There is no mobile phone signal at the cave, but the attendant's hut contains an emergency telephone
► Limited on-site facilities include a basic toilet building, changing screens and a very small shop
► The paths are rocky, steep and slippery: use a comfortable rucksack to transport your equipment and make two carries rather than struggle with a heavy load
► A hood is required in all seasons, but gloves are not essential during the summer
► The Resurgence and the White Horse Pool have no permanent lines as they would be destroyed by floods: nylon or sinking lines should be 4mm diameter and belayed at regular intervals using snoopy loops
► Clothes peg line markers are required for the cave upstream from the Tradesman's Entrance

chamber will be cramped. Remember that air in minute airbells such as this can rapidly become depleted of oxygen: keep your regulator in your mouth.

With sufficient diving gas, the next major landmark is Four Ways Airbell, approximately 50m further in. This has a more substantial air surface, with a trickle of water splashing in from a heavily calcited fissure overhead. Again, it is difficult to get out of the water as it is deep.

Less than 10m beyond lies a significant junction where the ongoing routes are both smaller. To the left a line leads to the diminutive, heavily silted and intimidating Top Entrance which, not surprisingly, is rarely used. To the right a strong flow emerges from a smaller tunnel, but be aware that the line in this relatively clean-washed passage is regularly damaged in high water. Approximately 40m from Four Ways Airbell another prominent junction is reached where the river emerges from the right; a tiny airbell (easily missed) is directly overhead, which is just about big enough for two divers to stand and talk.

This marks the start of Esser's Passage and the Lower Cave Series – the passage to the left is the route to the Upper Cave Series, which lies beyond a cobble restriction some 8m further on. This is a confusing part of the cave as some of the water emerging from Esser's Passage heads west, initially towards the Upper Cave Series, meaning that this last 8m section flows downstream. Few people venture to either Esser's Passage or the Upper Cave.

Air supplies

Bristol Channel Diving, Unit 3, The Timber Yard, East Moors Road, Cardiff CF24 5EE
Tel: 029 2046 4846
www.bristolchanneldiving.co.uk

Emergencies

Emergency contacts: see Appendix A
Nearest hyperbaric centre: Plymouth
Nearest hospital: Morriston Hospital, Heol Maes Eglwys, Morriston, Swansea SA6 6NL
Tel: 01792 702222

Further reading

FARR, Martyn. *The Secret World of Porth yr Ogof*, Gomer, Llandysul (1998)
PRICE, Duncan (comp). *Welsh Sump Index*, Cave Diving Group, 3rd edn (2006)
STRATFORD, Tim. *Caves of South Wales*, Cordee, Leicester (1995)

Beyond Rawlbolt Airbell in upstream Porth yr Ogof

Pwll-y-Cwm

Clydach Gorge, South Wales

FULL

Backmount

Objective

Pwll-y-Cwm only offers very limited potential for a cavern dive, but a significant and committing 650m long and 23m deep dive may be made into the hillside, eventually entering the cave of Daren Cilau. Anyone contemplating this major undertaking should be fully cave certified and proficient in side-mount techniques. As well as extensive diving experience, caving ability is also required to tackle this site.

Access

No permission is required.

Location

Pwll-y-Cwm is a prominent resurgence in the bed of the River Clydach, situated between Gilwern and Brynmawr in South Wales, and is the main rising for two major caves that lie beneath Llangattock Mountain to the north. Park your vehicle either in a layby on the A465 Heads of the Valleys road almost opposite the Drum & Monkey public house, or near the pub itself (gained via the parallel 'old road' running through Blackrock).

Immediately adjacent to the pub a prominent footpath leads south beneath the A465 down to the Devil's Bridge. Cross the river to the south bank and walk upstream for 80m. The resurgence, in the middle of the river, is protected by a low retaining wall which prevents debris from being washed into the flooded shaft in times of high water. The walk from the nearest parking area should take no more than six minutes and the pool has plenty of dry ground alongside it for kitting up.

Scheduled roadworks may alter the parking at this site, but the footpath to Devil's Bridge will be kept open.

The resurgence pool of Pwll-y-Cwm in the bed of the River Clydach. When the flooded shaft was dug open, a dam was constructed on the upstream side to prevent debris being washed back in

History

Pwll-y-Cwm is the principal resurgence for the internationally acclaimed caves Agen Allwedd and Daren Cilau. A dive was attempted here in 1961, but the flooded shaft proved to be completely blocked by debris at a few metres' depth. A route into the mountain was discovered in 1974 when Martyn Farr dived the nearby restricted Elm Hole. He subsequently explored the tunnel from both Elm Hole and Daren Cilau and connected them in 1986.

Sporadic attempts to clear the true resurgence had begun in 1985, but the project did not reach fruition until 1993 when Duncan Price

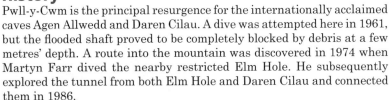

became the first person to pass between Elm Hole and Pwll-y-Cwm. Considerable engineering skills, a vast amount of manpower and the novel technique of using an air-lift to remove gravel were involved in opening the resurgence. It is interesting to reflect that over 10m depth of debris and countless tons of rocks have been removed from this hole to create the access we now enjoy.

Diving

The upwelling water emerges from a spacious shaft which leads to a steeply descending silt- and rubble-covered floor at 12m depth. The

PWLL-Y-CWM
Clydach Gorge, South Wales

Pwll-y-Cwm | main road | Elm Hole | squeeze | gravel squeeze −17m | −23m (max depth) | Daren Cilau dive base

0   100m   EXTENDED ELEVATION

tunnel retains substantial proportions as it slopes down to an abrupt restriction at −17m. Diving to this point is a straightforward cavern dive, but the squeeze and everything beyond requires a side-mounted configuration – it is a place only for highly experienced, fully certified cave divers.

The route forward is easily detected by the flow, which emerges over clean-washed gravel beneath rounded and smooth rock walls. Divers going through the flat-out squeeze must install their own line from the surface to beyond the gravel restriction and note that it frequently requires excavation in order to pass through.

Now at 18m depth, pay close attention to the lines – one leads to the extremely constricted neighbouring cave of Elm Hole and the other towards Daren Cilau.

The committing gravel squeeze at −17m

Both destinations are highly committing undertakings and thorough research and planning should be made before attempting to visit either. An insight to the nature of Elm Hole may be gained by walking a few metres from Pwll-y-Cwm down the northern bank of the Clydach to look at the entrance. This is not a pleasant dive site!

The major, underwater tunnel leading to Daren Cilau reaches its maximum depth of around 23m within 100m of the squeeze, but does not become significantly shallower until beyond 250m. This point is about halfway through the sump in terms of air consumption. The total distance from the surface in Pwll-y-Cwm to air in Daren Cilau is 650m. The water temperature is 8°C and the visibility is rarely better than 2m year-round.

Established thinking is that divers should not attempt to make the through-dive to Daren Cilau unless they are familiar with the dry cave system beyond – in the event of equipment problems preventing a safe return dive, visitors should be capable of making their own exit via the dry cave, rather than initiating a rescue callout. This would entail at least four hours of gruelling caving, assuming that you know the route, plus a 4km walk over the hill to return to your vehicle.

Air supplies

Bristol Channel Diving, Unit 3, The Timber Yard, East Moors Road, Cardiff CF24 5EE
Tel: 029 2046 4846
www.bristolchanneldiving.co.uk

Emergencies

Emergency contacts: see Appendix A
Nearest hyperbaric centre: Plymouth
Nearest hospital: Nevill Hall Hospital, Brecon Road, Abergavenny NP7 7EG; tel: 01873 732732

Further reading

FARR, Martyn. *Darkworld – The Secrets of Llangattock Mountain*, Gomer, Llandysul (1997)
PRICE, Duncan (comp). *Welsh Sump Index*, Cave Diving Group, 3rd edn (2006)

Coordinates

Dive site	NGR	Lat/Long
Pwll-y-Cwm	SO 2149 1244	51° 48′ 17.90″ N, 03° 08′ 24.92″ W

Further considerations

► Given the openness of the dive base, consider the security of any clothes or bags left on the surface
► The water flowing down the River Clydach may be polluted. However, although the water emerging from the cave looks brown and dirty, it is merely stained with natural tannins derived from distant peat-covered moors

White Lady Cave

Neath Valley, South Wales

Objective

INTRO

White Lady Cave, a large flood resurgence at the head of the Neath Valley, connects with a deep chasm up-valley known locally as Cwm Pwll-y-Rhyd or The Abyss. The site offers a shallow through-dive of some 45m and a maximum depth of 5m in large passage, suitable for introductory cave divers, with the option of climbing to the surface at the far end. This distance and depth may not appear unduly challenging, but the spectacular geography of the locality and the general cleanliness of the cave makes White Lady well worth a visit.

Access

A nominal goodwill fee is required to cross the land, payable at Blaen Nedd Isaf Farm at the end of the single-track lane, 500m due north from the parking area.

Location

The approach to White Lady Cave from the parking area at Bridge Cave (SN 912140) involves a scenic trek of about 400m that takes ten to fifteen minutes. Shorter routes may appear viable on the map, but this is the easiest, safest and, most importantly, the agreed access route. The path is very uneven and the rocks, particularly in the gorge down-valley from Cwm Pwll-y-Rhyd, are very slippery.

From the car park, step over the two stiles on the eastern bank of the river and follow the obvious path south down the valley. After 150m a hollow against the cliff face to the left marks where the water sinks; hopefully, any flowing water in the riverbed disappears here and beyond this point the bed remains dry. Some 100m later the path, still on the east bank, veers up a slope to the left, away from the river. Follow the path over the top of a small bluff (an ascent of less than 10m), then descend carefully beyond. Do not follow the valley bottom as the route is impassable, being blocked by the impressive chasm of Cwm Pwll-y-Rhyd, visible to the right (SN 9114 1380; 51° 48′ 43.91″ N, 03° 34′ 49.86″ W). Follow the floor of the dry valley over another stile, through a very slippery, muddy gorge-like section, until a 2.5m vertical drop brings you directly to the obvious White Lady Cave on the right. A small trickle normally issues from the entrance.

The dive base in White Lady Cave

History

White Lady Cave and Cwm Pwll-y-Rhyd have been known locally for hundreds of years. The first diving connection between the two was achieved in June 1960 by Charles George and Brian de Graff, who used rebreather equipment. Further extensions in the main side tunnel were made by John Parker in 1968 and Martyn Farr during the 1970s.

Diving

The prevalent water conditions underground may be assessed by examining the river beneath the bridge at the car park: if water is flowing, access to the White Lady dive base may be difficult or impossible and

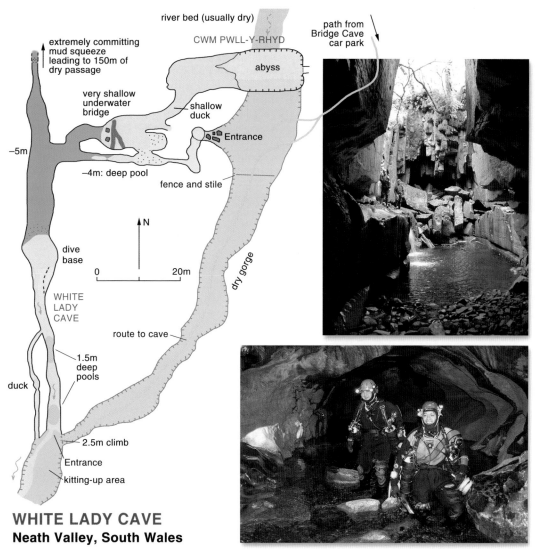

river bed (usually dry)

CWM PWLL-Y-RHYD

path from Bridge Cave car park

extremely committing mud squeeze leading to 150m of dry passage

abyss

very shallow underwater bridge

shallow duck

Entrance

−5m

−4m: deep pool

fence and stile

↑N

dive base

0   20m

dry gorge

WHITE LADY CAVE

route to cave

1.5m deep pools

duck

2.5m climb

Entrance

kitting-up area

WHITE LADY CAVE
Neath Valley, South Wales

a reconnaissance is therefore advisable. If water is flowing more than ankle deep from the White Lady Cave entrance, reaching the sump may be difficult; if it is knee-deep, reaching the sump will be impossible. Also consider that water levels may change rapidly – flood debris in the system indicates that levels can rise by more than 4m – so take close account of weather conditions.

Most of the kit preparation and checks may be undertaken outside the cave, as the final approach to the dive base consists of traversing an easy, clean-washed walking-sized tunnel. Some 70m of passage, including two sections of waist- to chest-deep water, leads to a fine circular chamber and a spacious sump.

Conduct the dive by following the right-hand (eastern) wall. Within 10m the cobble slope bottoms out at a depth of 5m and the nature of the passage

The entrances to Cwm Pwll-y-Rhyd and White Lady Cave

Coordinates

Dive site	NGR	Lat/Long
White Lady Cave	SN 9111 1368	51° 48′ 40.01″ N, 03° 34′ 51.29″ W

Air supplies

Bristol Channel Diving,
Unit 3, The Timber Yard,
East Moors Road,
Cardiff CF24 5EE
Tel: 029 2046 4846
www.bristolchannel
diving.co.uk

Emergencies

Emergency contacts:
see Appendix A
Nearest hyperbaric centre:
Plymouth
Nearest hospital: Morriston
Hospital, Heol Maes
Eglwys, Morriston,
Swansea SA6 6NL
Tel: 01792 702222

Further reading

PRICE, Duncan (comp).
Welsh Sump Index,
Cave Diving Group,
3rd edn (2006)

changes to become a fine circular tunnel over 3m in diameter where the visibility is generally about 2m. Despite a dusting of very fine silt, there is relatively little mud or debris along the main tunnel and, even after several divers have passed through, visibility is not significantly reduced.

Pass a corner after about 20m into the flooded passage – the tunnel continues to the right. Following the wall closely, after a further 15m it may be possible to surface to air directly ahead unless this is prevented by accumulated flood debris. A few metres before this point the normal route to Cwm Pwll-y-Rhyd consists of a spacious, clean-washed, cobble-floored tunnel towards the left which is easily negotiable.

After a further 20m this leads to a boulder restriction at floor level, where a direct ascent can be made to a wide lake cavern that is often festooned with floating debris. Dry land (and a safe, dry route back to the surface) lies a few metres to the right, while ahead, through a low airspace on the left, a short stretch of waterway reaches the foot of the Cwm Pwll-y-Rhyd chasm. It is possible to regain the surface from this point, though the climb is more exposed and slippery than the one at the entrance to White Lady Cave.

A side passage leads off the main sump in the left-hand (western) wall; this is low and very muddy and should be avoided as, within a short distance, it degenerates to extremely claustrophobic proportions and the ensuing retreat will be in a blackout.

The temperature is rarely less than 7°C and may rise to 10°C after an ingress of warm water in the summer months.

Gliding over the cobble floor in White Lady Cave

Further considerations

▶ This area has no mobile phone signal
▶ A short length of rope is useful at the 2.5m drop for lowering and hauling equipment, and to assist less-agile team members
▶ A 30m rope left hanging at Cwm Pwll-y-Rhyd will aid an exit, in case anyone is unable to make the return dive. The rocks are very slippery here and this access route is rarely used
▶ A hood and gloves are essential in all seasons
▶ The cave has no permanent line; a nylon line at least 4mm thick should be laid and recovered afterwards
▶ Use a comfortable rucksack to transport your equipment: make two carries to the dive site, rather than struggle with a heavy load
▶ Be mindful of fresh flood debris – the dive leader should carry a wire cutter to use in any ensnarement

Hurtle Pot

Chapel-le-Dale, Yorkshire Dales

Objective
Given the spacious nature of the upstream tunnel, the site may be used by all levels of ability, from cavern diver to fully certified cave diver, with a maximum depth of −35m.

Access
No formal access procedures are required. The cave lies on private farmland and visitors should abide by general rules of access and consideration for local residents: close gates (and do not obstruct these or passing places), avoid damage to walls, keep noise to a minimum and pick up any litter.

The entrance to Hurtle Pot: the sump pool at the base of the deep depression and the cave under flood conditions, when water spectacularly resurges over the surface

Location
Hurtle Pot is situated at the head of Chapel-le-Dale, around 4 miles/6km north-east of Ingleton in North Yorkshire. The site lies 2.5 miles/4km from White Scar Cave, near a small church on the west side of the valley directly adjacent to and on the right-hand side of the narrow approach lane. There is limited space for parking vehicles on a sloping patch of grass directly north of Hurtle Pot; a better recommendation is to use the church car park a short distance back down the narrow road at the valley bottom.

   Access to the dive base is via a small gate at the edge of the plot of grass. Descend to the lower side of the sheer-sided depression then carefully negotiate a steep muddy slope, where a rope is normally left as a handline.

History
Systematic exploration and surveying of this major network commenced in the early 1980s, when Hurtle Pot was first connected to Midge Hole after a 440m long dive by Jonny Shaw and Rupert Skorupka in 1982. Bryan 'Scoff' Schofield and Brian Smith then connected Hurtle to Jingle Pot after a 350m dive in 1986, and later joined Jingle to Weathercote Cave.

Diving
The impressive hole at Hurtle Pot is thought to have formed when the roof of a large submerged tunnel collapsed. The static pool at the bottom leads to a substantial complex over 2km long stretching both up- and down-valley. Little flow is apparent, but the discreet waterway passing through Hurtle is the main artery from caves upstream such as Jingle Pot and Weathercote Cave. Downstream, the water finally resurges at God's Bridge, having taken a devious route through Midge Hole and Joint Hole.

   The main route leads spaciously to the right from the dive base, trending upstream to the north. The passage descends a wide, clean-washed boulder slope and within a short distance enters a massive tunnel which continues to slope away at a gradual angle; at 70m from base the depth is 18m. The descent levels off and a line junction to

At a depth of 18m in
Hurtle Pot

Upstream

CAVERN

FULL

Downstream

FULL

Backmount

the right leads into the Eastwall Outlet Series – a side passage which, although straightforward in its early stages, becomes more challenging after 65m. This tunnel forms an escape route for water into the main surface valley during times of extreme flood.

Continuing past the Eastwall Outlet, the line runs along the right-hand wall in the main tunnel, descending steadily to –28m after a further 60m. This leads to a major landmark, the Hindenburg Wall, where at 130m from dive base the route up-valley suddenly ascends over bare, clean-washed rock. First-time visitors may find this a suitable turning point.

With due consideration to the line condition, visibility, distance and decompression, experienced divers may continue to the head of the ramp, where the depth shallows to 10m. The cave now quietly descends once more until it reaches Jingle Junction at –17m. Directly ahead, northwards, the tunnel continues its gradual descent to a low, sandy-floored, rounded roof arch at a depth of 23m. The route is now conspicuously smaller than hitherto (side-mounts are essential) and leads towards the next landmark, the Blottapress Squeeze at –27m, now some 250m from dive base. The cave continues in a fine passage, The Deep, but it is now both deeper and more committing.

At Jingle Junction, progress to the right is also a serious undertaking: the fixed line is regularly broken by floods. After a further 30m the passage leads very steeply up to Frog Hall airbell and onwards towards Jingle Pot; it is evident that this takes a dramatic flow in wet weather. Local divers have discovered that no line – be it an 11mm rope or even steel wire – can withstand the ravages of the water here. For those suitably prepared to replace lines it is possible to continue beyond Frog Hall, to eventually surface at Jingle Pot (SD 738774) after a traverse of about 350m. The route is complex and the exit is not easy, involving a sheer-sided, 12m pitch requiring ladders or a rope.

The Hurtle downstream section begins at the same dive base, where the outlet for the underground flow is on the left-hand side (to the south-west). However, the narrow passage is generally badly obstructed within 20m of the surface: this route is potentially hazardous due to unstable boulders and only highly experienced cave divers with side-mounted configurations should venture into this part of the complex. This said, after suitable planning and several dives repairing or replacing lines from either end, it is possible to make a through-trip of about 400m to Midge Hole (SD 737770). Depths in this part of the complex touch 22m.

In all cases, consult a weather forecast when planning. Heavy or prolonged rainfall will lead to flooding and, at the very least, poor visibility. In extreme conditions floodwater fills the depression and overflows onto the surface from the entrance. The Chapel-le-Dale waterway is normally heavily tannin-stained and visibility may be less than 2m, but after a long freeze or during lengthy dry periods in summer Hurtle Pot is spectacular, with visibility reaching 6m to 10m. Regardless of the weather, the water is a bracing 6°C year-round.

Hurtle Pot entrance

Air supplies

Capernwray Diving Centre, Jackdaw Quarry,
  Capernwray Road, Capernwray, Carnforth LA6 1AD
  Tel: 01524 735132; www.dive-site.co.uk
  Closed Mondays other than bank holidays

Emergencies

Emergency contacts: see Appendix A
Nearest hyperbaric centre: Wirral
Nearest hospital: Westmorland General Hospital,
  Burton Road, Kendal LA9 7RG; tel: 01539 732288

Further reading

MONICO, Paul (comp). Northern Sump Index, Cave
  Diving Group, 2nd edn (1995)

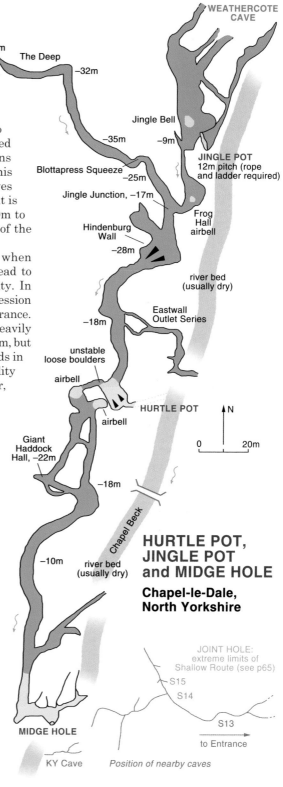

WEATHERCOTE CAVE

−35m
The Deep
−32m

Jingle Bell

−35m
−9m

JINGLE POT
12m pitch (rope and ladder required)

Blottapress Squeeze
−25m

Jingle Junction, −17m

Frog Hall airbell

Hindenburg Wall
−28m

river bed (usually dry)

Eastwall Outlet Series

−18m

unstable loose boulders

airbell

HURTLE POT

airbell

N

Giant Haddock Hall, −22m

0   20m

−18m

Chapel Beck

−10m
river bed (usually dry)

HURTLE POT, JINGLE POT and MIDGE HOLE

Chapel-le-Dale, North Yorkshire

JOINT HOLE: extreme limits of Shallow Route (see p65)

S15

S14

S13

to Entrance

MIDGE HOLE

KY Cave   Position of nearby caves

Shafts of sunlight filter
through green water in the
entrance pool

Coordinates

Dive site	NGR	Lat/Long
Hurtle Pot	SD 738773	54° 11' 26.20" N, 02° 24' 11.72" W

Further considerations

► Hurtle Pot is one of few caves in Britain where back-mounted cylinders may be worn, though most cave divers prefer side-mounted configurations owing to the ease of transport

► Wear sturdy footwear with a good tread to reach the entrance; the path is rocky, steep, muddy and slippery, and is particularly challenging when wet

► Lines are normally left in place, but they are frequently broken or badly damaged by floods; check lines carefully and repair or rebelay them where necessary

► Take a line reel for repair purposes. Nylon, or sinking lines, should be at least 4mm diameter and belayed at regular intervals using snoopy loops. Do not use thin technical line

► Clothes peg line markers are required for the junctions at the Eastwall Outlet and Jingle Junction

► The use of 12 litre cylinders is advisable for dives beyond the Hindenburg Wall

Joint Hole

Chapel-le-Dale, Yorkshire Dales

Objective
Although this is not a cavern site, it is appropriate for introductory cave diving training with side-mounted configurations. Experienced, fully certified cave divers will also find opportunities for some very lengthy and challenging diving. While the further reaches of the cave are complex, the initial dives are comfortable and straightforward with a maximum depth of 10m – an experience to savour.

Access
Other than parking with discretion without blocking the farmer's gates, no formal access procedures were required until 2012 when the owner changed and a new access agreement was required. Hopefully, access will be restored for all, but please check for online updates (see p2) and with the Cave Diving Group for current information.

Location
Joint Hole is located at the head of Chapel-le-Dale, just over 3 miles/5km north-east of Ingleton in North Yorkshire. The small layby, just off the main road exactly 2 miles/3km from White Scar Cave, has space for several vehicles. The approach is through the gate and downstream, directly alongside the streambed. The actual entrance, less than 200m from the parking area, is easily missed, being a relatively small opening set in the meadow beneath the east bank.

The hole is a wet weather resurgence for the subterranean flow running from Hurtle Pot – which lies further upstream (see p61) – to God's Bridge, a short distance down the valley. Under normal or low water conditions the entrance is marked by a small, cobble-floored pool a couple of metres beneath a rock shelf.

History
The entrance to Joint Hole was originally very restricted in size and the first recorded dive was made by Tom Brown in 1970. In 1976 Bob Hryndyj and Steve Thorpe excavated a substantially larger route into the flooded cave and, over a series of dives, reached a point over 260m from the entrance in Sump 3. In the years that followed, access difficulties arose and it was not until 1983 that a wave of exploration by a host of explorers began. The known system steadily expanded through a maze of over 800m of sumps and dry passage to within metres of Midge Hole (SD 737770).

Diving
The entrance pool consists of a small but comfortably sized, clean-washed opening dipping gradually from the surface over a

INTRO

Backmount

Contacts
Cave Diving Group of Great Britain
www.cavedivinggroup
.org.uk

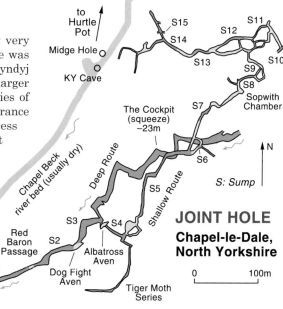

JOINT HOLE
Chapel-le-Dale,
North Yorkshire

0   100m

Water levels at the entrance vary enormously

Following the line in Sump 1

shingle and gravel floor. Some 10m inside, at the bottom of the slope, the depth reaches 9m where the passage levels out at a junction and it becomes larger. To the right a small opening, frequently obstructed by stone cobbles, marks the downstream continuation: this is not for the faint-hearted as it involves some very committing squeezes.

Upstream is a cave diver's delight. Sump 1 is pleasantly wide, at least a metre high and, given the floods which ravage the cave on a regular basis, beautifully clean with very little silt (which means that visibility should remain good for the exit – a very reassuring feeling when you are some distance from home). The depth is 10m at maximum.

A boulder slope heralds the ascent into a wide bedding which gradually surfaces to air in Red Baron Passage after 165m. This sump may be shorter under very low water conditions, when stooping and crawling for a short distance are required to reach the ongoing flooded sections. Under high water, however, the Red Baron airbell is small – about 3m long, 2m wide and only 0.5m high.

Sump 2 continues in a tunnel that is strewn with large boulders. As in Sump 1, the maximum depth is 10m for the 95m swim to the next landmark at 260m from dive base: Dog Fight Aven. This is an impressive air surface gained via a steeply inclined fixed jump line. The chamber is very spacious, over 15m long, 4m to 5m wide and some

Coordinates

Dive site	NGR	Lat/Long
Joint Hole	SD 735766	54° 11' 05.76" N, 02° 24' 26.73" W

Further considerations

▶ This site is not suitable for cavern diving or back-mounted cylinders
▶ Take a reel with 4mm line and snoopy loops in case the main line is broken or requires repair: do not use thin technical line

10m high. It is possible to stand at ease on a rocky floor, chat with a fellow diver and take the time to admire a fine cluster of straw stalactites on the ceiling.

Below and just a few metres before this point the underwater tunnel continues while only slowly deepening. Some 60m beyond Dog Fight Aven the Deep Route and the Shallow Route diverge at a major junction in an area of vertical rock fissures (cross-joints). Both passages present exceptional diving.

Nearing the surface at the end of Sump 2

Ahead and veering left is the Deep Route, which becomes progressively more challenging in every respect, while to the right lies the Shallow Route. Over the course of about 10m via a chaotic slope of boulders, the latter rises from 13m depth to the next impressive air surface: Albatross Aven. Beneath a short vertical jump line, Sump 4 continues for 55m and thereafter the diver has access to a most extensive, very complex series of passages running up-valley with a further eleven sumps interspersed with short air surfaces.

The average visibility is perhaps 2m, but may exceed 6m under optimum conditions. The temperature is a cool 6°C year-round.

Air supplies

Capernwray Diving Centre, Jackdaw Quarry, Capernwray Road, Capernwray, Carnforth LA6 1AD
Tel: 01524 735132; www.dive-site.co.uk
Closed Mondays other than bank holidays

Emergencies

Emergency contacts: see Appendix A
Nearest hyperbaric centre: Wirral
Nearest hospital: Westmorland General Hospital, Burton Road, Kendal LA9 7RG
Tel: 01539 732288

Further reading

MONICO, Paul (comp). *Northern Sump Index*, Cave Diving Group, 2nd edn (1995)

Section two

EUROPE

Cavern and Cave Diving

EUROPE'S widely differing environments and sometimes great range of climatic conditions make its cavern and cave diving sites as demanding as those in the UK. Depending upon the location, both the visibility and water temperature may vary considerably, so that when it comes to planning a visit – in addition to the information provided here – local contacts will prove invaluable for day-to-day updates.

The majority of the sites outlined in this book are located in southern Europe; they are acknowledged as the classic areas for cavern and cave diving and all offer a great day's activity. Divers usually base themselves in one area while away from home, consequently the dive sites in this portion of the guide have been gathered into sections defined by country or region. For mainland Spain, for example, chapters include the Costa Blanca, Costa Brava and Murcia: all are standard holiday destinations and visiting divers should liaise closely with a dive centre. The Balearic and Canary islands, the Greek island of Zante, the Palinuro headland in Italy and the Fethiye and Ölüdeniz region of Turkey are similar: diving

The Goul du Pont in the Ardèche, France

involves reliance upon a local operator or dive shop, especially where a boat is required, and selecting the best of these will require some careful consideration. Language barriers are no longer a major issue at most of the dive centres in southern Europe, but effective planning still depends heavily upon local knowledge and advice.

Many excellent dive sites are situated in France, but without question the foremost area lies around the Lot and Dordogne rivers in the south-west of the country. Unlike most others in Europe, this is an inland region and therefore the diving is in fresh water. The principal caves with relatively easy access are covered here and a number are suited to cavern diving – indeed, this magnificent area offers immense challenges to activists at every level. Divers return year after year, progressing ever further in their penetration of the caves and developing their experience.

Cavern dives in short tunnels can also be found in quarries and mines across Europe but, as with marine settings, conditions may be variable. The benign surface environment at inland sites presents significant advantages and better protection from the elements; however, the water may be susceptible to a greater range of both temperature and visibility. More serious as dive sites, owing to their depth and cold water, are the mines of Scandinavia. Ojamo Limestone Mine in Finland is by far the most notable site in northern Europe and divers considering a visit to this and other such locations must liaise with the controlling body to arrange legal access; for this reason Ojamo is detailed separately in Appendix B.

◀ The spectacular phreatic tube in Sump I of the Font del Truffe in France

Caves of the Ardèche

Bourg-St-Andéol, France

THE Ardèche is a popular area for cave diving. Two important cave diving sites – the Goul de la Tannerie and the Goul du Pont – lie within the town of Bourg-St-Andéol at the western edge of the Rhone valley in southern France. Together known as the Gouls de Tourne, they form the principal outlets for water draining from the St Remèze plateau, many kilometres to the west, and, most unusually, the two resurgences lie within 70m of one another. Despite their close proximity, no connection is known between the two systems and both offer magnificent diving with little or no silt. They are among the finest, most challenging and the most accessible sites in the country, as well as being two of the most beautiful locations that a diver could ever wish to visit.

Late spring, summer and autumn are the recommended times for diving here – conditions are reasonably assured between April and October, with water at about 13°C. In summer, the flow is generally light or non-existent and the visibility is good to excellent.

Access
Permission is required to dive in either cave; this may be obtained from the town hall (tel: 04.75.54.85.00) or the Services Techniques (04.75.54.50.53). Advance notice is requested.

It is also *protocol* (a local law) to inform the town *gendarmerie* before and after the dive.

The old Lavoir building and, beside it, the access road to the dive site of the Goul du Pont, taken from the Goul de la Tannerie (*bottom*) in Bourg-St-Andéol

Location
From the square at the centre of Bourg-St-Andéol, follow the signs for Val de Tourne, which lead down a one-way street, the Avenue Marc Pradelle. At the bottom of a slight descent, on the right-hand side of the road, is a magnificent, classical-style antiquity – the Lavoir, a nineteenth-century wash-house. Immediately preceding this, on the same side, is the entrance to a small town park. A shallow valley extends to the right; the caves lie directly adjacent to and at the far side of the intermittent stream course.

Once permission has been gained and the barrier key obtained, a telescopic barrier set directly adjacent to the Lavoir can be opened to allow vehicular access to a parking area. If there is a problem opening the barrier or should the parking spaces be unavailable, additional parking is located

Further considerations
▶ Plenty of excellent camping and accommodation is available in the area
▶ Respect the peaceful activities of other park visitors: do not disturb local residents
▶ Do not operate a compressor
▶ During the height of summer, an early morning start is highly desirable to mitigate the effects of the intense heat during your carry
▶ The town can be busy in summer months: consider the security of unattended bags

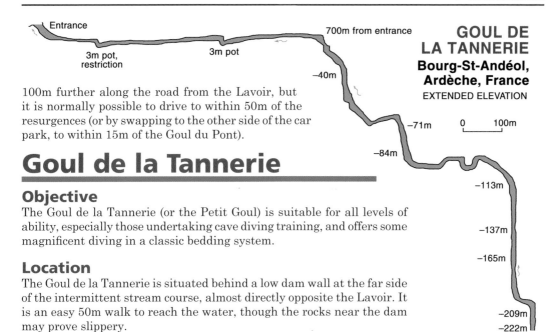

GOUL DE LA TANNERIE
Bourg-St-Andéol, Ardèche, France
EXTENDED ELEVATION

100m further along the road from the Lavoir, but it is normally possible to drive to within 50m of the resurgences (or by swapping to the other side of the car park, to within 15m of the Goul du Pont).

Goul de la Tannerie

Objective
The Goul de la Tannerie (or the Petit Goul) is suitable for all levels of ability, especially those undertaking cave diving training, and offers some magnificent diving in a classic bedding system.

Location
The Goul de la Tannerie is situated behind a low dam wall at the far side of the intermittent stream course, almost directly opposite the Lavoir. It is an easy 50m walk to reach the water, though the rocks near the dam may prove slippery.

History
This major site has been the scene of many audacious explorations. In 1972 a team from the Groupe d'Etudes et de Plongée Souterraine from Marseille reached a depth of 40m in a shaft some 700m from the entrance – it was hailed as a world record penetration. Then, over the course of five dives in 1978 a Swiss team from the Groupe Lémanique de Plongée Souterraine took the cave to 820m, with a depth of 71m, and in 1980 Francis Le Guen descended further to –84m.

CAVERN

The clear water of the Goul de la Tannerie

A LA MEMOIRE DE
BERTRAND LÉGER
1947 - 1984
SPÉLÉONAUTE - CINÉASTE
EXPLORATEUR ET TOPOGRAPHE
DE LA RÉSURGENCE DE TOURNE
EN 1983

Further considerations

▶ A pair of 12 litre cylinders should prove sufficient to reach the 700m shaft

▶ While back-mounted cylinders may be used, divers will find side-mounted configurations highly practical

Two years later Bertrand Léger, using trimix, mounted two explorations that penetrated to 1,020m from base and a depth of 113m. The Swiss diver Jacques Brasey dived to –137m in 1992, then another Swiss, Olivier Isler, continued the descent in 1996, supported by a strong team, and reached a depth of 165m.

In 2003 French diver Sylvain Redoutey dived to –180m using a semi-closed rebreather and subsequently progressed to –209m in 2004. Then, in 2008, Rick Stanton – assisted by John Volanthen – made a descent to –222m.

A plaque on a wall close to the Tannerie commemorates the major contributions to cave exploration made by the late Bertrand Léger.

Diving

Under normal conditions the water is effectively static at this spring. A slope of cobbles and coarse silt is descended, with the line beginning within the daylight zone about 10m inside the entrance against the right-hand wall. The route quickly passes through the somewhat murky surface water to enter the crystal clarity of the cave.

A wonderful bedding complex follows. This is an absolutely delightful passage over 3m wide and generally less than 1m high. The rock is superbly sculpted; the white limestone, complete absence of silt and the clear water make for, in cave diving terms, a stress-free environment.

Owing to the ravages of floodwater, a very sturdy line has been installed for over 200m – the line is robust and exceptionally well laid throughout the cave. At around 100m a pot about 3m deep leads directly to a cobble-floored restriction which, at times, may require enlargement to allow back-mounted divers to pass. Immediately beyond, the passage gains larger proportions and for the next few hundred metres is about 1m high by 6m wide. The depth remains fairly constant at around 11m, until a 3m pot in the floor is found at 500m from base. Thereafter, the bedding character reasserts itself at a slightly more comfortable 1.5m high all the way to 700m.

Here, quite abruptly, the floor disappears into a very impressive deep shaft and the cave becomes completely transformed. In crystal clarity a spectacular descent follows and, in a series of steps, the depth rapidly increases to 222m.

The Tannerie presents some fabulous diving in a benign setting, but – as elsewhere – divers should restrict their penetration to within the limits of their training. Unless actually undergoing training, cavern divers should remain within 60m of the dive base and all diving (at whatever level) should be firmly constrained by the rule of thirds.

Goul du Pont

Objective

The Goul du Pont (or the Grand Goul) offers superb diving opportunities for training dives and is a perfect venue for more technical practitioners undertaking progressive penetrations to depth. Cavern divers will be limited by the cobble squeeze some 30m in from the surface, but those with appropriate training and experience will find this site, just as at the Tannerie, enchanting.

Location

The Goul du Pont is situated approximately 70m up-valley (north-west) from the Goul de la Tannerie, directly beneath a railway bridge and less than 15m from the closest part of the parking area.

The bridge (or *pont*) over the Goul du Pont

Descending the
first shaft at the
Goul du Pont

CAVERN

Coordinates

Both sites are located on the French IGN 1:25,000 map no. 2939 OT (Top 25): Gorges de L'Ardèche
IGN maps include a blue grid that enables WSG84 coordinates to be looked up directly
For conversion to UTM data, this area lies in Zone 31T

Dive site	WSG84 coordinates	Lat/Long
Goul du Pont	6307 49143	44° 22' 13.50" N, 04° 38' 27.71" E
Goul de la Tannerie	6308 49142	44° 22' 10.82" N, 04° 38' 29.47" E

History

This second major site has witnessed a similar exploration history to the Tannerie, but although early dives progressed steadily, a subsequent blockage at the entrance severely restricted access for a number of years.

In the 1950s local cavers from Bourg-St-Andéol excavated and opened the underwater entrance. Albert Casamatta and his colleagues were supplied with diving equipment by the Lyon fire service, while their suits were home-made. They passed a restriction at 12m depth and gained the top of a shaft at around –19m, some 75m from base.

In 1972 Claude Touloumdjian and the Groupe d'Etudes et de Plongée Souterraine from Marseille reopened the cave and extended the exploration to a depth of 85m. In 1981 Eric and Francis Le Guen, together with Véronique Borel, continued to –97m and the following year, using a heliox gas mix, a Swiss team from the Groupe Lémanique de Plongée Souterraine continued to –115m. Four years later, in 1985, the German diver Joseph Schneider reached –135m at a point 330m from the cave entrance.

Between 1985 and 2000 the cave remained closed to all comers due to a formidable blockage at the entrance. Over the following two years a major clearance of the entrance restriction took place and in May 2002, Xavier Méniscus continued to a depth of 140m, now 380m from the entrance; in January 2003 he continued to –153m and 450m from base. A few months later, Jérôme Meynié reached –178m and 560m from the entrance, then on a return in 2006 he gained –180m and 570m. A couple of months later in 2006 Xavier returned and descended to –185m.

Diving

Under normal summer conditions the water at this spring is static. Descend in a rounded, smooth-walled tunnel with a slope of cobbles which leads quickly to a restriction at a depth of 12m. This may require excavation by pushing aside some of the stones, but within a couple of metres the tunnel returns to its prior dimensions. A gently dipping, flat-floored bedding passage about 3m wide by 1.5m high leads to the lip of a fine shaft at around 19m depth some 75m from the entrance.

The crystal-clear water in the shaft draws divers downwards, directly to –33m, with the passage being well equipped with a heavy duty, well-belayed 11mm thick rope. The depth now increases rapidly, dropping from one shaft to the next in a series of straightforward steps. At –60m the route becomes more awkward in a smaller passage, then a modest horizontal gallery is entered at –79m before the route continues its descent to a point 210m from the entrance where the depth is 110m. The narrow, winding and difficult passage now trends ever deeper, leading to a depth in excess of 185m some 575m from the entrance.

Air supplies

No air supplies are available in the town of Bourg-St-Andéol or the neighbouring environs; take your own compressor or make prior arrangements for refills.

Emergencies

Emergency contacts:
  see Appendix A
Nearest hyperbaric centre:
  Avignon, Marseille or Montpellier
Nearest hospital: Centre Hospitalier d'Ardèche Méridionale, Hôpital d'Aubenas, 16 Avenue Bellande, 07200 Aubenas Tel: 04.75 35.60.60
International telephone country code: +33;
  drop the preceding zero from the local number

Entrance
restriction, –12m
–19m
–60m
–79m
–110m
–140m
0   100m
–185m, 575m from entrance

GOUL DU PONT
Bourg-St-Andéol, Ardèche, France
EXTENDED ELEVATION

Based on surveys by Jean Marc Belin, David Bianzani, Xavier Méniscus, Jérôme Meynié and Frank Vasseur

Caves of the Lot and Dordogne

France

FRANCE has many excellent sites for cave diving, but the area centred on the Lot and Dordogne rivers in south-west France is the most popular for cavern and cave diving in the whole of Europe. Places such as the Émergence du Ressel, the Trou Madame, the Fontaine Saint-Georges and the Font del Truffe rate among the finest, most challenging and most accessible in the country.

The surface topography of the region is fairly uniform, consisting of an undulating limestone plateau incised by beautiful valleys flanked by precipitous cliffs. The easiest caves to enter lie in the valley floors, where substantial springs emerge. These resurgences often possess comfortably large passages with relatively small amounts of silt and little in the way of the unpleasant organic debris that is characteristic of stream sinks.

Late spring, summer and autumn are recommended for diving because conditions are reasonably assured between April and October, with the water being at about 13°C. However, the weather (and hence the water levels) may be variable in spring, and even at the height of summer localised thunderstorms can occur which may reduce the visibility. At these times caves such as Saint-Georges and the Gouffre de Cabouy suffer badly and diving may become impractical. Even at the Ressel, generally regarded as one of the least affected sites, visibility may occasionally drop to less than 1.5m. Nevertheless, while conditions may be poor in one area or valley, local operators can usually suggest another where you will find near-perfect conditions.

Sump 1 in the Font del Truffe

The distance from vehicle to water is typically less than 200m at nearly all the locations, though parking space may be limited (in particular at the Source de Landenouse and the Trou Madame). Gas fills can be purchased in Gramat and at the Lot Cave Diving Centre in Frayssinet, but to avoid daily travel and sometimes lengthy journeys consider taking a small compressor (but do not disturb local residents with its use). Plenty of excellent camping and other accommodation is available in the area.

In busy periods several groups a day may visit some of these springs, such as the popular Ressel and the Trou Madame, so plan accordingly. Early morning starts during the height of summer are highly desirable to mitigate the effects of the intense heat later in the day.

None of these sites have any facilities. First-time visitors should head for the Trou Madame, the Ressel and perhaps the Font del Truffe; Saint-Georges, the Cabouy and the Source de Saint-Sauveur also present excellent diving, though they involve greater depths. For side-mount practitioners, the Oeil de la Doue, the Émergence de Crégols and the Source du Marchepied offer superb underground adventures. All the sites are clearly marked on 1:25,000 maps; see p102 for their coordinates.

Numbers with headings relate to locations on the area map (opposite)

(1) Doux de Coly

CAVERN

Objective

The beautiful spring at the Doux de Coly was the scene of world record penetrations in the 1980s and it presents golden opportunities to divers of all levels of ability. The entrance area is perfect for cavern divers and the general nature of the cave is ideal for progressive operations.

Access

Permission is required to dive at the Doux de Coly, but at the time of writing this is being denied to all divers. However, it appears likely that access will reopen, so details of this important site are included in the hope that this occurs.

Location

The Doux de Coly is located approximately 20km south-west of Brive-la-Gaillarde, 3km to the south-east of the village of Coly and directly adjacent to the D62 between La Cassagne and Le Lardin-St-Lazare. The large, 45m diameter, shallow pool lies behind a low wall less than 2m from the road. Parking is limited on the roadside, other than outside the mill building.

History

The first determined assault on the Doux de Coly was made by Pierre-Jean Debras who, in 1971, reached 365m from the entrance and 52m depth. In 1981 a Swiss team from the Groupe Lémanique de Plongée Souterraine, including Jean-Jacques Bolanz, Cyrille Brandt, Olivier Isler and

The Doux de Coly entrance pool

continues to 5,880m
−53m

−6m

The Shaft   −50m
−57m

to Coly   −10m
−60m

mill

D62 road

N

oxbow

DOUX DE COLY
La Cassagne, Dordogne, France

0   100m

surface pool

to La Cassagne

Claude Magnin, dived to 1,760m at −56m. Spearheaded by Isler, the team went on to advance the known limits to 3,100m in 1983 and 1984 and in 1998 Isler attained 4,250m.

The German-based European Karst Plain Project (EKPP) team, consisting of lead divers Reinhard Buchaly and Michael Waldbrenner, subsequently continued exploration and in August 2003 reached 5,880m from the surface.

Diving
The mill pool, fringed with luxuriant pondweed, descends gradually into a spacious, cobble-floored entrance at 5m depth. Immediately inside, the passage size increases to over 6m wide by at least 3m high with a floor of clean-washed boulders and sand; the depth averages around 6m to 8m. The line starts just inside the entrance and is easy to follow in such a regular and accommodating passage. These dimensions remain fairly constant for the next 300m to an abrupt and very spectacular shaft.

Floating out over the top of the shaft is an awesome experience,

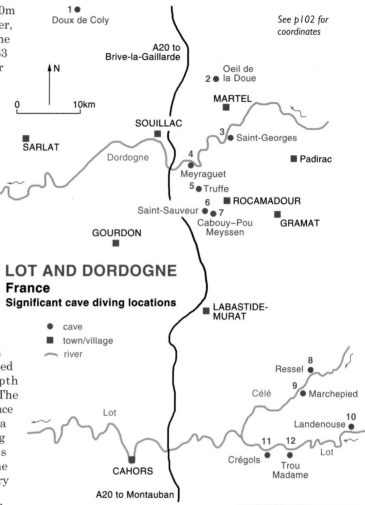

See p102 for coordinates

LOT AND DORDOGNE
France
Significant cave diving locations

- cave
- town/village
- river

René Houben entering the Doux de Coly

Further considerations
▶ The D62 road forms a narrow bend around the mill and the spring: beware of vehicles on the road
▶ Do not assume that access is permitted: take local advice and do not attempt a dive that may destroy negotiations
▶ Gloves are required on all but the shortest of dives
▶ Visibility may occasionally be reduced to 5m or less

Approaching a habitat for decompression after a long dive

Some of the Doux de Coly veteran divers: John Volanthen (left), Jason Mallinson, René Houben, Rick Stanton and Olivier Isler

with the cave below – over 5m in diameter – dropping sheer into blackness. Beyond a ledge at –35m the cave descends rapidly to –57m, then levels out and maintains a near-constant depth for well over 2km. The final section is at –64m, leading to the limit of exploration at 5,880m.

(2) Oeil de la Doue

Objective

INTRO

The Oeil de la Doue provides interesting and exciting opportunities for introductory and fully certified cave divers, in particular for those wishing to make longer penetrations. Passing Sump 1 to view the large dry cave beyond with its spectacular streamway is justifiable in its own right. However, at high water levels and in clear conditions the site can be appropriate for cavern diving.

Access

No permission is required.

Location

The Oeil de la Doue resurgence is located 3km north-west of Martel. From Martel, take the D23 north for 2km, then turn left towards Hôpital-St-Jean, still on the D23. Follow this downhill for just under 2km to the Doue stream and immediately on the far side of the bridge turn left onto a track. Pass the Moulin de Murel, which lies to the left, and continue for a further 300m to where the track turns abruptly right. Park at this spot beside a low cliff, from where a 550m walk on foot westwards along the valley bottom takes only ten minutes to reach the resurgence at the base of an impressive rockface.

History

A series of six sumps, interspersed with 'dry' cave, has been passed in this challenging system. Various French teams progressively explored the cave and in 2000 Patrick Bolagno and Marc Douchet reached a terminal depth of 52m at a low shingle bedding plane about 100m into Sump 5. In the mid-2000s British divers Rick Stanton and John Volanthen took up the gauntlet. The pair passed Sump 5 in 2006, together with Sump 6 to reach a short, dry extension ending at a massive boulder blockage some 3,350m from the entrance, involving just over 3km of diving.

Diving

The line is tied to the Oeil de la Doue cliff face at the far right of the entrance pool and the visibility, while often appearing slightly milky, generally ranges from 5m to over 15m. The water level fluctuates markedly by up to 2m depending upon rainfall, causing Sump 1 to vary significantly in length. At high level the entrance is submerged and a shallow lake forms on the surface, while at low level the initial sump may be very short. In extreme drought an airspace exists throughout Sump 1, although to reach the normally 'dry' cave beyond visitors still have to swim through deep water in the latter part.

The entrance to the Oeil de la Doue in high (normal) and low (dry) conditions

When water levels are high a flooded portion perhaps 75m long and 5m deep leads to a 60m long and 3m deep canal followed by a 20m long and 6m deep dive. You emerge to a vastly different environment than you might expect. From the calm of the sump you surface to a lofty cavern with a strong current zipping towards you as you stand waist deep in a narrow canyon. Care must be exercised not to drop your mask, fins or any other item of equipment. For the next 30m to 50m the floor presents a network

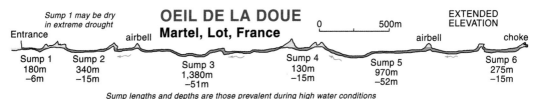

OEIL DE LA DOUE
Martel, Lot, France

EXTENDED ELEVATION

Sump 1 may be dry in extreme drought

Entrance

airbell

0 ____ 500m

airbell

choke

Sump 1	Sump 2	Sump 3	Sump 4	Sump 5	Sump 6
180m	340m	1,380m	130m	970m	275m
−6m	−15m	−51m	−15m	−52m	−15m

Sump lengths and depths are those prevalent during high water conditions

Further considerations

▶ Check the water level and visibility before carrying equipment to the cave
▶ It is easier to tackle the cave in high water, because carrying dive equipment between the sumps is strenuous in low conditions

Following the line in Sump 1 of the Oeil de la Doue, and the start of Sump 2

of small, shallow potholes formed by the swirling water: care is required here too. Thereafter the route is 3m to 5m wide and perhaps 10m high.

The journey eases the further upstream you progress until you arrive at the large sand-floored cavern that marks the start of Sump 2. This next dive is a true delight. Sump 2 dips away very gradually, perhaps 10m wide and at least a couple of metres high with a sand floor; it is 340m long with a maximum depth of 15m. Sump 3 is longer and more challenging. It descends rapidly to 15m, then surfaces in an airbell after about 100m; the total length is about 1,380m with a maximum depth of 51m.

A short section of walking-sized passage then ends at Sump 4, which is 130m long (maximum depth 15m), followed by some more walking-sized streamway and Sump 5, being 970m long with a maximum depth of 52m. A short stooping passage leads to the 275m long Sump 6, then 40m of dry passage reaches the terminal choke.

(3) Fontaine Saint-Georges

Objective

CAVERN

The Fontaine Saint-Georges is suitable for all levels of ability; the cave descends fairly rapidly to a maximum depth of 29m in Sump 1.

Access

No permission is required.

Location

The large and well-known entrance to the Fontaine Saint-Georges nestles discreetly below and 1km from the small, picturesque village of Mont-valent, which itself lies some 9km north of Rocamadour. Having passed through the village on the main road to Martel, after 1km take the first

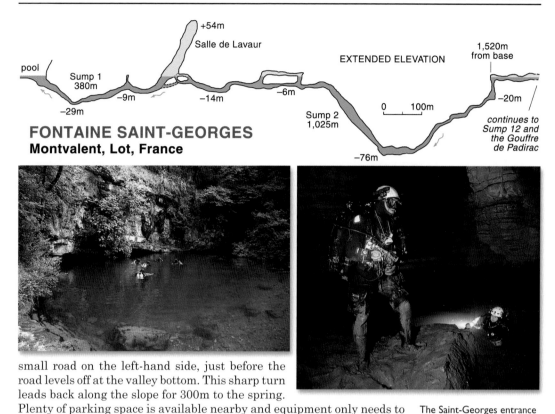

FONTAINE SAINT-GEORGES
Montvalent, Lot, France

small road on the left-hand side, just before the road levels off at the valley bottom. This sharp turn leads back along the slope for 300m to the spring. Plenty of parking space is available nearby and equipment only needs to be carried for less than 100m to the water's edge.

The Saint-Georges entrance pool, and surfacing in the Salle de Lavaur

History

The first exploration at this major spring was made by the French cave diving pioneer Guy de Lavaur in 1948, who reached a depth of 29m after several operations. In 1973 Sump 1 was eventually passed by Bertrand Léger after a total distance of 380m and a maximum depth of 29m. In subsequent years a long series of investigations was undertaken, but it was the Swiss diver Cyrille Brandt, supported by a strong team of divers from the Groupe Lémanique de Plongée Souterraine, who eventually passed Sump 2 in 1987.

Frenchman Francis Le Guen furthered the work in 1989, then another strong French team – including Marc Douchet and Bernard Gauche – took over to reach a restriction in Sump 7. British cave divers Jason Mallinson and Rick Stanton continued the exploration with two trips during 2002, but it was Stanton who, on a solo trip in 2003, carried on into a twelfth upstream sump and eventually made a connection to the fifth downstream sump in the Gouffre de Padirac.

Diving

The water in Saint-Georges is normally somewhat milky, with visibility generally less than 8m. The cave is entered at about 10m depth, heading down a gradual slope in a very wide, clean-washed passage of ample height and passing over and between massive, well-rounded rocks and boulders. Below –20m the dimensions begin to shrink and the floor changes to one of progressively smaller deposits of gravel.

At 60m from the entrance an abrupt U-bend at –29m leads into a different environment: the ascending passage quickly assumes very large

Reduced visibility in the Fontaine Saint-Georges

Further considerations

▶ A pair of 12 litre cylinders should be sufficient to reach the Salle de Lavaur

proportions with copious quantities of mud and silt. First-time visitors will feel an apprehensive, perhaps ominous sense of remoteness here; some have described agoraphobic feelings.

After a penetration of 150m the cave shallows to less than 20m depth, thereafter rising very slowly. At 270m the depth is 9m, at a point where a small, deep water airbell may be entered but with nowhere to leave the water. Continue in the main tunnel – the route deepens to 13m, then a line junction against the right-hand wall is reached at 380m from base where the depth is 11.5m. Here you can surface, being careful not to disturb the silt, and land on a steep slope in the Salle de Lavaur – a very large and impressive lake chamber with a high aven. It is easy to leave the water and explore a short, clean, dry passage at the far side of the chamber.

The main route onward into Sump 2 begins at the underwater junction at 380m. The sump runs at a shallow 10m depth for over 500m to reach a steep ramp descent that leads to an elbow at −76m and another air surface at 1,025m from the junction. A further ten sumps follow to the connection point with the Gouffre de Padirac.

(4) Émergence de Meyraguet

Objective

INTRO

The Émergence de Meyraguet is suitable for introductory and fully certified cave divers. The fine passage and gradual deepening of the cave make it ideal for divers extending their experience.

Access

Air quality

Depending on which route to the cave is taken, permission may be required. In November 2003 two Swiss divers died in the airbell beyond Sump 1 when, it is believed, they became critically hypoxic as a result of breathing the air in the enclosed space. Subsequent analysis of the gas in this chamber showed an oxygen content of only 8%, well below that required to sustain life. Warning plaques have now been erected in the entrance passage.

Location

The Émergence de Meyraguet is located in the west (left) bank of the Dordogne river, 1.5km north-west of Lacave and around 8km north-west of Rocamadour. From the village of Lacave follow the D23 in a westerly direction. After crossing the Ouysse river, take the D43 towards Belcastel and continue on the same road into the small village of Meyraguet approximately 1km

Entering the Émergence de Meyraguet

beyond. The cave itself is about 140m south-east of the church.

Reaching the 6m high and 2m wide entrance can be a challenge, as divers must negotiate the main river with its variable flow. The most convenient point of access, via a private property almost directly above, requires prior planning and permission. Here, a flight of steps and a short rigid ladder lead to a bare rocky platform at the water's edge, from which the cave entrance is approximately 30m upstream. If permission is not sought beforehand the alternative is a swim/wade of the order of 440m from a parking area at the side of a track to the north-west. The prominent entrance, popular with passing canoeists, lies at the base of the cliff some 40m upstream from a conspicuous steel cable which spans the river.

History

Belgian divers originally explored the area beyond a depth of 43m.

Diving

A beautiful smooth-walled phreatic tube meanders for 100m to the first sump, which is about 50m long, less than 5m deep and has a visibility generally in excess of 4m. The substantial 20m long airbell beyond is notable for its bad air. Be warned: various incidents have happened at this point and deaths have occurred. The line continues through the airbell into Sump 2.

The warning sign at Meyraguet

Sump 2 slopes gradually to −25m at about 80m distance, then reaches −30m at 110m. There follows about 100m of passage at the −20m level, beyond which a ramp descends to −43m. At 220m from the Sump 2 dive base the passage

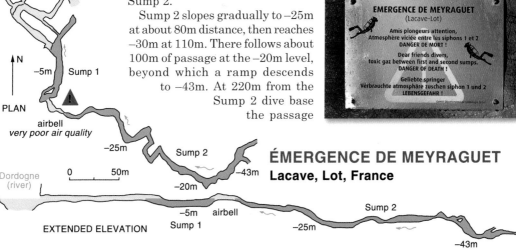

ÉMERGENCE DE MEYRAGUET
Lacave, Lot, France

Further considerations

▶ The roadside near the church has ample parking, but please be considerate of the villagers
▶ Consider carefully the strenuous nature of the river
▶ There are no limitations with regard to equipment use
▶ Take a reel in case a line needs to be laid
▶ The cave was still being explored during 2012
▶ Remember: *Keep your regulator in your mouth at all times*

lowers and splits. The passage size remains roughly the same as the –43m level, but the further you go in Sump 2 the more silt you encounter.

Several lines have been laid in the further reaches and a couple of short side leads loop back to the main tunnel. Care is required when marking the route to avoid confusion.

(5) Font del Truffe

Objective

INTRO

The Font del Truffe offers spectacular diving to introductory and fully certified cave divers, but is not a cavern diving site. The maximum depth is 13m in Sump 1.

Access

No permission is required.

Location

Situated around 6km north-west of Rocamadour, the Font del Truffe can be approached from two directions. The first route is via the D673 trending west from Rocamadour, leading down a small winding road for about 12km to a bridge over the Ouysse river. Turn right just before the bridge and follow the valley downstream, staying on the east bank of the river (due north); the route soon degenerates to a track (the GR6). Around 3km from the turning off the D673, the Truffe is found directly beside the track on the right-hand side. Space is normally available for several cars to park about 20m from the water.

The alternative is to travel up-valley from Lacave, a village on the Dordogne river. Follow the GR6 south along the Ouysse valley, along the way memorably passing through a narrow opening beneath a local residence. Some 2.5km from the start of the GR6 track, spot the Truffe on the left.

The surface pool is in a conical depression; the water level varies. Under high water

to Lacave

Entrance

Sump 1

continues to
three short
sumps

track
(GR6)

150m
−13m

to D673
and
Rocamadour

Sump 2
150m
−12m

Sump 3
85m
−15m

Northern Sump

FONT DEL TRUFFE
Lacave, Lot, France

Based on survey by Michel Verlhac

Sump 4
118m
−7m

N

0   100m

The entrance pool

Sump 5
continues to Sump 13

levels in spring it may flow over the concrete spillway, while under low flow the level may drop by over 2m. The pool may not appear to be clear on first inspection, but inside the cave the visibility is always excellent.

History

Local divers from Brive-la-Gaillarde are believed to have made the first investigations in the Font del Truffe, but in 1975 Daniel Andrès and Bertrand Léger passed Sump 4 and discovered 500m of dry passage beyond. Later, Jean-Charles Chouquet, Patrick Penez and Frédéric Vergier extended the cave to Sump 11 and Fred Swierczynski subsequently passed this and made a 40m foray into Sump 12.

Exploration was furthered by Bernard Gauche and Ludovic Giordano, who terminated their activities at −30m in Sump 12. This was later passed by Rick Stanton and John Volanthen in 2007 and they both went on to pass a thirteenth sump, but found no obvious continuation. The end of the cave is about 3,300m from the entrance, of which 2,110m is flooded and just under 1,200m is dry passage.

Diving

The line is usually belayed at the far side of the pool. Follow a steady slope into the hillside and pass to the left of a boulder to reach a restriction within a few metres. At about 1.2m wide and less

Further considerations

▶ The first two sumps can be passed using 12 litre back-mounted configurations, but it is less stressful, more comfortable and more enjoyable wearing side-mounted cylinders

▶ A pair of 7 litre bottles are more than adequate for a first visit and should allow divers to reach the end of Sump 2

▶ Divers may find themselves panting abnormally in the dry passage beyond Sump 2 due to a raised level of carbon dioxide; while this is somewhat uncomfortable, be reassured that it is not life-threatening

▶ Wetsuits are advisable for penetrations beyond Sump 2 because of the restricted passage size and the dry caving involved after Sump 3

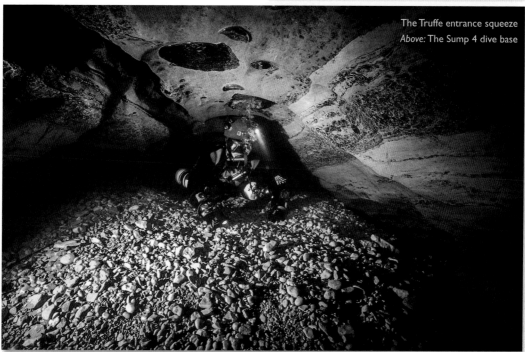

The Truffe entrance squeeze
Above: The Sump 4 dive base

than 0.6m high, this may prove interesting for those at the rear of the party as visibility on the outer side can be reduced to 0.3m.

Once beyond this point, now at 6m depth in low water conditions and 8m in high water, the cave opens out into substantial proportions in near-perfect visibility. Ahead lies one of the best examples of a phreatic tube that divers will ever encounter. The roomy sump meanders onwards, with next to no silt, touching a maximum depth of about 13m before rising to an air surface at 150m.

In low water a very short climb makes the exit slightly awkward; with higher levels it is much easier, as is the subsequent approach to the second sump which is found within a few metres in the comfortably sized passage to the right (the side passage on the left after Sump 1 leads to a set of three small sumps). In low water one may huff and puff to gain Sump 2 as the preceding canal may contain less than 30cm of water.

Sump 2 is a smaller version of Sump 1: the passage is about half the size, though it is completely clean-washed with no silt, making the visibility better than in the first sump. The depth briefly dips to a similar depth of around 12m before surfacing steeply to air after about 150m. In the summer months a fair-sized airbell is normally found just before the end of the dive at between 6m and 8m depth; it has been formed by divers' exhalations becoming trapped in a well-sculpted section of passage. The twists and turns in this sump are a real delight.

A short section of dry cave passage leads to Sump 3 (85m long, –15m); a lengthy series of ten more sumps lies beyond.

◀ Sump 2 in the
Font del Truffe

Font del Truffe
Sump length and max. depth

Sump 1:	150m	−13m
Sump 2:	150m	−12m
Sump 3:	85m	−15m
Sump 4:	118m	−7m
Sump 5:	200m	−11m
Sump 6:	170m	−15m
Sump 7:	60m	−6m
Sump 8:	270m	−8m
Sump 9:	20m	−6m
Sump 10:	255m	−15m
Sump 11:	270m	−30m
Sump 12:	260m	−32m
Sump 13:	90m	−15m

Source de Saint-Sauveur   (6)

Objective
The Source de Saint-Sauveur has a large and impressive pool which does not disappoint divers making a visit. It is suitable for all levels of ability, though the cave rapidly descends to below 40m depth.

CAVERN

Access
No permission is required.

Location
Saint-Sauveur is a primary tributary to the Ouysse river, situated 4km to 5km west-south-west of Rocamadour. It is best approached by following the D673 road south from the village of Calès to the network of small country roads south of the river. Around 500m after passing through the hamlet of Les Vitarelles the road turns abruptly east (signposted Rocamadour); turn off at this corner onto the road straight ahead towards Les

The Source de Saint-Sauveur; enter the water on the far side

Granges-de-Bonnecoste. Approximately 2.5km from the junction turn left onto a track that leads due north for a further 1km down a wooded valley directly to the resurgence. Plenty of parking space is available about 100m beyond a heavy metal gate (please close it after use) and some 60m from the entrance pool.

History
The first recorded dive at the Source de Saint-Sauveur was made by Yves-Henri Dufour and Guy de Lavaur in 1954. A major advance was achieved by the brothers Eric and Francis Le Guen in 1980 when they penetrated the site to 350m, reaching –78m in

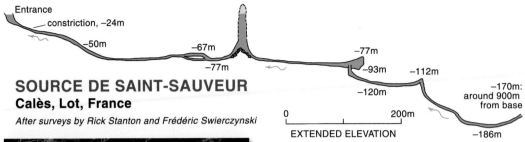

Entrance
constriction, −24m
−50m
−67m
−77m
−77m
−93m
−112m
−120m
−170m:
around 900m
from base

SOURCE DE SAINT-SAUVEUR
Calès, Lot, France
After surveys by Rick Stanton and Frédéric Swierczynski

0   200m

EXTENDED ELEVATION   −186m

a vast, level gallery. Later, in 1986 Xavier Goyet died when returning from his exploration.

During the 1990s a team including Hubert Foucart and Patrick Jolivet (of the Fédération Française d'Études et de Sports Sous-Marins, Languedoc-Roussillon Midi-Pyrénées section) made progress to 580m from the entrance, at which point they were at −92m. During the latter part of the decade an FFESSM team made determined efforts to locate the way on, but it was not until 2001 that British diver Rick Stanton located a new lead and continued to −103m, now 610m from the entrance.

In March 2004 Jacques Berou gained a depth of 110m, then that September Stanton returned to descend to −120m. In 2007 Stanton attained −186m on a dive lasting 16 hours and 40 minutes – he took the length of Sump 1 to about 900m. The cave appears to be trending upwards beyond the limit reached.

Further considerations

▶ The permanent dive line begins close to the restriction at −24m and is easily reached by following the sandy floor downwards

▶ An easy walking path leads to the Gouffre de Cabouy, around 1.25km to the east, but it is not practical in a car

▲ The entrance pool at the Source de Saint-Sauveur

Diving

The visibility in the Source de Saint-Sauveur is usually excellent. From the entrance pool the floor rapidly falls away over banks of sand and gravel, then at about 15m depth the route funnels inwards, leading to a restriction at −24m. At times the sand restriction in this section has proved a major limitation to some equipment configurations, but generally this obstacle presents little deterrent.

Beyond 24m depth the gravel disappears and the cave is savagely clean-washed – clear evidence of a very strong flow at times of flood. After 40m depth the descent is steeper over well-scalloped bedding slabs, then beyond 60m depth the inclination of the passage is more gradual, while the dimensions increase to about 2m high and over 5m wide. About 200m from the surface the depth levels off at 68m and from here onwards the route enlarges to about 5m by 5m, until at 350m a short shaft leads to −75m. Some extremely deep penetrations have been made beyond this point.

(7) Gouffre de Cabouy and Gouffre de Pou Meyssen

INTRO

Objective

The Gouffre de Cabouy is suitable for all levels of ability, though the cave descends fairly rapidly to the deepest point of 31m, so it has limited scope for cavern divers. Completing a through-dive to the associated Gouffre de Pou Meyssen is an exciting challenge.

Access
No permission is required.

Location
The Gouffre de Cabouy is a major flood resurgence at the head of the Ouysse river, 3km south-west of Rocamadour. It is approached from Rocamadour on the steeply descending and narrow D32 road, heading initially towards Couzou. A map will prove invaluable for navigating the numerous junctions and switchbacks on the circuitous route, which terminates at a water pumping station. During the summer months the Cabouy appears to be a static pool mainly covered with pondweed; the water is easily entered approximately 50m from the large parking area.

Around 675m due east from the Cabouy lies the Gouffre de Pou Meyssen, a small static pool situated beneath a low crag in the valley bottom. It is reached via a fairly level walk through woodland of just over 800m along a good, straightforward path from the parking area at the Gouffre de Cabouy. The Pou Meyssen leads downstream to the Cabouy and upstream to another major complex of passages.

History
Determined exploration and recording of the Cabouy–Pou Meyssen complex commenced in the mid-1970s when a French Fédération Française d'Études et de Sports Sous-Marins (FFESSM) team consisting of Gilbert Francziakis and Claude Touloumdjian dived 300m downstream from Pou Meyssen towards the Cabouy in 1974. Some 275m of progress was also made upstream, then the next year the same pair continued downstream to 510m. Following the death of Francziakis, Touloumdjian carried on with the project alone, establishing a connection between the two caves in 1976. The first traverse of the then major sump was undertaken by Touloumdjian and Patrick Penez in 1979.

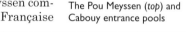
The Pou Meyssen (top) and Cabouy entrance pools

Further successive penetrations upstream from the Pou Meyssen entrance by Touloumdjian in 1976 took him to 850m from base. In 1978 he used a scooter and after 1,190m the lone explorer passed the sump to enter a long canal. A Swiss team from the Groupe Lémanique de Plongée Souterraine consisting of Olivier Isler and Claude Magnin reached Sump 2 after another 400m and later the same year passed this after 40m to discover a long, dry gallery. In 1988 members of the FFESSM gained Sump 3, now 2,700m from the surface, and the following year progressed to 3,000m.

GOUFFRE DE CABOUY

EXTENDED ELEVATION

GOUFFRE DE POU MEYSSEN

0   100m

−20m   −20m   −16m   −18m   continues to
Sump 3
−31m   at −120m

GOUFFRE DE CABOUY–GOUFFRE DE POU MEYSSEN
Rocamadour, Lot, France

Further considerations

▶ The lines are frequently in poor condition

▶ Personalised line markers will be useful

▶ Use a sack truck or wheelbarrow to carry equipment on the long walk to the Pou Meyssen

▶ The water conditions for the Pou Meyssen are best determined by diving in the Cabouy

In 1991 Frédéric Bernard and Marc Douchet found a promising lead at a depth of 35m in Sump 3. Over a series of dives from 2000 to 2005, Jason Mallinson and Rick Stanton explored beyond this point and Stanton subsequently reached −120m depth at about 550m from dive base, with the passage left ongoing.

Diving

The water at the Gouffre de Cabouy is notoriously murky with a deep orange-brown tint and visibility very rarely betters 6m. A dive line is normally tied off above water at the far end of the pool. A slope of deep sand quickly leads from the surface to a maximum depth of 31m at floor level. The entrance is over 10m wide by perhaps 6m or more high, but only once you are inside and looking back from beneath the rounded roof can you really appreciate its impressive size. Onwards, a very large, well-sculpted and clean-washed tunnel, in excess of 6m in diameter, leads upstream. Conditions only rarely allow you to experience the finer qualities of this tremendous cave; most of the time it is a big, gloomy void. The tunnel shallows very gradually, until at about 450m it abruptly ascends to about 5m depth, which is the midpoint between the Cabouy and the Pou Meyssen.

Diving at the Pou Meyssen end of the system requires more effort because of the walk involved. The entrance pool is below a short mud slope and is awkward to access. The rope generally left *in situ* will prove invaluable, but it is impossible to avoid disturbing the silt at this point. The water flow is imperceptible and divers need to exercise caution following the line in reduced visibility. The downstream tunnel is roughly 16m deep and this area may have several different lines of dubious condition running in close proximity: take care.

Broken or multiple lines

Each summer, technical divers from throughout Europe descend upon the area and the 900m through-dive between the two sites is increasingly popular – but always check the route from either end before attempting a crossover, especially when using open-circuit equipment. The lines are often broken after floods and divers should always be watchful for badly frayed sections. Common sense dictates that these should be repaired wherever possible.

The Pou Meyssen also offers superb opportunities for a lengthy penetration upstream, where a 1.2km long dive with a maximum depth of 21m leads to a substantial 600m long section of mainly canal cave passage ending at Sump 2. This is 40m long and 6m deep, and is followed by 400m of dry passage to Sump 3, which reaches 120m depth and 550m from base.

(8) Émergence du Ressel

CAVERN

Objective

The Émergence du Ressel is suitable for all levels of ability and the large numbers of visitors to this spring is a clear indication of its popularity. The site is extremely convenient and offers everything an aspirant cave diver could wish for. Understandably, divers often return here year after year.

ÉMERGENCE DU RESSEL
Marcilhac-sur-Célé, Lot, France

Lac Isler, 1,875m from base

Célé (river)

Shallow Route

Deep Route

Sump 1

bypass

−44m

Sump 1

−42m

−80m

EXTENDED ELEVATION

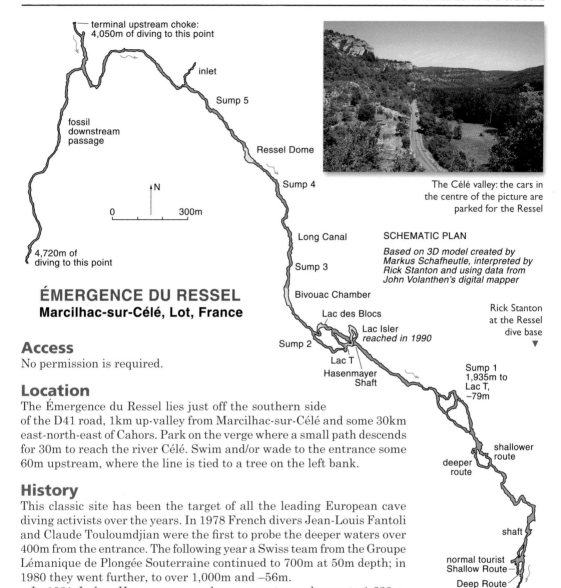

terminal upstream choke:
4,050m of diving to this point

inlet

Sump 5

fossil
downstream
passage

Ressel Dome

↑N

0 ——————— 300m

Sump 4

The Célé valley: the cars in
the centre of the picture are
parked for the Ressel

Long Canal

SCHEMATIC PLAN

*Based on 3D model created by
Markus Schafheutle, interpreted by
Rick Stanton and using data from
John Volanthen's digital mapper*

4,720m of
diving to this point

Sump 3

ÉMERGENCE DU RESSEL
Marcilhac-sur-Célé, Lot, France

Bivouac Chamber

Lac des Blocs

Rick Stanton
at the Ressel
dive base
▼

Lac Isler
reached in 1990

Sump 2

Lac T
Hasenmayer
Shaft

Sump 1
1,935m to
Lac T,
−79m

Access
No permission is required.

shallower
route

deeper
route

Location
The Émergence du Ressel lies just off the southern side
of the D41 road, 1km up-valley from Marcilhac-sur-Célé and some 30km
east-north-east of Cahors. Park on the verge where a small path descends
for 30m to reach the river Célé. Swim and/or wade to the entrance some
60m upstream, where the line is tied to a tree on the left bank.

shaft

History
This classic site has been the target of all the leading European cave
diving activists over the years. In 1978 French divers Jean-Louis Fantoli
and Claude Touloumdjian were the first to probe the deeper waters over
400m from the entrance. The following year a Swiss team from the Groupe
Lémanique de Plongée Souterraine continued to 700m at 50m depth; in
1980 they went further, to over 1,000m and −56m.

normal tourist
Shallow Route—

Deep Route

Entrance

In 1981 Jochen Hasenmayer made a momentous advance to 1,620m,
touching a depth of over 80m while using a revolutionary new rebreather
– and a couple of days later he progressed to 1,755m, now at −20m, using
open-circuit equipment. However, the honour of passing Sump 1, which
ended only a short distance further on, fell to Olivier Isler in 1990.

In 2000 British divers Jason Mallinson and Rick Stanton continued the
exploration and after 4,050m of diving reached a boulder choke in Sump 5.
The following year Stanton, accompanied by John Volanthen, discovered
a new passage close to the end of Sump 5 and followed this for 800m.

Then, in 2012 the pair
continued for a further
70m to a dangerously
unstable gravel slope
after 4,720m of diving
from the entrance. This
significant new passage

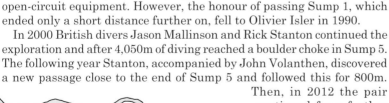

ump 2   Sump 3   Sump 4

Sump 5   blocked

0 ——————— 200m

Further considerations

▶ The Ressel can be very busy during summer months
▶ Elevated levels of carbon dioxide may occur beyond the first sump, affecting the quality of the cave air
▶ Divers with sensitive ears should use ear drop medication, which is available from local pharmacies

is a shallow, fossilised downstream development, thought to be the original course of the water before the current active network was formed, and presumably once ran to a second entrance further downstream in the Célé valley. Including the canals, oxbows and dry boulder chambers, the system is estimated to be around 6,830m long.

Diving

Under normal conditions the clear flow of the spring emerges invisibly to mix with the turbid water of the Célé a little over 6m below the surface. Descending steeply to the modest entrance, divers quickly leave the warm river water for the often crystal-clear clarity of the cave.

Directly inside, at the foot of a gravel slope, the width of the tunnel increases to very generous proportions. A fixed line, well-positioned and distance-marked, runs into the hillside at a depth of 10m. This is an impressive passage over 5m high by more than 8m wide with a large, boulder-strewn floor and little or no silt present.

The depth remains at about 12m for the next 170m to a junction: to the left lies the Shallow Route, while directly ahead is the Deep Route. The former is a fine phreatic tube, generally over 3m diameter, which carries on at the same depth until, about 330m from the entrance, the two routes reunite at a step-like shaft at −24m. Here, the tunnel regains its former magnitude, gradually deepening to an even more spectacular shaft some 30m further on.

The Shallow Route in the Ressel, the dive base in Bivouac Chamber beyond Sump 2, and Jason Mallinson at the camp

From now onwards the cave descends to over 40m and the diving becomes more committing. At 440m the passage veers to the left at a distinct corner where gas reserves should be assessed – this is frequently a turning point for divers using open-circuit configurations. The enormous tunnel continues, finally reaching air after a total distance of 1,875m and a maximum depth of 80m. This extensive cave has four further sumps.

◀ Jiří Huráb at the shaft 400m into Sump 1

(9) Source du Marchepied

FULL

Air quality
beyond
Sump 1

The Marchepied dive base

Cruising the clay floor 150m
into Sump 1 at 16m depth

Objective

The Source du Marchepied presents some stunning underwater scenery to fully certified cave divers using side-mounted equipment; the maximum depth in Sump 1 is 17m.

Access

In 2012 the regional government (Conseil Général du Lot) acquired ownership of this spring with the intention of allowing cave divers full access. As this book goes to print a project is scheduled to investigate potential instability in the entrance area and, if necessary, make it safe for entry.

Location

The Source du Marchepied is situated 1.5km south-south-west of Marcilhac-sur-Célé on the eastern (left) bank of the river Célé, about 28km east-north-east of Cahors. In Marcilhac cross the river to the east side, turn right and follow the small country road due south-west. Remaining close to the valley bottom, follow signs via the hamlet of Sarrou (600m from the river crossing) towards Doujac, a farm approximately 1.5km further along the dead end road. Some 500m from Sarrou the road runs very close to the river on the right; park after another 300m where there is plenty of room for several vehicles. The Source du Marchepied lies less than 100m away on the lower side of the road.

History

British divers Tim Chapman and Clive Stell 'discovered' the spring in the early 2000s and, following determined excavations, by August 2002 they could see into open passage. Entry was gained in 2003 and the pair progressed their exploration to approximately 770m from dive base in

Near the bottom of the Marchepied entrance slope

Célé (river)

−6m −2m

surface pool

−8m

Sump 1, 510m

to Marcilhac-sur-Célé

to Doujac (dead end)   small road   −16m

SOURCE DU MARCHEPIED
Marcilhac-sur-Célé
Lot, France

−4m

−17m

⚠ airbell: may contain bad air

↑N   −8m

−3m   end of Sump 1   0   50m

Based on survey by Nadir Lasson

⚠ very poor air quality

Sump 2, 28m   About 30m from dive base in Sump 1

−5m   canal   Sump 3 ▼

continues 668m to boulder choke, max depth 69m ↘

2007. In the spring and summer of 2008 French diver Pierre-Eric Deseigne laid 450m of line on two operations to reach 1,220m from the entrance at −58m. British diver Rick Stanton continued from this point early in July 2008, achieving a maximum depth of 69m before ascending a shaft to encounter a boulder blockage approximately 1,400m from the entrance.

Diving

The line is tied off at the entrance and the small, stone-walled resurgence pool dips at a fairly steep angle into a restricted, low passage floored with cobbles and gravel. Care is required to ensure that debris does not compromise a restriction at 6m depth. Beyond this point the passage levels off and in good solid rock follows a narrow but somewhat awkward fissure. Then, at 40m from dive base, at 8m depth, the passage becomes significantly larger. The continuing route, often 3m to 4m high and at least 2m wide, is one of the finest, most beautifully sculpted tunnels imaginable.

The visibility is crystal clear and Sump 1 offers an outstanding dive with a maximum depth of 17m. After 260m or so the passage slowly begins to rise and some airbells are found about 440m from dive base. Sump 1 effectively ends at 510m when you have to get out of the water for 20m or so. Be warned: the air quality here is very poor and visitors have found the effort of moving between one sump pool and the next to be distinctly worrying when attempting to breathe the cave air. It is important to maintain composure at such places and once back in the water, breathing once more from your dive kit, the stress will quickly disappear. Sump 2 is 28m long followed by about 80m of canal to Sump 3. This sump is over 660m in length, with a maximum depth of 69m and finally terminates at a boulder blockage at 57m depth.

Further considerations

▶ Avoid causing loose material to collapse or slump into the water in and around the surface pool; it could be critical if any debris drops into the entrance when a diver is inside

▶ This is not a cavern site: side-mounted cave divers only

(10) Source de Landenouse

Objective

INTRO The Source de Landenouse offers an exceptional dive site for introductory and fully certified cave divers, with roomy passages and excellent visibility. The depth increases only very gradually and long penetrations are possible.

Access

No permission is required.

Location

Around 35km east of Cahors, close to the north bank of the Lot river, is the resurgence of Landenouse. It lies just over 1.5km east of Cajarc, directly alongside the D662 road heading towards Montbrun and Figeac. The entrance is easy to locate, lying in a large unroofed concrete water tank immediately below the road on the right. A significant landmark is a large house and outbuildings situated just beyond, the only such structures on this stretch of road. Parking nearby is very limited and visitors may have to leave vehicles some distance away to avoid blocking access to the fields – take care not to inconvenience the local landowner.

History

While French divers from the Groupe Spéléologique Auvergnat made the initial explorations of this magnificent cave, it fell to the German diver Jochen Hasenmayer to make a most audacious advance in 1980. Equipped with a revolutionary, custom-built rebreather, Hasenmayer reached a gravel restriction at 88m depth and 1,240m from the entrance. Rick Stanton passed Hasenmayer's terminus in 2002, progressed further on a series of dives in 2005, and reached –120m and 1,430m from the entrance in 2007.

Diving

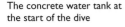

The concrete water tank at the start of the dive

The water level in the tank varies, but last-minute kitting up is always undertaken in deep water, so careful thought needs to be given to this beforehand.

Access to the water is via a pair of fixed ladders attached to the walls and equipment is usually lowered and hauled up with ropes. Rigging a pulley system to assist this is advantageous, but not essential; a couple

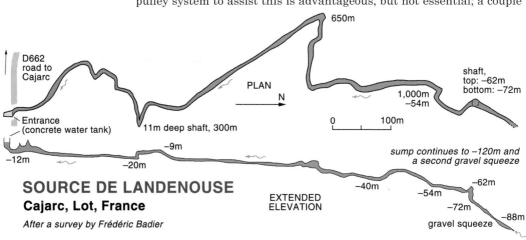

650m

D662 road to Cajarc

PLAN

N

shaft, top: –62m bottom: –72m

1,000m –54m

Entrance (concrete water tank)

11m deep shaft, 300m

0   100m

–9m

sump continues to –120m and a second gravel squeeze

–12m

–20m

SOURCE DE LANDENOUSE

Cajarc, Lot, France

After a survey by Frédéric Badier

EXTENDED ELEVATION

–40m

–54m

–62m

–72m

–88m

gravel squeeze

Spacious passage at 15m depth in the initial section of the Source de Landenouse

of strong people can easily manage one set of equipment at a time. Whatever approach is adopted, take a few extra karabiners and slings to speed things up and for attaching items in an orderly fashion at water level. The water is roughly 2m to 3m deep in the summer and the sides are sheer and smooth (in flood, the place overflows at the lip – a very impressive sight). The nylon line is tied off in the daylight zone.

Passing through a vertical cleft in the bottom of the tank, you land on a slope of large, clean-washed cobbles at about –12m, where there is ample room to leave a decompression cylinder if required. After a further descent of about 3m the floor levels and you enter the passage, which is spacious and unobstructed by rocks or debris. Visibility is always excellent, in excess of 8m, unless the silt has been disturbed by heavy diver use. The tunnel, floored with sand, gravel and fine silt, meanders steadily in a northerly direction; it is generally 5m to 6m wide and about 3m high. The character remains the same and the depth increases only very slowly, reaching –20m after about 270m distance.

Quite suddenly, at the 300m mark, a shaft approximately 2m in diameter takes the diver up to –9m, then after a few twists and turns the cave begins a gradual descent once more. By 1,000m the depth is around 50m, beyond which the descent accelerates, passing Hasenmayer's gravel restriction (–88m) at 1,240m and leads ultimately to a more committing terminal restriction at –120m and 1,430m from the entrance.

Further considerations

► Relationships are delicate between divers and the local farmer; please respect his position, in particular concerning his access to his fields
► The technical difficulty of lowering and raising equipment to and from the water requires careful planning

Émergence de Crégols (11)

Objective

The Émergence de Crégols presents some remarkable underwater scenery for introductory and fully certified cave divers using side-mounted equipment. The maximum depth is 3m in Sump 1, while Sump 2 descends rapidly to over 40m.

INTRO

Backmount

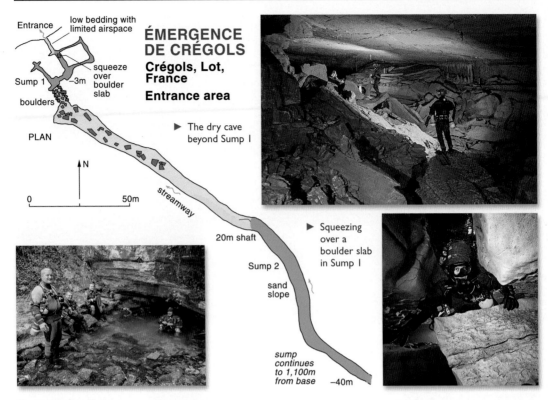

ÉMERGENCE DE CRÉGOLS
Crégols, Lot, France
Entrance area

PLAN

Entrance — low bedding with limited airspace

squeeze over boulder slab

Sump 1 — −3m

boulders

0 ___ 50m

▲N

streamway

20m shaft

Sump 2

sand slope

sump continues to 1,100m from base   −40m

▶ The dry cave beyond Sump I

▶ Squeezing over a boulder slab in Sump I

The entrance to the Émergence de Crégols

Access
No permission is required.

Location
The small village of Crégols lies on the southern bank of the river Lot some 3km up the main valley from the well-known beauty spot of St-Cirq-Lapopie and around 20km east of Cahors. On the western edge of the village a small concrete building beneath a cliff face about 100m west of the church serves as a pumping station and takes water from the cave. Park directly adjacent to the building where there is ample space for several vehicles. The unimpressive low bedding entrance to the resurgence lies almost directly below the pump house.

History
For many years the Émergence de Crégols comprised only 10m of crawling-sized passage and a 40m long sump that surfaced at a massive above-water boulder choke. In 1993 Jean-Marc Lebel, accompanied by Stéphane Guignard, broke through the choke to discover a substantial chamber followed by Sump 2, which Lebel dived the following year for 450m until it closed down. British divers, Rick Stanton in 2002 and together with John Volanthen in 2004, extended a major side passage to about 1,100m from base.

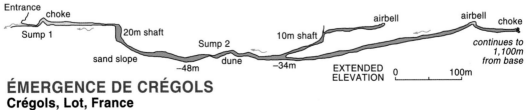

Entrance
choke
Sump 1
20m shaft
sand slope
−48m
Sump 2
dune
−34m
10m shaft
airbell
airbell
choke
continues to 1,100m from base
EXTENDED ELEVATION   0 ___ 100m

ÉMERGENCE DE CRÉGOLS
Crégols, Lot, France

Crégols Sump 1

Diving

Crawl into the cave in a variable depth of water to reach a crystal-clear, silt-free sump within 10m. The lined sump begins with a squeeze over a large boulder, then enlarges into a comfortably sized phreatic tube. After meandering through a shallow tunnel at a maximum depth of 3m, you will surface some 40m from the dive base. The far side of the sump is marked by a major boulder fall.

Dekit and climb up for about 3m; this ascent is awkward to negotiate with dive equipment, but quickly gives access to an enormous cavern. Cross the muddy boulders with care to regain the water about 120m from Sump 1, where a deepening canal heralds the approach of the next flooded portion. Sump 2 begins as a splendid shaft dropping to a sand slope at 20m, then continuing to descend in a tunnel floored with course silt deposits. At about 35m depth the passage enlarges to perhaps 10m wide by 10m high; the depth quickly reaches 40m and the imposing tunnel carries on at a maximum of –48m for many hundreds of metres. This is a truly sensational excursion that will quickly take the diver into decompression.

Further considerations

▶ The zigzag descent path to the cave is about 100m long: sturdy footwear is recommended

▶ Side-mounted equipment is essential in Sump 1

▶ Take a line reel in case the line in Sump 1 is broken

▶ Passing the boulder choke requires care; for this and the dry cavern beyond appropriate footwear is strongly recommended

(12) Trou Madame

Objective

INTRO

The Trou Madame offers wonderful opportunities for long, roomy and shallow penetrations for introductory and fully certified cave divers; however, it is not generally regarded as a cavern diving site and certainly not in high water conditions.

Access

No permission is required.

Location

The Trou Madame is situated a short distance south of Cénevières, which lies in the Lot valley 25km east of Cahors. About 1km from the crossroads in the village, heading south towards Limogne-en-Quercy on

Entrance

high water dive base

low water dive base

*water emerges
from entrance
during high water*

Sump 1

95m
–5m

↑N

Sump 2
265m
–5m

0   100m

TROU MADAME

Cénevières, Lot, France

*Based on a survey by Jacques Brasey
and Vincent Durant, 1987*

Sump 3
10m
–2m

Sump 4
350m
–10m

Sump 5
8m, –2m

Sump 6
200m, –14m

Sump 7

*continues
to Sump 9*

17m
–4m

◀ The entrance to
the Trou Madame

The dive base in low
water conditions
and a group of divers
beyond Sump 3
▼

The approach to Sump 4

the D24, a small and easily missed track leaves the road on the right-hand side just before the 'zigzag bends for 8km' road sign. The narrow and rough track crosses a small stream, le Girou, which is the outflow from the cave; follow the track at valley floor level for 250m. Park beside a small, low rock face on the right – however, space is only available for two cars, so please park considerately.

The footpath to the cave lies 5m further down the track, on the left (towards the east). After 75m the path converges with the small stream and follows it on the right-hand side – another 25m reaches the large cave entrance. The last section in the slippery, rocky streambed is awkward underfoot. You can change in comfort at the cave mouth beneath a large overhang.

Further Considerations
▶ Take care not to obstruct the parking area
▶ There are no equipment limitations, but it is easier to make two carries to the entrance
▶ Carbon dioxide may be detected in areas where activities are strenuous, but it is not as noticeable as in other caves in the region

History
The major cave diving site of the Trou Madame has witnessed many explorations, notably during the 1970s: first by Bertrand Léger and later by Francis Le Guen and a large team of divers from the Spéléo-Club de Paris. The latter team passed the 1,285m long and 30m deep Sump 8 to discover an active stream passage involving a cascade, which led to Sump 9. They dived this for 210m at a maximum depth of about 12m, reaching a terminal boulder blockage in August 1979. The total distance to the 'end' is about 2.5km.

Diving
If water levels are high, the dive base lies 10m inside the cave within sight of daylight, but under normal or low water conditions the sump begins after a further 50m and equipment has to be carried in through a short stooping-cum-crawling section. Once in the water, the visibility is very good, the depth is shallow and it is possible to dive for as far as you feel comfortable in a series of spacious sumps. The cave trends steadily south-east as a straightforward, single passage with no route-finding difficulties or complications.

In low water the dive begins as a 75m long stretch of deepening canal. Sump 1 is generally over 3m high and about 10m wide, with very little silt. After 95m, at a maximum depth of 5m, the surface is gained in a gloomy 15m long canal. The water, under low conditions, is standing depth with about 2m of airspace.

Sump 2 is about 265m long at a similar depth and surfaces in a small airspace, while Sump 3 is very shallow at only 2m and is merely 10m long. In practical terms, Sumps 2 and 3 are best regarded as a single dive and the next distinct landmark is some 40m to 50m of canal passage, mostly over 2m wide with over 3m of airspace.

The cave now becomes altogether more varied and interesting, with short shafts and some boulders. A further

A short distance into Sump 1 in the Trou Madame

six submerged sections follow, the longest of which is Sump 8 at 1,285m and 30m maximum depth. In all but extreme drought, the air chambers leading to Sump 7 may be easily passed by swimming. However, the approach to Sump 8 is noteworthy in that it involves a relatively strenuous 30m or more scramble over sharp and slippery rocks. These further reaches are not travelled on a regular basis, so the condition of the line will warrant very close attention. Sump 9 ends at a boulder blockage after 210m.

Coordinates

Map numbers refer to the following French IGN 1:25,000 maps:

2035 E (Série Bleue): Terrasson-Lavilledieu

2136 ET (Top 25): Rocamadour, Padirac, Vallée de la Dordogne

2138 OT (Top 25): Cahors, St-Cirq-Lapopie, Vallées du Lot et du Célé

2238 O (Série Bleue): Cajarc

IGN maps include a blue grid that enables WSG84 coordinates to be looked up directly. For conversion to UTM data, this area lies in Zone 31T

Dive site	Map No.	WSG84 coordinates	Lat/Long
1 Doux de Coly	2035 E	3655 49917	45° 04' 00.63" N, 01° 17' 35.70" E
2 Oeil de la Doue	2136 ET	3886 49800	44° 57' 54.88" N, 01° 35' 14.75" E
3 Fontaine Saint-Georges	2136 ET	3910 49716	44° 53' 22.00" N, 01° 37' 08.35" E
4 Émergence de Meyraguet	2136 ET	3848 49676	44° 51' 09.89" N, 01° 32' 31.87" E
5 Font del Truffe	2136 ET	3855 49645	44° 49' 29.49" N, 01° 33' 02.94" E
6 Source de Saint-Sauveur	2136 ET	3867 49606	44° 47' 25.40" N, 01° 34' 08.00" E
7 Gouffre de Cabouy	2136 ET	3880 49606	44° 47' 24.95" N, 01° 35' 03.79" E
7 Gouffre de Pou Meyssen	2136 ET	3887 49607	44° 47' 26.31" N, 01° 35' 34.65" E
8 Émergence du Ressel	2138 OT	4025 49350	44° 33' 42.95" N, 01° 46' 21.99" E
9 Source du Marchepied	2138 OT	4019 49326	44° 32' 22.51" N, 01° 45' 51.91" E
10 Source de Landenouse	2238 O	4098 49266	44° 29' 15.66" N, 01° 51' 56.39" E
11 Émergence de Crégols	2138 OT	3965 49235	44° 27' 25.76" N, 01° 41' 55.29" E
12 Trou Madame	2138 OT	4009 49227	44° 27' 02.49" N, 01° 45' 15.07" E

Contacts and air supplies

Lot Cave Diving Centre, La Forge, Pont de Rhodes, 46310 Frayssinet
  Tel: 05.65.31.77.48; www.lotcavedivingcentre.com
  Lat/Long: 44° 40' 17.14" N, 01° 28' 41.50" E

Air Supplies – Station de Gonflage:
  André Grimal, Bournazel, 46500 Gramat
  Tel: 05.65.38.75.36; mobile: 06.80.33.82.16; www.gonflage.com
  Lat/Long: 44° 47' 23.85" N, 01° 43' 44.63" E

Emergencies

Emergency contacts: see Appendix A

Nearest hyperbaric centre: Toulouse

Nearest hospitals: Centre Hospitalier Jean Coulon, avenue Pasteur, 46300 Gourdon; tel: 05.65.27.65.47
  Hôpital Louis Conte, 150 avenue François Souladié, 46500 Gramat; tel: 05.65.38.73.50
  Centre Hospitalier Jean Rougier, 335 rue du Président Wilson, 46005 Cahors; tel: 05.65.20.50.50
  Hôpital de Figeac, 33 rue des Maquisards, 46100 Figeac; tel: 05.65.50.66.26

International telephone country code: +33; drop the preceding zero from the local number

The high water dive base in the Trou Madame

Further reading

FARR, Martyn. *The Darkness Beckons,* 2nd edn, Diadem, London (1991); 3rd edn postscript, Bâton Wicks, Macclesfield (2000)

WARD, Andrew. *Underwater Guide to the Lot & Dordogne France,* 2nd edn, Aven International, Swindon (2003)

The Island of Zante

Greece

Objective
The island of Zante (or, in Greek, Zakynthos) is a superb venue for cavern diving that will also entertain cave divers wishing to explore further.

Access
No permission is required, but diving certification must be carried at all times.

Location
Zante is one of the principal islands in the Ionian chain off the west coast of Greece's Peloponnese peninsula. Situated in the Ionian Sea, this small island lies directly south of Cephalonia, itself a site worth visiting for its caverns and caves. As a tourist destination, each year the island comes alive in May, but everything closes down at the end of October. Outside the main holiday season, flights to Zante are via Athens (45 minute transfer). A regular car ferry runs from Kyllini harbour in the north-west part of the Peloponnese to Zakynthos harbour (one hour).

Environmentalists will be quietly drawn to Zante by the annual influx of the rare, protected species of loggerhead sea turtles, *Caretta caretta*. After many years wandering the eastern Mediterranean, the turtles arrive on the southern beaches of Zante in April and hatchlings appear in late August and September. Historically, this is their most important breeding site.

The coast has four areas of caves: Marathia, Keri and White Reef, close together in the south, and Skinari in the north. A boat is required in order to reach the first three, whereas Skinari Cave is a shore dive.

Other Greek destinations offering cavern diving include Lesbos (see: www.lesvoscuba.gr).

History
The earliest exploration of the caverns on Zante was undertaken by visiting Italian open water divers, using their own scuba equipment, during the early 1980s. Diving was not a popular activity on the island and it was not until February 1998 that Fanis Nikoloudakis and Antonis Synetos made the first dives in Skinari Cave.

CAVERN

Entering Keri caves

Diving

Only a twenty-minute boat journey south-west from the principal tourist centre of Laganas lies the beautiful and fascinating area of **Marathia** on the south coast. A network of six short caverns and caves are sited along a 200m stretch of cliff, either side of and in very close proximity

A rift in White Reef Caverns

to a 15m high limestone arch. Marathia presents beautiful and intriguing cavern diving in water less than 12m in depth. None of the tunnels are likely to take a novice beyond his or her comfort zone, but streamlined cave diving specialists would no doubt wish to negotiate the restrictions and explore further.

The most interesting cave lies on the westerly side of the prominent natural arch, where a large cavernous opening leads within 30m to an inner chamber with a thick layer of milky-coloured water suspended like a cloud above the diver's head. By rising through this, it is possible to surface in a small enclosed chamber where the acrid smell of sulphur is immediately apparent and, indeed, almost overpowering: divers should not remove their mouthpieces here, as the air quality is so poor.

Just 20m to 30m from the sunshine and the warm, clear water of the open sea, this chamber could be used as a sci-fi movie set. The ceiling contains curious encrustations of yellow sulphurous matter and life forms adapted to the alien conditions swim in the milky water. A shallow, low and constricted cave passage leads on – it has been tentatively explored for a short distance in extremely poor visibility.

Geological quirks such as this are comparatively rare in limestone caves and it is worth reflecting that the island was devastated by an immense earthquake in 1953 – this fissure is clearly an outlet for some deep-seated geothermal emission.

Approximately 2km south-west of Marathia, an area abounding in rocky clefts, ravines, caverns and caves at the southern extremity of the island is known as the **Keri** caves; boat access is again required. One cave here extends for 50m

Contacts and air supplies

Diver's Paradise, Louis Zante Beach Hotel, Kalamaki, 290 92 Zakynthos
  Tel: 2695 051918; www.diversparadise.gr

Emergencies

Emergency contacts: see Appendix A
Nearest hyperbaric centre: Athens (40 minutes by helicopter)
Nearest health centre: General Hospital of Zakynthos, Agios
  Dionisios, 29 100 Zakynthos; tel: 26950 59100 or 26950 42514
Nearest hospital: Naval Hospital of Athens, 70 Dinokratous,
  115 21 Athens; tel: 21 07216166
International telephone country code: +30

Coordinates

Dive site	Lat/Long
Keri caves	37° 38′ 48.02″ N, 20° 50′ 34.76″ E
Marathia caves	37° 39′ 41.22″ N, 20° 51′ 30.89″ E
Skinari Cave	37° 56′ 00.50″ N, 20° 41′ 53.53″ E
White Reef Caverns	37° 38′ 43.13″ N, 20° 49′ 47.99″ E

or more from an entrance at 30m depth; the water is unbelievably clear and contains thousands of shrimps. Another, much larger but shallower cave surfaces to a large, deep lake that is dimly illuminated by a small skylight some 15m or 20m above the water. The ravines and caverns are generally less than 12m deep with shoals of small sardine-like fish and walls padded with colourful arrays of orange and yellow sponges. The Arc de Triomphe, the roof of which lies at 12m, is clearly a popular landmark and presents a memorable, if short, swim-through.

Only 1km further west, the superb 70m to 80m long **White Reef Caverns** (another site requiring boat access) runs westwards through a headland at a relatively shallow depth of around 12m.

At the northern tip of Zante, some 27km north-west of Laganas, the island of Cephalonia looms large across the sea 15km distant. Sight-seeing tourists may be attracted to the renowned boat trip to the nearby Galazia Spilia or Blue Caves, which are spectacular in their own right. Caves and caverns abound in the north, the finest of which is **Skinari Cave**, accessed by a shore dive from the embarkation point for visiting the Blue Caves. Skinari has an absolutely enormous entrance, well over 20m square, and an ongoing passage that leads for perhaps 50m at 20m depth to a much larger cavern which has an opening to daylight high above.

On surfacing through a halocline, the topmost 2m will be found to comprise fairly fresh water. Not much light penetrates the depths from the 5m diameter skylight, but enough is present to create a dramatic impression, especially when looking back through the haze towards the main entrance.

Further considerations
▶ A knowledgeable guide will help in locating the various sites
▶ The water temperature varies from 12°C in winter (it is coldest in February and March) to over 22°C in late summer, and it may reach 30°C
▶ A 5mm wetsuit is ample in the summer
▶ Divers familiar with cold water diving will find a hood and gloves unnecessary in summer
▶ The visibility is 20m or more

▲ The Arc de Triomphe at Keri caves

The huge tunnel continues on the right-hand side of the chamber at a depth of 30m, terminating abruptly perhaps 75m later where the passage splits into two much smaller silty tubes at the same depth. A dive deep into the main cave will require decompression. At least two other significant caves are located between Skinari's entrance and the point of entry to the water – there is little doubt that more caves such as these remain to be discovered and explored.

The Caves of Cong

Co. Galway and Co. Mayo, Ireland

NOWHERE in Ireland can a more intriguing set of risings and associated caves be found than at Cong. These offer interesting possibilities for all levels of ability from cavern divers through to fully certified cave divers with, mostly, a maximum depth of less than 24m.

Other caves exist in the Cong locality, but they are not described here as they either lie on private property with restricted access, involve greater technical difficulty to enter, or are simply blind pools of water.

Access

Permission is not required at any sites listed here, but please be discreet when changing and avoid disturbance to local residents. Park vehicles with consideration for farmers and other road users.

Location

Cong lies in the west of Ireland, on the border between Co. Galway and Co. Mayo. Some enormous upwellings of water are located virtually in the centre of the small village, and this then flows south to feed Lough Corrib. The source of the water is several kilometres to the north at Lough Mask, which acts as if it is a giant colander. Millions of litres of water a day flow into Lough Mask and disappear underground at a series of sinister-looking whirlpools and small sinks at the lake's southernmost edge.

The water also reappears at some impenetrable springs in the Cong area. Between the sinks and resurgences a maze-like network of inter-connecting flooded caves remains largely unexplored. Seven areas are of interest, some with more than one dive site.

History

Martyn Farr and the Dark Shamrock cave diving team started working at Cong in the early 1980s.

Cong village, surrounded by forest and dive sites

Further considerations

► Strong currents are a feature of the caves in and close to Cong: be careful
► Do not use thin technical line
► Water temperatures vary according to season, from perhaps 6°C to 19°C
► The visibility is rarely better than between 3m and 4m, and is frequently less

Hatchery Rising

CAVERN

Objective
Hatchery Rising is an open water site; no overhead environment certification is required.

Location

Hatchery Rising

Hatchery Rising is the most impressive of the risings in the village of Cong, situated directly alongside a large, factory-like building with a domed roof. Access to the water is over the low wall from the pavement.

Diving
It is possible to descend into the funnel-like depths to some 22m. Here, powerful flows of water emerge from between massive boulders and prevent any further progress. The visibility is around 4m in summer, at which time the temperature may rise as high as 19°C.

Duck Pond Rising

CAVERN

Objective
Duck Pond Rising provides limited opportunities for cavern diving.

Location
Duck Pond Rising lies near Hatchery Rising, behind the garage and filling station in Cong; it is also known as Mill Rising.

Diving
A powerful flow mushrooms and ripples the surface of the rising, but the opening is more restricted than at the Hatchery. At a depth of 15m, water forces upwards from a distinct vertical fissure that deepens to the northern end and in which, due to a gradual narrowing of the route, no progress has been made below −22m.

Duck Pond Rising

Lost World

Objective
Dives suited to cavern divers, introductory divers and fully certified cave divers are available at Lost World.

Lost World: The Pit

Location

At the eastern approach to the village of Cong a large public car park is situated directly adjacent to the river that flows away from Duck Pond Rising. A separate watercourse lies on the other side of the car park from the main river, immediately beyond the route of the infamous, long-abandoned Cong Canal, and for most of the summer this contains a few limpid pools of tranquil water. However, a slight flow in the waterway represents water which passes

LOST WORLD
Cong, Co. Mayo, Ireland

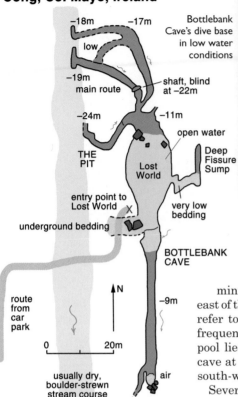

-18m   -17m

low

Bottlebank
Cave's dive base
in low water
conditions

-19m
main route

shaft, blind
at -22m

-24m   -11m

open water

THE
PIT   Lost
World

Deep
Fissure
Sump

entry point to
Lost World   X

very low
bedding

underground bedding

BOTTLEBANK
CAVE

route
from
car
park

N

-9m

0   20m

usually dry,
boulder-strewn
stream course

air

too tight

through a wonderful little area for cavern and cave diving: Lost World.

Lost World, as the name implies, is not easy to find – it is a circular, 20m diameter rock-walled depression overhung by trees, about 250m and seven minutes' walk from the car park and some 15m to 20m east of the dry, boulder-strewn stream course. Local residents refer to this site as Mark Anthony's, a place occasionally frequented by local fishermen. An impressively large rising pool lies at the northern edge and a walk-in stream sink cave at the southern side; entry to the depression is at the south-west corner.

Several dives are possible at Lost World, including two at The Pit (the rising) and one at Bottlebank Cave (the sink).

Diving: The Pit

CAVERN

The Pit offers an exhilarating cavern dive with a strong flow in a cave typical of the area, descending to a maximum depth of 24m. The spacious passage is diveable in virtually all conditions, with a visibility of between 3m and 4m.

The dive is set against the left-hand (western) wall of Lost World, where a fixed line may be followed until, at 11m depth, the boulder slope channels into a smaller passage in solid rock. A strong current emerges here and within a few metres a short vertical descent gives way to a silt-covered floor at 20m – the narrowing passage ends abruptly at a low gravelly squeeze at 24m depth.

The return to the surface will be made in greatly reduced visibility, but back at –11m the sheer size of the cavernous entrance can be appreciated and a safety stop will reveal a wealth of fish life including perch, trout and eels.

Diving: Lost World northern passages

The second location in Lost World is at the northern side of the cavernous rising, where a separate short network of flooded passages may be explored to a maximum depth of 22m. This is a much more challenging dive involving low bedding passages, high currents and the presence of silt and

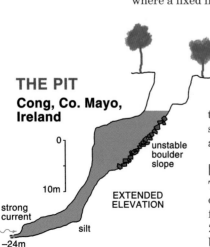

THE PIT
Cong, Co. Mayo, Ireland

0

unstable
boulder
slope

10m

strong
current

EXTENDED
ELEVATION

silt

-24m

should only be tackled by side-mount divers with an introductory or fully cave certified level of training; this is not a suitable site for cavern divers.

Access can only be made under low flow conditions: if Bottlebank Cave – the sink for Lost World – is inaccessible then so will be this section. Descend steeply over boulders in the main tunnel, passing a low side passage on the right-hand side at –13m, until it levels off at a depth of 17m. After a couple of familiarisation set-up dives, ensuring that the lines are securely belayed, it may be possible to complete a short round-trip through an intimidating low section which connects the two tunnels. Dive the main tunnel first (i.e. clockwise), so that if required a return can be made without attempting the tight section.

A shaft dropping from floor level in the main tunnel at –17m leads to a very silty dead end at –22m.

Diving: Bottlebank Cave

Bottlebank Cave offers a lovely cavern dive, descending to a maximum of 9m in a fine, clean-washed oval tunnel.

Water flowing from The Pit sinks into a walking-sized cave at the southern edge of Lost World. Some 7m from the outside world a slight descent leads to a downstream sump which should *not* be attempted under high water conditions. Visitors must be very cautious if water is pouring directly into the sump pool as it may not be possible to fight back out against the current.

INTRO

Backmount

CAVERN

BOTTLEBANK CAVE
Cong, Co. Mayo, Ireland

very small airspace

0

WARNING
Think carefully
about your exit
if water is flowing

underwater bridge

EXTENDED ELEVATION

outlet

10m

–9m

Entering The Pit at 10m depth

However, under low flow summer conditions, this downstream site offers a perfect training dive. The tunnel drops steeply to –9m, then rises gradually to a small air surface 45m from dive base. Until 2007 this furthermost section was a separate cave and open to the surface but, sadly, it has been infilled, leaving just enough space for two divers – three if very friendly – to surface and briefly chat about their inward dive. As it has been used in the past as a refuse dump (hence the name Bottlebank), visitors should be wary of broken glass.

Bunnadober Cave

CAVERN

⚠️

Unstable rocks on entrance slope

Objective

This fine cavern dive reaches a maximum depth of 23m and offers an experience in crystal-clear, static cave water.

Access

Bunnadober Cave lies on land belonging to Mr Pat O'Connor – there are no access difficulties, but out of courtesy ask for permission to visit before crossing the land. Heading from Clonbur to Ballinrobe, take the last lane on the right before the cave, towards Castletown and the village of Neale. Call at the bungalow 1km/0.6 mile on the right-hand side.

Bunnadober Cave. The restriction lies at the foot of the slope beyond the disturbed silt; the alternative route lies directly ahead at the level of the diver's exhaled bubbles

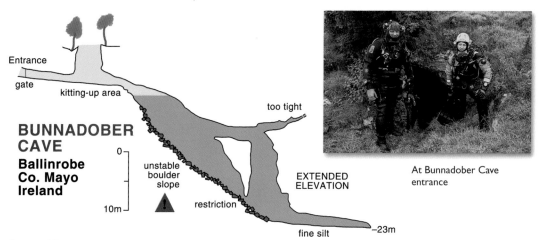

At Bunnadober Cave entrance

BUNNADOBER CAVE
Ballinrobe
Co. Mayo
Ireland

Entrance
gate
kitting-up area
too tight
unstable boulder slope
restriction
fine silt
EXTENDED ELEVATION
0
10m
−23m

Location
Bunnadober Cave lies some 7km/4.5 miles north of Cong and just over 2km/1.2 miles before the T-junction in Ballinrobe on the road from Clonbur; it is situated 30m from the southern side of the road. Ensure that all gates are kept closed and remain unobstructed.

The cave entrance is marked by a small clump of stunted trees and hazel scrub in a gently rising green field – it is all but invisible until the last few paces. The cave is fitted with a heavy metal gate which visitors should secure firmly at the close of their trip.

The crystal-clear sump pool is easy to reach, just over 10m inside the comfortable, walking-sized cave. Divers are asked to kit up and dekit about 5m inside the cave in a small chamber with a skylight opening, rather than doing so on the surface

History
Bunnadober Cave was first dived by Martyn Farr in 1983.

Diving
From the dive base, negotiate a steep rocky slope down the right-hand wall, being careful not to dislodge rocks onto any divers below. This leads to a minor, localised constriction at 15m depth which can be passed with care using conventional back-mounted equipment, but an alternative and easier route is to swim up and over the restriction then descend immediately beyond into what appears to be a large, ongoing tunnel. However, the passage only continues for 20m to an abrupt, restricted and very muddy end at a depth of 23m. The water temperature is 9°C.

The silt is easily disturbed in this tunnel. Inexperienced cave divers are strongly advised not to proceed beyond the bottom of the rocky slope at −20m.

The River Run

Objective
The River Run is a great cave where experienced side-mount divers at both introductory and fully cave certified levels can undertake some exhilarating diving; this is *not* a cavern dive site.

Access
There are no access difficulties.

INTRO

Backmount

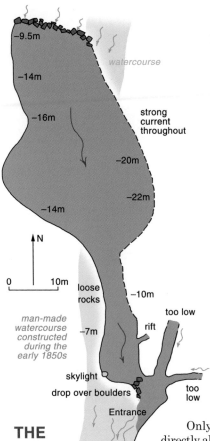

-9.5m

watercourse

-14m

-16m

strong
current
throughout

-20m

-22m

-14m

N

0   10m

loose
rocks   -10m

too low

man-made
watercourse
constructed
during the
early 1850s   -7m   rift

skylight

drop over boulders   too
low

Entrance

**THE
RIVER
RUN**

**Cong,
Co. Galway,
Ireland**

Location

Directly behind the largest of the Cong risings, Hatchery Rising, a salmon ladder produces a cascade into an enormous whirlpool-like feature directly below. Scuds of foam rotate in this dark pool and, 7m beneath the surface, a good proportion of the Hatchery water sinks between debris-strewn boulders. There is no open passage here, which is perhaps just as well!

A man-made cutting, dating from the era of canal construction in the nineteenth century, leads from the pool to the south and about 50cm depth of water courses down this overflow channel en route to Ashford Castle and Lough Corrib. Some 80m to 90m from the whirlpool, against the left-hand (eastern) bank, a powerful flow resurges from beneath a rocky ledge. This marks the low, obscured entrance to The River Run, offering a challenging dive back upstream towards the river sink.

History

The River Run was discovered and first dived by Martyn Farr in the summer of 2007.

Diving

Given that the entrance is low, heavily obstructed with boulders and discharges a very powerful flow, side-mounted equipment is required to gain entry and even then access is only possible in low flow conditions. In summer the temperature here can be a balmy 18°C or 19°C and visibility between 3m and 4m.

Only 2m inside the bedding plane entrance, a junction leads directly ahead into a very low passage that terminates in boulders after 15m, while immediately to the left a strong flow emerges from a restricted hole: the flow here is breathtaking. Begin the descent carefully, mindful that the boulders have sharp edges, and within a couple of metres enter an impressive tunnel trending north. This is clearly a very ancient passage, in places 30m wide by some 5m high, and it can be followed for 80m through a similarly enormous passage back to the source of the whirlpool inflow.

The maximum depth is 16m along the lined western wall, but the depth and silt deposits increase significantly on the eastern side of the tunnel. Be particularly wary of the current and do not accidentally dislodge any unstable rocks lining the left-hand (western) wall.

Two Counties Cave

Objective

FULL

Backmount

Two Counties Cave is a site for experienced, fully cave certified divers using side-mounted equipment; it is not suitable for a cavern dive.

Access

There are no access difficulties, but please park vehicles with consideration and change with discretion.

Location

Between the Thatched Cottage and Nailan's public house on the Cong one-way road system, a small bridge leads into the salmon hatchery enclosure.

The bridge lies across the county boundary between Co. Galway and Co. Mayo – Two Counties Cave is found in an inconspicuous pool a few metres upstream, below a small outflowing cascade from the hatchery.

History
Two Counties Cave was discovered and first dived by Martyn Farr in the summer of 2007.

Diving
In high water conditions Two Counties Cave acts as a resurgence, while in low water the entrance area has no flow and the cave is very silty. Regardless of water levels, the cave has a very strong sinking current and in the further reaches water flows away from the point of entry.

   The cave is over 110m long and comprises a descending silty tunnel leading to a restriction at a depth of 33m. At about 100m from the dive base a very strong current enters from some narrow roof fissures on the right and the flow surges into a restriction at 110m.

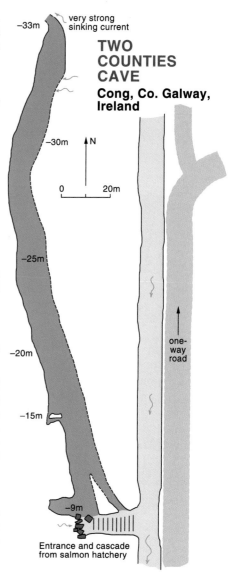

Pigeon Hole

Objective
Pigeon Hole is a challenging site that offers a taster of diving in a constricted bedding passage with a strong flow. It is suitable only for fully certified cave divers using side-mounted equipment, as all the diving, both upstream and downstream, is of a very serious, committing nature. This is *not* a suitable site for trainees at any level.

Access
No permission is required, but diving is only possible under low flow summer conditions – if water is flowing down the cave at the bottom of the entrance steps, no dive should be attempted.

Location
Pigeon Hole is a well-known tourist attraction some 1.5km/1 mile west of the village of Cong. Take the R345 heading for An Fhairche (Clonbur),

Coordinates
All the sites described in this chapter are located on the Ordnance Survey Ireland, 1:50,000, Discovery Series map, no. 38

Dive site	Grid ref	Lat/Long
Bunnadober Cave	M 168624	53° 36′ 16.77″ N, 09° 15′ 28.92″ W
Duck Pond Rising	M 148555	53° 32′ 33.83″ N, 09° 17′ 10.46″ W
Hatchery Rising	M 147555	53° 32′ 34.87″ N, 09° 17′ 18.30″ W
Lost World	M 150556	53° 32′ 37.34″ N, 09° 17′ 00.90″ W
Pigeon Hole	M 134554	53° 32′ 31.47″ N, 09° 18′ 26.28″ W
The River Run	M 146554	53° 32′ 31.11″ N, 09° 17′ 21.13″ W
Two Counties Cave	M 146553	53° 32′ 29.73″ N, 09° 17′ 18.47″ W

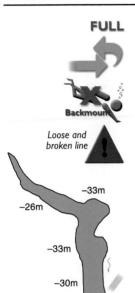

FULL

Backmount

Loose and
broken line

−33m

−26m

−33m

−30m

−25m

road

−20m

**Upstream
Sump**

−10m

water pipe

Entrance

pass the entrance to the active quarry on your right, then take the first road on the left. Park in the clearly signposted layby on the left-hand side some 500m further on at the edge of Pigeon Hole Wood. Follow the footpath down a slope for 200m to the conspicuous, fenced-off entrance.

A steep flight of well-worn steps leads down to a large, cavernous passage about 15m wide by 5m high. An obvious sump pool on the left contains some water extraction pipes – this is the flood rising for water flowing from Lough Mask and is hopelessly blocked by boulders. The only viable diving sites lie to the right of the main entrance.

History

The cave has been the site of major exploration since the 1980s. Downstream Sump 1 was passed by Martyn Farr and Nick Geh in 1991 and Sump 2, via Jacuzzi Shaft, was first explored by Farr in 1992. The upstream cave network was discovered by Farr in the summer of 2006.

Diving

The underwater passages are constricted, involve dangerously strong flows of water and some areas are very unstable. The depth and poor visibility further exacerbate the inherent dangers at this site; the maximum depth upstream is 33m and downstream, 38m.

This is a cave only for the most experienced of side-mount divers and it is mentioned here purely to dissuade those who might be encouraged to take a look at what they perceive to be an accessible dive site.

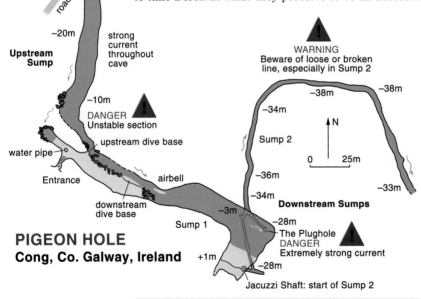

strong
current
throughout
cave

DANGER
Unstable section

upstream dive base

airbell

downstream
dive base

PIGEON HOLE
Cong, Co. Galway, Ireland

Sump 1

−3m

+1m

WARNING
Beware of loose or broken
line, especially in Sump 2

−38m   −38m

−34m

N

Sump 2

0   25m

−36m

−34m   −33m

Downstream Sumps

−28m
The Plughole
DANGER
Extremely strong current

−28m

Jacuzzi Shaft: start of Sump 2

Contacts and air supplies

Scubadive West, Renvyle, Co. Galway
  Tel: 095 43922; www.scubadivewest.com

Emergencies

Emergency contacts: see Appendix A
In the event of an incident call the Garda (999 or 112) and ask for the Irish Cave Rescue
  Organisation or the Irish Coast Guard
Nearest hyperbaric centre: Portadown
Nearest hospital: University Hospital Galway, Newcastle Road, Galway; tel: 091 544544
International telephone country code: +353; drop the preceding zero from the local number

The Green Holes of Doolin

Co. Clare, Ireland

Objective

Numerous swim-throughs, caverns and caves may be found off the rugged coasts of Ireland, but the most extensive and certainly the most interesting and accessible lie in the west near Doolin in Co. Clare. The submarine network of caves, collectively known as the Green Holes, presents some of the finest cavern and cave diving sites in Europe, offering exceptional opportunities at all levels of ability. The complex amounts to over 2km of passage with three separate parts – the Reef Caves, Hell and Mermaid's Hole – as well as the more isolated Urchin Cave.

The water clarity in the Green Holes is excellent, depths are shallow and the main tunnels are generally spacious with a maximum depth of 17m. The marine life is colourful and varied – urchins, sponges and anemones proliferate, seals are common, and basking sharks and porpoises may occasionally be seen.

The karst scenery of the nearby Burren is stunningly beautiful

The Pól na Mongach entrance to Hell

Access

No permission is required to dive in these coastal caves.

Location

The Green Holes area centres upon Doolin Point just north of Doolin Pier, a small harbour at the south-western edge of the Burren karst area (R 0575 9705; 53° 00′ 56.29″ N, 09° 24′ 13.49″ W).

Under optimum conditions – prevailing winds from the east – the diving is of the highest quality and the caves can be accessed from the sea or by land, but in both cases the weather and sea conditions must be assessed very carefully. Currents, particularly around the small Crab Island and the Reef Caves, can exceed five knots and this, in conjunction with turbulent surface swell, has resulted in numerous deaths. Be warned: a long swim underwater may be required to avoid surfacing in hostile conditions. Divers generally approach the area of the reef by entering the water just beyond the toilet building at the western end of the car park in Doolin.

History

The submarine entrances were discovered by open water divers in the 1960s, but systematic exploration and surveying in the main sites – the Reef Caves, Hell and Mermaid's Hole – did not begin until the late 1970s. The longest cave in the Green Holes, Mermaid's Hole, has been progressively explored by various divers including Martyn Farr, who reached a tight squeeze

▶ All sites can be reached by foot (Mermaid's Hole with difficulty)

▶ All are rich in marine life, but warnings due to currents apply across the board

Hell
CAVERN

Mermaid's Hole
CAVERN

Reef Caves
All except Through Cave
FULL

Backmount

Reef Caves
Through Cave
CAVERN

Urchin Cave
INTRO

Backmount

at 900m in 1991. Brian Judd passed this to gain the 935m point in 1993, while Artur Kozłowski pushed on through a hideously silty passage to reach 1,025m in the winter of 2008. Kozłowski also connected the network of passages in Hell to Robertson's Cave in the Reef Caves section in August 2007.

Diving

The **Reef Caves** comprise a complex of some 250m of passages that are best found and entered by diving from the vicinity of Doolin quay, only a couple of hundred metres away. Visitors should pay very close attention to the sea conditions as, apart from the strong currents, thick swaying kelp overhangs the ledges here, so it may take a while to become orientated.

The openings are situated at between 13m and 17m depth. Harbour Hole, Chert Ledge Cave, Lobster Pot Cave and Robertson's Cave are small and only suitable for fully trained cave divers using a side-mount configuration: these are not appropriate sites for cavern diving. However, Through Cave (R 0541 9731), one of the furthest from the quay, possesses a substantial entrance and, as the name suggests, provides a fine 20m traverse suitable for cavern divers.

The **Hell** complex, situated directly adjacent to the Reef Caves, is a larger network that is suitable for all levels of ability. Cavern divers should not stray beyond the limits of their certification.

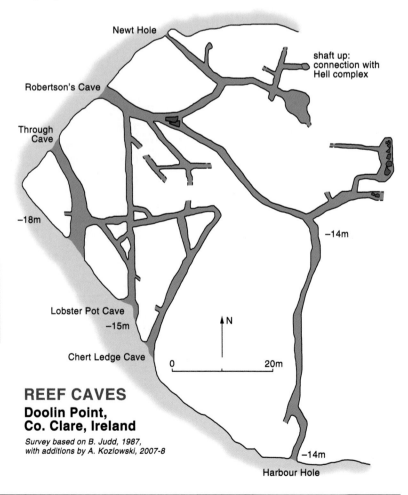

Newt Hole

shaft up: connection with Hell complex

Robertson's Cave

Through Cave

−18m

−14m

Lobster Pot Cave
−15m

N

Chert Ledge Cave

0   20m

REEF CAVES
Doolin Point,
Co. Clare, Ireland
Survey based on B. Judd, 1987,
with additions by A. Kozlowski, 2007-8

−14m

Harbour Hole

HELL COMPLEX
Doolin Point,
Co. Clare, Ireland

Sian and Sarah's Teashop
Lost Entrance
Pól na Mongach
Bedding Cave
−12m
−12m
−13m
J.B. Entrance
Brittlestar Boulevard
Hell's Kitchen (Entrance)
↑N
Honey Pot Chamber
0   20m
−10m
connection with Robertson's Cave
Hall of the Beast
−5m
Melting Pot

Lowering diving kit at Urchin Cave, the approach to Mermaid's Hole and the chamber within Mermaid's: Pirate's Paradise

Hell is normally entered via a massive fissure, Hell's Kitchen, on the storm-scoured limestone platform a few metres above and just a few metres from the sea. However, although the trench-like entrance to this underwater world is sited on dry land, this does not mean that it is an all-weather point of entry. In calm seas the water gloops and slops gracefully around the foot of the 6m deep boulder climb, but if conditions are rough it is a different situation: Hell is aptly named. As the water surges through the cleft, time your entry to the water with considerable care and be mindful about how you will get out again.

In good conditions this is the finest cavern dive in the British Isles. Shortly after submerging into the dark cleft, a dim, distant patch of blue becomes visible – the Pól na Mongach exit to the sea, a superb 30m to 40m long through-dive at a maximum depth of 13m. Just prior to reaching the opening, a large tunnel crosses the route at right angles. To the eastern side on the right, a loop leads to another surface entrance, Bedding Cave, while to the left a complicated area of large westerly trending

Coordinates

All the sites described in this chapter are located on the Ordnance Survey Ireland, 1:50,000, Discovery Series map, no. 51

Dive site	Grid ref	Lat/Long
Hell	R 0552 9734	53° 01′ 08.50″ N, 09° 24′ 23.17″ W
Mermaid's Hole	R 0565 9750	53° 01′ 13.68″ N, 09° 24′ 17.02″ W
Reef Caves	R 0550 9760	53° 01′ 04.64″ N, 09° 24′ 22.32″ W
Urchin Cave	R 0576 9778	53° 01′ 20.02″ N, 09° 24′ 12.84″ W

Entering Hell in good conditions

A low, sandy section in Mermaid's Hole

passageways gradually goes deeper. The other openings in this western area are very difficult to access because they are below cliffs, so these do not make suitable entrances or exits to the Hell complex. One passage heads southwards, and from here a tight connection is possible with Robertson's Cave, but only experienced side-mount divers should attempt this.

Beyond Pól na Mongach, a small north-easterly trending bay edged by low, limestone cliffs contains **Mermaid's Hole** – a suitable cave for divers at all levels of ability to tackle and the longest and most challenging site discovered at Doolin. At low tide the entrance is situated in about 10m depth of water and unless a boat is available, gaining access is awkward under all conditions.

The bay faces west and anything more than the slightest breeze renders exit difficult, if not downright dangerous, and many divers have experienced perilous moments here attempting to regain land. Calm, stable weather is essential for exploration of Mermaid's Hole, but even so it is advisable to take an old climbing rope and perhaps a caving ladder to aid entry and exit – just in case! This is all made much easier with side-mounted equipment. Some visitors have been known to dekit on the seabed and have their surface support team haul it up while they use a ladder. A further possibility is to swim to Pól na Mongach, although exiting at this point cannot be assured in turbulent conditions.

Just inside the entrance to Mermaid's the water becomes noticeably murky; further on, divers will meet an abrupt thermocline and, at a low section about 90m from the entrance, distinctly shimmering and ice-cold water can occasionally be found. This is a freshwater resurgence, fed by a normal cave stream flowing from the hills of the Burren.

The first 100m of Mermaid's Hole consists of a substantial tunnel, but beyond this the passage dramatically reduces in size and side-mounts become essential. At about 300m take the first major junction on the left, where an experienced cave diver can follow the winding route towards Pirate's Paradise, a short length of passage which at low tide reveals 'dry' land and a chamber well adorned with stalactites. This requires a 430m dive from the entrance – the remainder of the system is highly prone to silting and any diving undertaken here is best conducted solo.

Further to the north lies the equally discreet **Urchin Cave**, a suitable site for introductory and fully certified cave divers using side-mounted equipment. The best time to dive is perhaps at low tide, when the main entrance is fully visible and accessible as a dry cave, though a 6m caving ladder and rope are required to descend the limestone cliff. Compared to the Hell complex and Mermaid's Hole, Urchin Cave is smaller in both passage size and overall extent.

Air supplies

Oceanlife, Kilkee, Co. Clare
Tel: 065 9056707
www.oceanlife.ie

Emergencies

Emergency contacts:
see Appendix A
In the event of an incident call the Garda (999 or 112) and ask for the Irish Coast Guard or the Irish Cave Rescue Organisation; the local coastguard station is at the eastern end of the Doolin car park, adjacent to the road and the entrance to the campsite

Nearest hyperbaric centre:
Portadown

Nearest hospital:
Ennis General Hospital, Ennis, Co. Clare
Tel: 065 6824464

International telephone country code: +353; drop the preceding zero from the local number

Clear water with urchins adorning the walls in the main passage of Hell

Further considerations

▶ Plan thoroughly and evaluate sea conditions carefully; the currents near the Reef Caves can be extremely strong and surface conditions are often hostile

▶ Doolin Pier is used regularly by many types of marine traffic, particularly during the holiday season; be aware of their swift approach

▶ A hood is required in all seasons; gloves are not essential during the summer months

▶ Use a comfortable rucksack to transport equipment to the caves: make two carries, rather than struggle with a heavy load

▶ The coastal platform is popular with tourists, so leave someone on the surface to supervise and tend personal belongings

▶ Given the exposed nature of the coast and the likelihood of damage from the surging current during stormy weather, be very wary of all lines

▶ Do not interfere with, or remove, any crustacean or fish; local fishermen rely upon these for their livelihoods

Grotta Giusti

Tuscany, Italy

CAVERN

Objective
Grotta Giusti is perhaps the most exotic and unusual cave diving site in Europe, being based in a hotel. A dive here makes for a thoroughly unique and unforgettable experience: this is cavern diving at its best, with a maximum depth of 30m.

Access
Permission is required to dive in Grotta Giusti – this is arranged by Mediterranean Dives & Tours, which operates the diving for the Grotta Giusti Terme Hotel. Divers must be qualified open water divers with at least four open water dives (qualifications, together with a declaration of health and fitness, have to be presented prior to the visit) and they must be resident in the hotel. All visitors are required to attend two briefing sessions, where the layout of the cave and its evolution is explained. To ensure that the pressure of use does not detract from the peaceful relaxation sought by hotel visitors, the party size and frequency of diving groups are limited.

Location
Grotta Giusti lies in the Tuscany region of west central Italy, one kilometre outside the small town of Monsummano Terme, which is some 40km away from both Pisa and Florence. The cave sits amid the rolling Apennines, a complex geological area where deep-seated primeval forces have produced geothermal heating along the line of a fault. As a result, the water in the cave is wonderfully clear and a stable 34°C year-round.

    The dive site is accessed directly from the ground floor of the hotel spa complex. From the rear of the building a carpet-floored corridor gradually descends into the cliff face. After about 10m to 15m this intercepts a much larger cave tunnel running at right angles, roughly parallel to the sloping ground surface. The rise in temperature at this point is marked: to the left the route leads to the aptly named Sala Inferno (a sauna) where the temperature is 36°C. An offshoot, also on the left, leads to the electrically illuminated Lago del Limbo which marks divers' access to the water.

Grotta Giusti Terme Hotel

History
Grotta Giusti was discovered by quarrymen in 1849, who – at the outset – believed they had located a new source of water. The landowner, Domenico Giusti, had the small hole enlarged and asked for volunteers to explore the cave. They returned from their investigations with wondrous tales of breathtaking beauty and suggestions of a 'miraculous atmosphere'.

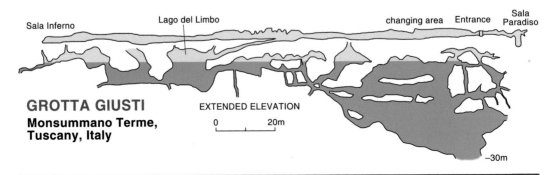

Sala Inferno   Lago del Limbo   changing area   Entrance   Sala Paradiso

GROTTA GIUSTI
Monsummano Terme, Tuscany, Italy

EXTENDED ELEVATION

0   20m

–30m

Domenico Giusti soon decided to build some treatment rooms, which have progressively transformed into the Grotta Giusti spa that exists today.

Dive exploration commenced in the 1980s. In 1997 an arrangement was made with the Grotta Giusti Terme Hotel, which owns and operates the spa sauna, to allow recreational access to the flooded section.

Diving

The normal ratio is two divers per instructor. Typically, one instructor leads the dive while a second brings up the rear; thus a group of three or four visitors may be safely supervised with no deterioration in visibility.

Divers are equipped with a single 10 litre cylinder and a stab jacket; the cylinder valve is fitted with two separate regulators capable of being shut down independently. Given the warmth of the water, wetsuits are not required and therefore nor are lead weights. To minimise diver abrasion and to make the harness more comfortable, visitors are encouraged to wear a T-shirt. Fins are not permitted and all divers should wear training shoes as the crystalline nature of the rock is unforgiving.

The absence of fins may feel odd at the outset, but after a couple of dives it is clear that underwater 'walking' has a lot to commend it – at least, in this environment. Your movement becomes cartoon-like, something akin to the exaggerated flying strides of Peter Pan and the effortless bounding along the passages gives the impression of walking on the moon. The walls are always within reach and convenient ledges allow divers to travel outward on one level and complete a circuit of roughly 200m by returning upon a different

Contacts

Mediterranean Dives & Tours; www.meditonline.it
Grotta Giusti Terme Hotel, via Grotta Giusti 1411, 51015 Monsummano
    Terme PT; tel: 0572 90771; www.grottagiustispa.com

Emergencies

Emergency contacts: see Appendix A
Nearest hyperbaric centre: Pisa
Nearest hospital: Ospedale del Ceppo,
    viale Matteotti 9/D, 51100 Pistoia PT; tel: 0573 3521
In an emergency, tel: 118; the operator will direct the call to the
    appropriate service
International telephone country code: +39; do *not* drop the preceding zero
    from the local number

one. Several lines can be followed – these are sturdy, firmly tied off and carry directional safety markers.

▲ The richly coated walls of the Grotta Giusti

Passing through a narrow section, you suddenly observe that the legs of the person in front of you are covered in minute bubbles of gas. In fact, everything seems to gather them. Remaining stationary for a moment reveals that a constant flow of effervescent gas is quietly rising past your mask. The analogy is like being inside a bottle of fizzy drink – because

Warm water prevails
in Grotta Giusti

Further considerations

► Very few items of dive equipment are required, but check with your host; expect to take your own mask and regulators, but all other equipment should be supplied

► No wetsuit or protective underwater garments are necessary, other than a swimming costume, T-shirt and training shoes

► Divers change into swimming costumes in special cubicles situated underground

this is carbon dioxide being released from the water.

The walls are encrusted in a hard, crystalline deposit and the lights of other divers sparkle and dance in the myriad of little gas pockets caught amid crystals on the ceiling. As in the above-water cave, at intervals large stalagmite structures come into view and it is interesting to reflect that these may have been formed below water.

When you surface at the dive base you realise that an hour has slipped past in this mysterious world, yet you have used much less than half a cylinder of air. You feel warm and relaxed; Grotta Giusti certainly offers the most fascinating and luxurious cave dive in the world.

Coordinates

Dive site	Lat/Long
Grotta Giusti	43° 52' 01.62" N, 10° 49' 55.73" E

Capo Palinuro

Campania, Italy

Objective
The Capo Palinuro headland presents opportunities for divers at all levels of experience, from cavern diver to fully cave trained, to explore its sea caves. Palinuro is one of Europe's best kept secrets and one of the best places to mount a diving holiday, as virtually every dive can incorporate a different cavern or cave spiced with interesting features, including stalactites and stalagmites, emissions of sulphur and a profusion of varied and colourful marine life.

Access
No permission is required.

Location
Capo Palinuro lies in the Campania region of south-west Italy, 100km to the south of Naples. It is a very spectacular limestone headland riddled with the most intriguing caverns and caves. The journey by road from Naples to the small fishing village of Palinuro takes about two-and-a-half hours.

History
Exploration of the undersea caves at Palinuro commenced in 1983 when Massimo Alvisi, Fabio Barbieri and Paolo Colantoni began a systematic programme of mapping and scientific study.

Diving
The diving season at Palinuro runs from Easter to the end of October; the water temperature in April is usually between 13°C and 14°C, but by the close of the season it has risen to about 23°C. The visibility is generally in excess of 30m.

All the caves are situated at the base of impressive cliffs and are accessed by boat within a relatively short distance from the harbour. For example, reaching **Cattedrale** (Cathedral Cave) only requires a five-minute cruise

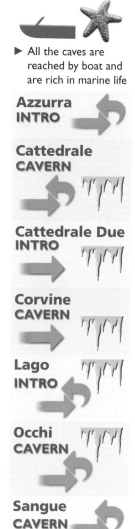

► All the caves are reached by boat and are rich in marine life

Azzurra
INTRO

Cattedrale
CAVERN

Cattedrale Due
INTRO

Corvine
CAVERN

Lago
INTRO

Occhi
CAVERN

Sangue
CAVERN

Grotta del Sangue
(Blood Cave)

Coordinates

Dive site	Lat/Long
Grotta Azzurra	40° 01′ 52.86″ N, 15° 16′ 08.04″ E
Cattedrale	40° 01′ 40.58″ N, 15° 16′ 08.06″ E
Cattedrale Due	40° 01′ 39.07″ N, 15° 16′ 09.72″ E
Grotta delle Corvine	40° 01′ 28.29″ N, 15° 16′ 07.57″ E
Grotta del Lago	40° 01′ 26.96″ N, 15° 16′ 55.21″ E
Grotta degli Occhi	40° 01′ 22.86″ N, 15° 16′ 36.51″ E
Grotta del Sangue	40° 01′ 26.18″ N, 15° 16′ 36.85″ E

Palinuro's sea life

Divers at Palinuro will enjoy seeing some of the finest marine life in the Mediterranean, with lots of variety and some unusual species. Common fish include greater amberjacks (*Seriola dumerili*), dentex (*Dentex dentex*), dusky and golden groupers (*Epinephelus marginatus* and *E. costae*) and brown meagres (*Sciaena umbra*). Beautiful red coral (*Corallium rubrum*) is in abundance, as are sea fans (*Eunicella cavolinii*, *Leptogorgia sarmentosa* and *Paramuricea clavata*) and spiny lobsters (*Palinurus elephas*). Some creatures are peculiar to this region, such as the purple starfish (*Ophidiaster ophidianus*), the ornate wrasse (*Thalassoma pavo*) and the star coral (*Astroides calycularis*).

With its sulphurous emissions from the hydrothermal springs, this is a fascinating area and other rare species have been noted. These include the black faufre (*Grammonus ater*), the leopard goby (*Thorogobius ephippiatus*), the cave spider crab (*Herbstia condyliata*) and the sponge *Petrobiona massiliana* that was long thought to be extinct.

The entrance to Grotta delle Corvine

▶ In the sulphurous area of Grotta Azzurra

around the first headland. This, like so many of the sites at Palinuro, presents a superb cavern dive. After dropping through the cobalt water, divers enter the cliff face at 19m depth, then quietly ascend to a much larger tunnel at −10m. To the right lies an enormous blue portal, a shallow return to open water for those so inclined. To the left a short length of tunnel leads to an air surface, a dark and cosily enclosed 'air bubble' decorated with a few humble and discoloured flowstone formations.

The **Grotta Azzurra** (Blue Cave) is literally a couple of minutes from the harbour and boatmen regularly take sightseers inside this dark but spacious cavern. The site is special in that the inner cave is illuminated by a deep blue glow of daylight permeating through a short length of flooded tunnel from the far side of the headland and the rich flow of water through the cleft supports some of the finest marine life in the Mediterranean. This part of the site is suitable for cavern diving.

From a divers' perspective, however, far more is of interest. To the landward (left-hand) side of the tunnel lies a huge void, one of the most intriguing places that any diver will visit. The cavern, at about 15m depth, is known locally as the Snow Room because, although the marine life decorating the lower walls is typical of any dark zone in the area, as divers rise through the water they gain entry to a wholly different environment.

A thin, wispy trace of cloud heralds both a halocline and a temperature gradient, above which it feels not only warmer but distinctly eerie. The undulating ceiling of this very large submerged cavern is plastered in a mat of sulphurous bacterial growth – it appears strange and almost alien. Examined closely, the rock surface looks as though it is carpeted with cream-coloured fine hairs about 5mm to 10mm long. As you progress into the cave, exhaled bubbles induce a fascinating effect – like a gentle

Rich marine life in Grotta Azzurra

Contacts and air supplies

Palinuro Sub Diving Center, via Porto snc,
  84051 Palinuro-Centola SA
  Tel: 0974 938509; www.palinurosub.it

Emergencies

Emergency contacts: see Appendix A
Nearest hyperbaric centre: Salerno
Nearest hospital: Ospedale San Luca, via Francesco
  Cammarota, 84078 Vallo della Lucania, Salerno SA
  Tel: 0974 711111. In an emergency, tel: 118; the
  operator will direct the call to the appropriate service
International telephone country code: +39; do not drop
  the preceding zero from the local number

Further reading

BARBIERI, Fabio. Palinuro Sub: Guida alle Immersioni –
  Diver's Guide, La Reclame, Trento (2001): dual language,
  Italian and English

snowfall from a windless sky, flakes of every size quietly drift into the blackness.

Remarkable it might be, but it is chilling to reflect that over the years four divers have perished here in two separate incidents when they became disorientated in the reduced visibility. Today, dive operators exercise a more responsible, proactive approach to diver safety and this inner, sulphurous Snow Room is deemed beyond the bounds of those trained only in cavern diving; introductory cave certification is fine.

These caves were once high and dry but, due to an earthquake that occurred millennia ago, the Palinuro land mass has been thrust downward, plunging the caves below sea level. It is along this massive fault plane that deep, thermally heated water finds its escape and the chemically rich sulphurous discharge now seeps quietly to the surface, emerging unseen from small fissures to warm several of the outlet caves to a constant 24°C year-round. The thermocline between the cave and surface water is only a degree or so in October, but in April, when the sea is at its coolest at 13°C to 14°C, this difference becomes a marked 10°C.

Cattedrale Due (Cathedral 2) is another long and deep network containing some very fine displays of stalactites and columns. For those suitably equipped and introductory cave qualified, it is possible to descend a 25m shaft at the furthermost point and then follow a straight passage at a maximum depth of 32m to emerge, via a slight restriction, at −30m in open water.

Grotta delle Corvine is a short cave for cavern divers possessing two fine entrances, a halocline and more speleothems; it is named after a fish – the brown meagre, *Sciaena umbra*.

A substantial 7m wide opening at a depth of 21m provides easy access to the cave, followed by a slow ascent through 30m of sloping passage to the level of the upper entrance. The passage is dominated by a group of 3m high stalagmites affectionately named the 'submerged monks'. Some 40m into the cave, divers can rise through a halocline to reach an air surface 7m long by 2m wide, where helictites and other formations are found. From this airbell an oblique tunnel, 10m long by 1.5m wide and 2m high, allows an exit to open water at a depth of 7.5m. A wide range of fauna lives throughout the cave, so the dive will be full of interest – watch out for boxer shrimps (*Stenopus spinosus*) in the lower levels, cardinalfish (*Apogon imberbis*) and scorpionfish (*Scorpaena notata*), as well as cowries (*Erosaria spurca* and *Luria lurida*).

Grotta degli Occhi (Cave of the Eyes) and Grotta del Sangue (Blood Cave) are two contrasting caves within easy swimming distance of one another that offer excellent cavern dives. The first, with a maximum depth of 14m, is a dual-entrance, ancient fossil cave containing speleothem formations and an air surface approximately 25m from the upper entrance. A dead end muddy offshoot passage at 10m depth is avoided by visitors to this fine and easy cave, but it was here in June 2012 that four divers, untrained and unaware of the specific requirements of cave diving, tragically perished when they lost their way in a silt-out. Their bodies were found less than 35m from the entrance.

Grotta del Sangue, 80m to the north, is a sporty, well-sculpted cave in relatively shallow water (8m depth) that was formed by wave action. A comfortably sized offshoot in the latter leads for about 30m to a very large lake chamber; amazingly, some seagulls that had fallen from some lofty perch in the darkness have been rescued alive from this pitch black cavern. Despite their entombment and lack of breathing apparatus, the birds survived several minutes underwater and were able to take to the air five minutes or so after regaining daylight at the surface.

Grotta del Lago (Lake Cave) is suitable for introductory and fully certified cave divers (but not those cavern-trained). It lies about fifteen minutes from the harbour, almost directly below the lighthouse on the headland. The small bay here is affectionately known as Stinky Bay after the distinct waft of sulphur that rises from the water. The cave is noteworthy not only for its sulphurous environment, but also because of its underwater traverse from the sea to a sizeable lake some 40m inside the cliffs. Here, superb arrays of calcite formations can be seen above and below water; the maximum depth is 12m.

One of the many caves entered only by boat, and beyond the sump in Grotta del Lago

There are very few places where a diver can appreciate such wonders without difficulty or risk of causing damage: Grotta del Lago is one of the most accessible in Europe.

Further considerations

- ▶ A 5mm wetsuit is preferable
- ▶ A hood and gloves are not required during the summer
- ▶ The smallest cylinders available for hire locally are 15 litre
- ▶ Always use a line in the dark zone

A stalagmite column forms a convenient belay in the sulphurous water of the Grotta del Lago

Sardinia

Italy

Objective

Almost everything that anyone could wish for during a diving or multi-activity holiday can be found on the Italian island of Sardinia. Surprisingly few British people seem to make the effort to visit the island, although it has superb opportunities for cavern and cave diving, suiting all levels of ability. Indeed, other than the Lot and Dordogne area of south-west France, the east coast of Sardinia is unrivalled in Europe.

Access

Other than at the showcaves of Grotta del Bue Marino and Grotta del Fico, no permission is required to dive in the sea caves. Some access restrictions exist at Dragon's Belly Cave because of the sensitive nature of the cave environment and diving is currently severely restricted at Su Gologone.

Location

An entrance typical of those found around the Sardinian coast: Grotta del Bue Marino, which can only be entered by boat

Sardinia is the second-largest island in the Mediterranean (after Sicily), lying to the west of mainland Italy and south of the island of Corsica. A profusion of cave diving sites can be found in the Gulf of Orosei on the eastern coast, south of the small resort town of Cala Gonone – all are only accessible by boat. Around 13km inland from this area is the resurgence of Su Gologone.

Further sea caves worthy of consideration are located in north-west Sardinia on the rocky headland at Capo Caccia, west of the town of Alghero, of which Grotta di Nereo is briefly mentioned here.

Diving

Diving is largely boat-orientated and weather conditions are therefore crucial. The sea temperature varies from around 14°C in January and February to about 25°C in late August; visibility is generally in excess of 30m. Inside the caves, especially if the site is a freshwater rising, there will often be a distinct halocline and associated thermocline. The temperature in fresh water is usually around 14°C to 15°C.

For divers making their initial foray into the world of overhead environment diving, **La Galleria** offers a simple but enchanting cavern dive. Situated in the Gulf of Orosei south of Cala Luna bay, this picturesque saltwater cave presents a network of beautifully rounded tunnels, accessed from a huge entrance set in bright turquoise water. With depths of less than 12m and sunlight streaming into the entrance, this is a wonderfully atmospheric site. Other than sand, there is no silt to be disturbed and scores of cardinalfish flit to and fro in the shadows; it is a joy to tour these tunnels. It only takes a few minutes to reach the furthest part of the cave, after which you can explore the nooks and crannies outside.

A short distance south along the coast, **Grotta del Bel Torrente** is regularly used for cavern and cave diving and is suitable for those of all levels of certification. This is one of several points in the area where fresh water draining from the bare limestone interior resurges in a submarine cave. Entered at a depth of less than 10m, the first section is eminently suitable for cavern diving as the tunnel is large and the water is shallow with an airspace above it.

Given the good visibility and the reassuring blue light permeating the cave for over 40m, this is an interesting place on several counts. For example, for divers who have never experienced a halocline before, the effects are very marked: suddenly, as you ascend, the visibility becomes obscured and your buddy, who a moment before was swimming alongside you, becomes a vague shape recognisable only because of his or her movement in the water. The water feels noticeably colder, perhaps by several degrees, as you pass from warm seawater into the outflowing and now brackish water above. Then, for a few moments, the visibility might clear again before you suddenly enter another patchy halocline. The first 300m to 400m of cave has a considerable amount of airspace over it; however, as this offers limited room beneath the passage ceiling, divers find it preferable to follow the lower level of the tunnel where the visibility is not impaired by the halocline.

At about 60m inside the cave a large pillar of limestone rock splits the passage and it becomes possible to ascend through the halocline to gain air at a substantial lake over 4m wide and more than 20m long, where arrays of stalactites drape from the roof a couple of metres above.

The further you proceed, the more stable the visibility becomes and, as the effects of the mixing zone diminish, the fresh water becomes purer and gin clear. The spacious tunnel continues at between 4m and 7m depth, the reassuring permanent guideline being periodically belayed to stalactites that formed during an earlier era when the cave was filled with air. At about 90m from the entrance a substantial slab of rock, like a broken column on the floor of some ancient Greek or Roman ruin, testifies to the earth movements which have taken place over the millennia. Frequent mirror-like air pockets and chambers appear overhead; these can be used by those of limited experience to communicate with their friends and they also present opportunities for viewing other stalactite grottoes that are still intact.

The first 500m to 600m of the dive are in a simple and straightforward tunnel with a maximum depth of 8m; at about 800m, however, the Ramo del Bue tunnel diverges on the left-hand side. From the cave entrance to the end of this branch requires about 1.5km of diving at a maximum depth of 24m; the furthest point was reached by the German diver Thorsten 'Toddy' Wälde in 2008. The crystal clarity of the water in this spectacular phreatic tunnel may be complemented by the sight of monk seal bones protruding from the sand – these have been dated at between 5,000 and 6,000 years old.

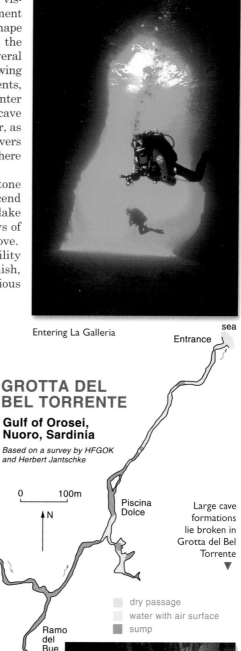

Entering La Galleria

Galleria HFGOK

sea

Entrance

GROTTA DEL BEL TORRENTE

Gulf of Orosei, Nuoro, Sardinia

Based on a survey by HFGOK and Herbert Jantschke

Grand Sifone Multiteco

Sifone Terminale Hasenmayer

500m long and 65m deep, leading to a 490m extension with a further sump

0   100m

↑N

Piscina Dolce

Large cave formations lie broken in Grotta del Bel Torrente ▼

Ramo del Bue

dry passage
water with air surface
sump

Sand ripples in the cavern of Grotta del Fico

Further considerations

▶ The diving season runs from Easter to the end of October

▶ A 7mm wetsuit is preferable for all dives of an hour or less, although gloves are not needed during the summer

▶ A drysuit and gloves are recommended in all seasons in the freshwater zone

▶ Some knowledge of Italian will prove immensely beneficial; few people speak English

The large main tunnel of Bel Torrente continues beyond the Ramo del Bue junction to reach a section of dry cave passage, Galleria HFGOK, at a distance of about 1.6km from the entrance. This furthest extent of the system was first explored by the renowned German diver Jochen Hasenmayer, but in 2008 an operation by Toddy and British diver Rick Stanton took the cave deep into the enormous Grande Sifone Multiteco. A subsequent dive by Stanton in 2010 passed this 65m deep sump after 500m, resulting in the discovery of 490m of dry cave extension and a further flooded section at the upstream limit.

Approximately 6.5km south-east from Bel Torrente another freshwater outflow occurs at **Grotta del Fico**. The site is easy to locate as del Fico is a commercial showcave that is only accessible by boat – permission to dive can be arranged at the local dive centre. Although tourists disembark at a small platform for the 15m stepped ascent to the large prominent oval entrance, divers enter an inconspicuous opening beneath an obvious fissure in the cliff face about 25m to the south.

The dive begins at 8m depth and follows a straightforward, gradually shallowing passage that runs directly into the hillside. The tunnel is about 4m wide and perhaps 6m high with miniature sand dunes and coarse silt on the floor. It surfaces in a large boulder chamber aligned along a very distinct 15m high fissure. A keen eye will spot an inaccessible metal walkway in the showcave high overhead, but unless tourists are present the chamber will not be illuminated.

Beyond this natural limit of cavern diving the ongoing cave takes a much smaller route to the right, dropping sharply to about 30m depth before ascending to air beyond. This section of cave is deemed suitable for fully certified cave divers and is considerably more complex than hitherto. A team of German divers made the first explorations of the cave in 1998 and 2006, but in 2008 Rick Stanton and Thorsten Wälde extended it to a total length of 2.2km.

Further south along the coast lies perhaps the most technical cave diving site on Sardinia. Here, two caves – **Grotta Utopia** and Risorgenza di Ispuligidenie (known locally as **Euphoria**) – have been connected to form a complex system of passages extending to over 4.2km in length. The majority of the exploration has been undertaken by the Höhlenforschungsgruppe Ostalb-Kirchheim (HFGOK) from Germany and depths of 107m have been reached in the further limits. Realistically, this system offers diving to introductory cave divers and above, though the entrance to Utopia is suitable for cavern diving.

Utopia begins as a large entrance at a depth of 12m. Within a few metres a shaft drops abruptly to about 28m depth and thereafter continues for much of its length through huge galleries at an average depth of 30m to 35m.

The entrance to Euphoria lies about 300m south from Utopia. The opening is about 2m in diameter at a depth of about 5m, where a substantial flow of fresh water is evident. Stalagmites and stalactites are found close to the entrance and, apart from their black coloration, the passage is very reminiscent of cenotes in Mexico. The depth in the initial section, which is some 1m to 1.5m wide, is less than 15m, but beyond the 150m mark the depth increases to over 45m. Diving is possible throughout with a back-mount configuration and stage tanks. With careful planning, it is possible to make a traverse underwater between these two caves in about one hour and twenty minutes.

The beach at Cala Luna, looking south

Another site that is well worth diving is the **Risorgenza di Cala Luna**. The cave is situated just around the first headland to the south of the beautiful valley and beach at Cala Luna – it is suitable for all levels of ability, but must be treated with caution. The entrance location appears to be nothing special; however, while swimming towards it from your boat you soon become conscious of having to fin with much greater effort. This is a major submarine resurgence which, being of clear water, is invisible against the normal turquoise colour of the sea. Entry to the cave can be a real struggle if the outflow is strong and under these conditions it is easier to pull yourself along the floor rather than expend excess energy finning, though due to the mixing effects of the fresh and salt water, the visibility is very poor. Under low flow the halocline is much less in evidence.

Less than 50m inside, a junction offers a bizarre experience: turn off the main route into the right-hand tunnel and you will no longer fight the outflowing current – in fact, quite the opposite. The flow here runs in the other direction, downstream. The waterway splits at this point and carries the diver, albeit with less intensity, away from the open sea! This is obviously a site to be wary of: it is extremely complex, more than one line may be in place and the ledges and floor contain plenty of silt that can be thrown up into the water.

The system has several major branches, with the longest penetration requiring a dive of about 1.5km from the entrance. One branch has beautiful phreatic tubes in pure white rock, another is riddled like a Swiss cheese while the main, longest tunnel is formed of very dark rock that readily absorbs light: conger eels have been sighted in the further reaches. The total length of this cave is over 3km, with a maximum depth of 35m.

The jewel in the crown of Sardinian caves lies around 3.5km south of Cala Gonone: it is the renowned and spectacular showcave, **Grotta del Bue Marino**. Behind the huge entrance lie over 17km of tunnels, forming the second longest cave on the island and currently the longest underwater system in Italy.

Bue Marino has featured on tourist itineraries since the 1800s and is only accessible by sea. Regular tours are conducted from Cala Gonone and the cave itself is well worth a visit even if you do not have permission to dive (this must be arranged well in advance at the local dive centre). The main showcave is breathtakingly beautiful. Some 900m of walkway in a huge tunnel in excess of 15m diameter lead to a simple rope barrier and a deepening canal of crystal-clear water that gives an indication of the nature of the diving

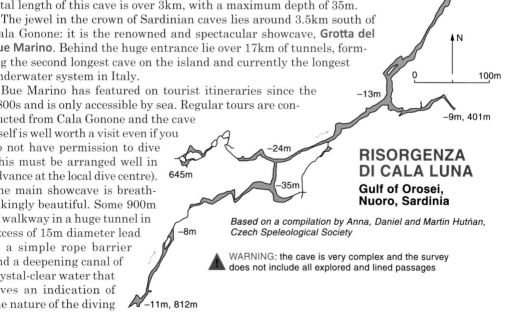

sea
Entrance
−4m

↑N

0   100m

−13m

−9m, 401m

−24m

645m

−35m

RISORGENZA DI CALA LUNA

Gulf of Orosei, Nuoro, Sardinia

Based on a compilation by Anna, Daniel and Martin Hutňan, Czech Speleological Society

−8m

⚠ WARNING: the cave is very complex and the survey does not include all explored and lined passages

−11m, 812m

that follows. It is suitable for all levels of experience, but in particular fully certified cave divers, and it really stirs the imagination – one can dream about undertaking some very long penetrations here.

In essence, this fabulous system has three separate branches. The Ramo Sud passage, trending predominantly southwards, continues (above water) from the lake at the end of the showcave; however, it is a considerable distance – at least an hour's caving – before the diving begins. In 1977 Jochen Hasenmayer passed the first sump after a 630m long and 35m deep dive. The French divers Eric Le Guen and Patrick Penez subsequently made further explorations beyond this in 1982, while Czech teams including Daniel Hutňan, Miroslav Manhart and Michal Megela made yet more advances in this sector in 2007.

The Ramo Nord passage presents another very complicated network of mixed and challenging terrain. Twenty-four dives lead to a 520m long and 35m deep sump, following which lie many more shorter sumps. Czech teams have made the greatest impact on this area, commencing with a major exploration by Lubomír Benýšek and Milan Slezák in 1993, then in 2006 and 2007 Jiří J. Čermák, Martin Hones and Miroslav Manhart added further significant extensions.

Between Ramo Sud and Ramo Nord lies the Ramo Mezzo. Jochen Hasenmayer explored the initial 650m of this middle branch, then fellow German Thorsten Wälde progressed to 2km in relatively shallow underwater passage in 2006. The following year Czech divers Radoslav Husák and Jan Žilina continued the exploration to 3.8km and a depth of 50m. Some 38 sumps have to be negotiated to reach this point!

It is conceivable that Bue Marino will eventually be connected with other extensive caves beneath the mountainous interior of the island. Geological and hydrological studies clearly suggest some tantalising possibilities, perhaps yielding a network over 70km long, and work is ongoing to achieve this.

Another very special coastal site is the little-known **Dragon's Belly Cave**, located not far north of Bel Torrente. Though short, nearly everything it contains will generate surprise and wonder. The entrance is small and inconspicuous, being situated on the face of an otherwise blank underwater wall. At a depth of just 4m, the opening is barely a metre in diameter and immediately inside drops about a metre to enter a comfortably sized, single-file tunnel that leads for just over 20m to an air surface. Here

The dive base in Bue Marino

Sifone Nord Grande (520m, –35m)

series of sumps

Ramo Nord

sea

N

0   1km

Entrance

series of sumps

GROTTA DEL BUE MARINO

end of showcave

Gulf of Orosei, Nuoro, Sardinia

Based on a compilation by Leo Fancello and Daniel Hutňan

Only the longest sumps are marked

Ramo Mezzo   lakes

Ramo Sud

–50m, 3.8km from entrance

Sifone Terminale (630m, –35m)

Formations in
Bue Marino

Beyond the sump in
Dragon's Belly Cave

divers must leave the water to see why the cave is so exceptional.

An awkward little climb of about one metre is required to gain dry land, then a hands-and-knees, crawling-sized muddy passage leads directly back into the cliff face. About 15m to 20m from the water a chamber permits standing and visitors can then take in one of the most spectacular arrays of speleothem formations that a diver will ever have the privilege of viewing. Directly in front lies a profusion of helictites bristling like hairs on the side of some giant inverted cactus – most of the smaller hair-like growths are pure white, glistening with drops of clear water. It is an amazing, absolutely awe-inspiring sight. The sensitive nature of this cave cannot be overstressed; it is for this reason that only fully certified cave divers are allowed entry and even then they must always be accompanied by a guide. There is relatively little room to move around and any further penetration into the tunnel requires even greater care due to the slippery, muddy conditions.

Su Gologone (aka Su Cologone) is an inviting inland site about 8km east-north-east of the small town of Oliena. It is a well-known beauty spot with a clear freshwater rising that discharges water from the major cave systems of Su Bentu and Sa Oche over 3km to the south-south-west. Starting in a narrow fissure, a 3m to 4m wide shaft drops sharply to –35m where divers enter a substantial chamber, some 20m to 30m high and between 10m and 15m

Coordinates and cave summaries

The most useful map of the area is Istituto Geografico Militare (IGM) map 500 (Nuoro Est) 1:50,000. Note that some older Italian maps use the Monte Mario in Rome (instead of Greenwich, as used in this guidebook) as the location for the prime meridian for longitude.

Grotta del Bel Torrente

Lat/Long: 40° 11′ 29.68″ N, 09° 37′ 44.51″ E	
Length: Over 3km	
Max. depth: Generally less than 15m, but deep inside at 60m or more	
Characteristics: A large tunnel with a halocline and many airspaces	

Grotta del Bue Marino

Lat/Long: 40° 14′ 26.07″ N, 09° 37′ 24.35″ E	
Length: Over 17km	
Max. depth: 50m	
Characteristics: An extensive, very complex system with large tunnels	

Risorgenza di Cala Luna

Lat/Long: 40° 13′ 24.62″ N, 09° 37′ 42.98″ E	
Length: Over 3km	
Max. depth: 35m	
Characteristics: Strong currents and silt mean great care is required	

Dragon's Belly Cave

Lat/Long: 40° 11′ 37.52″ N, 09° 37′ 44.02″ E	
Length: 25m dive with 40m dry cave beyond	
Max. depth: 5m	
Characteristics: A short dive leading to a spectacular dry cave	

Grotta del Fico

Lat/Long: 40° 08′ 21.70″ N, 09° 39′ 38.30″ E	
Length: 2.2km	
Max. depth: 30m	
Characteristics: A complex system with both wide and narrow passages	

La Galleria

Lat/Long: 40° 11′ 54.46″ N, 09° 37′ 39.64″ E	
Length: 50m	
Max. depth: Less than 12m	
Characteristics: Spacious saltwater cavern with little silt	

Su Gologone

Lat/Long: 40° 17′ 19.39″ N, 09° 29′ 49.97″ E	
Length: 370m	
Max. depth: 138m	
Characteristics: A complex freshwater cave with a steeply descending passage	

Grotta di Nereo

Lat/Long: 40° 33′ 43.10″ N, 08° 09′ 41.51″ E	
Length: 350m	
Max. depth: 32m	
Characteristics: An extensive sea cave with large tunnels and many entrances	

Grotta Utopia–Euphoria (Risorgenza di Ispuligidenie) system

Lat/Long (Utopia): 40° 07′ 53.97″ N, 09° 40′ 10.85″ E	
Lat/Long (Euphoria): 40° 07′ 45.41″ N, 09° 40′ 16.48″ E	
Length: Over 4.2km	
Max. depth: 107m	
Characteristics: A complex and deep cave system	

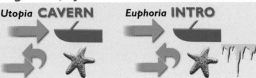

Bue Marino

wide. Beyond, the cave narrows and drops relatively quickly to a depth of 138m, a point reached in 2010 by Alberto Cavedon. The total length of passage at this spring is about 370m.

Unfortunately, due to the relative ease of access and the attractive size of the entrance tunnel, several fatalities have occurred in Su Gologone and access is restricted.

On the other side of the island, **Grotta di Nereo** is the most renowned cave at Capo Caccia, west of Alghero on the north-west coast. This multi-entranced network is situated in the cliffs of a major promontory and offers an excellent tour at depths of between 15m and 32m. Numerous other cavern diving sites also exist in this area.

Contacts and air supplies

▶ East Sardinia
ProTec Sardinia SAS, via Collodi 9, 08020 Cala Gonone NU
  Tel (mobile): 3351 680168; www.protecsardinia.com
  Services: boat, equipment hire, guide, air, oxygen, helium, rebreather friendly

▶ North-west Sardinia
Blue Service Alghero Diving Center, via Lido 18, 07041 Alghero SS
  Tel: 079 987197; www.blueservicealghero.com
Capo Galera Diving Center, Località Capo Galera, Fertilia, 07041 Alghero SS
  Tel: 079 942110; www.capogalera.com

Emergencies

Emergency contacts: see Appendix A
In an emergency, tel: 118; the operator will direct the call to the appropriate service
International telephone country code: +39; do *not* drop the preceding zero from the local number

▶ East Sardinia
Nearest decompression chamber: La Maddalena (30 minutes by helicopter)
Nearest hospital: Ospedale San Francesco, via Mannironi, 08100 Núoro NU; tel: 0784 240237

▶ North-west Sardinia
Nearest decompression chamber: Sorso
Nearest hospital: Ospedale Civile, via Don Minzoni, 07041 Alghero SS; tel: 079 9955111 or 079 987161

Cavern Dives of Gozo and Comino

Malta

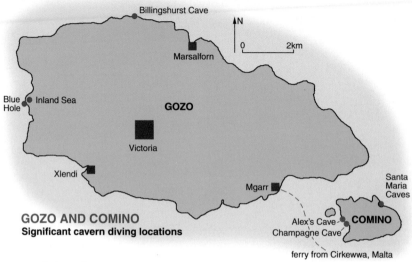

Billingshurst Cave

Marsalforn

Blue Hole · Inland Sea

GOZO

Victoria

Xlendi

Mgarr

Santa Maria Caves

Alex's Cave · **COMINO**
Champagne Cave

ferry from Cirkewwa, Malta

GOZO AND COMINO
Significant cavern diving locations

N
0   2km

CAVERN

All the caves
on Gozo and
Comino are
suited to cavern dives and
are rich in marine life

Billingshurst Cave

Objective

Malta is an excellent venue for cavern diving, and a few classic sites are situated around the coast of the associated islands of Gozo and Comino. The visibility is exceptional and the maximum depth for these dives is 30m.

Access

No permission is required to dive at any site, but Malta does have diving regulations that need to be followed. Before diving anywhere on the islands you must register at a dive centre where you will have to complete a self-declaration medical questionnaire. A doctor's certificate or a local examination will be required for divers with specific conditions. Divers also need a certain level of qualification in order to dive without an instructor.

Location

Situated in the central Mediterranean, the Maltese islands lie 90 km south of Sicily. They principally consist of three separate land masses: the main island of Malta, Gozo to the north-west (a half-hour crossing by regular ferry service) and, sandwiched between the two, the tiny island of Comino. Significantly, bar Comino, all the sites listed here may be entered from the shore, which substantially increases the flexibility of activities.

History

Malta's caverns have long been explored by adventurous open water divers. The longest and most challenging, Billingshurst Cave, was discovered and explored in the early 1990s by members of Billingshurst Sub Aqua Club, based near Crawley in the UK.

Diving

Sea temperatures range from 15°C in January and February to a peak of around 27°C in August and this, combined with

The Azure Window sea arch and the Blue Hole in the foreground; diving here is superb

exceptional visibility, makes for some of the finest diving conditions in the Mediterranean.

The most famous landmark of the islands, that seen in all tourist brochures, is the spectacular Azure Window on the western coast of Gozo. This is also the location of the **Blue Hole**, a fine circular shaft situated very close to the foot of the window. To dive in the clear blue water of the entrance with sunlight streaming in from above will set a scene to last a lifetime and, viewed from the darker recesses of the cavern, the sculpting of the natural rock arches and the shafts of light piercing the ethereal haze are nothing short of magical.

Walk-in access to the water is straightforward and equipment only has to be carried approximately 130m from the car park. No specialist equipment, not even a line reel, is required to explore and savour this site by day (as anywhere, things are totally different by night): the cavern only stretches back for 25m at 15m to 20m depth and the magnificent blue portal provides a constant safety beacon. A short distance away along the rugged underwater cliffs other delights such as the Chimney will enrich any underwater tour from the Blue Hole.

CAVERN

If conditions are too rough to access the Blue Hole, the **Inland Sea** lies only a few minutes' drive away and will provide an equally enjoyable all-weather alternative. Here, equipment can be transported right to the water's edge. Divers can enter a narrow tunnel with an air surface leading for some 105m through the imposing cliffs that line the north-west part of the island, to emerge upon stark, sheer walls at around –25m. Remaining at a safe and sensible depth is imperative at all times – an ascent to the surface along the cavern's length must be considered carefully and is generally not advisable. The surge between the narrow walls can be frightening in any swell, while in calm conditions a multitude of small boats ply the dark stretch of waterway on sightseeing tours to and from the open sea. At depth, which varies between several metres in the Inland Sea to 25m or more at the northern exit, divers are spared such hazards.

CAVERN

The Inland Sea

There is always sufficient illumination to find your way, although – as with all sites – carrying a handheld light is essential to see details in the walls and for use in an emergency.

Taking careful heed of local advice and when conditions permit, one of the best dives on Gozo is **Billingshurst Cave** on the northern coast, about 2.5km to the west of Marsalforn. Once again,

Coordinates

Dive site	Lat/Long
Alex's Cave	36° 00' 38.10" N, 14° 19' 31.71" E
Billingshurst Cave	36° 04' 52.17" N, 14° 14' 08.04" E
Blue Hole	36° 03' 10.01" N, 14° 11' 18.17" E
Champagne Cave	36° 00' 35.93" N, 14° 19' 37.45" E
Inland Sea	36° 03' 14.68" N, 14° 11' 28.28" E
Santa Maria Caves	36° 01' 05.00" N, 14° 20' 25.00" E

CAVERN

you can drive very close to the water. As you stand directly above the cave on some intriguing man-made salt pans that date back to Roman times, nothing indicates the presence of a spectacular and enormous tunnel below your feet. The stride-entry to Billingshurst is committing; once you are in, you are in! The swell sloshes noisily into undercuts and climbing out again is nigh on impossible – everyone involved must be clear as to the direction and nature of the exit point from the sea, which is over 100m away to the east.

As you descend from the surface, a grey shape immediately appears in the cliff. The ceiling of this wide tunnel stretches back at 15m depth, but the bottom lies at –30m where a succession of pebble ridges runs from wall to wall, conveying the clear impression that this rugged coast is not always so calm. Eventually, perhaps 40m or 50m from the entrance, the pebbles give way to finer silts.

Champagne Cave

By now, your eyes will be more accustomed to the lower light levels. This is an awesome void: the tunnel is perhaps 25m wide and more than 10m high; it seems to be a long way back to the entrance, especially if you only have a single cylinder. Divers have perished here, so it is prudent to curtail further penetration unless the dive has been planned very carefully for the next section. Ahead, massive boulders rear up in the darkness and good lighting is essential. This is a place where the reassurance of a line is appreciated and a permanent one has been installed on the left-hand side.

About 100m from the entrance the vast tunnel rises to air in a huge lake chamber and, surprisingly, this marks the conclusion of the cave. The darkness may appear oppressive, but if all the lights are turned off, the dim and distant glimmer of the surface world becomes visible. It feels like a remote spot – as if it is a long way from home, especially considering that you have another fifteen minutes to swim from the entrance to where you can leave the water. A 15 litre cylinder should be considered a minimum for this superb dive.

Many caverns and challenging dives are dotted around the three islands, but if time is short and you wish to tour somewhere very, very special and less committing than Billingshurst, take a boat to Comino and visit **Santa Maria Caves**. These lie on the north coast, some half-hour's journey from either of the two larger islands. The caves are sited in less than 15m of water and the principal swim-through is magnificent. This is holiday diving at its best.

CAVERN

Champagne Cave

On the western side of Comino lie two more beautiful dive sites close to the southern extremity of the famous Blue Lagoon. The first – **Alex's Cave** – is located on the south side of the large islet almost exactly 750m north of Lantern Point. The substantial entrance has a water depth of about 14m and sufficient airspace to accommodate small boats taking tourists a short way into the tunnel. Underwater, the tunnel progressively loses its natural light and when it reaches a dead end at about 10m depth it is possible to surface to a chamber large enough for six or more divers to congregate. If you have the time or the inclination, you can dekit and pass a narrow fissure leading out to dry land and the sunshine.

CAVERN

The second dive site is perhaps more enchanting. **Champagne Cave** or Comino Caves lies in the south-western flank of the large peninsula approximately 160m to the south-east of Alex's Cave. A superb passage over 3m in diameter leads for 70m directly through the peninsula at a depth no greater than 14m.

CAVERN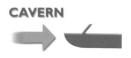

Further considerations

► Information about Maltese diving regulations is available from the Professional Diving Schools Association, (see Contacts)

► Remember to take your diving certification and, if relevant, your doctor's medical certificate

► During summer months a 5mm wetsuit is adequate and a hood and gloves are unnecessary; a vest or even a drysuit might be required at other times of the year

► Other than at Billingshurst Cave, no sea caves have lines installed

► Do not leave valuable possessions in your vehicle

► English is widely spoken

Contacts and air supplies

Malta and Gozo have a lot of diving stores; these are registered with the Professional Diving Schools Association, PO Box 12, St Paul's Bay, Malta www.pdsa.org.mt
St Andrew's Divers Cove, St Simon Street, Xlendi Bay, XLN 1302, Gozo; tel: 2155 1301; www.gozodive.com

Emergencies

Emergency contacts: see Appendix A
Nearest hyperbaric centres: Victoria (Gozo) and Msida (Malta); Gozo's is never further than a fifteen-minute drive away from a shore dive
Nearest hospital: Gozo General Hospital, Victoria, Gozo Tel: 2156 1600
International telephone country code: +356

Mallorca

Balearic Islands, Spain

Objective

CAVERN INTRO

As will be seen by a visit to the famous showcaves, Cuevas del Drach, Mallorca has a dimension that extends beyond a holiday destination; as well as sunshine and scenery, it provides a superb location for cavern and cave diving activities. Some of the caves on the island possess excellent displays of flowstone formations and these stalactites, stalagmites and columns extend below water. Like the submerged blue holes of the Bahamas or the tropical cenotes of the Mexican Yucatán, the caves in the Balearic Islands were formed or were later modified in an air-filled environment, where streams once flowed and calcite was deposited.

Then, over 10,000 years ago at the close of the last ice age, the great polar ice caps and glaciers of the world began to recede; the level of the oceans rose, Britain was severed from the continent of Europe and many caves at low altitude close to the coast were invaded by the sea. When it comes to pure beauty, only the caves in and around the Caribbean stand any comparison to those of Mallorca.

A traverse of Cova dets Ases will prove a real adventure and is suitable for full cave divers and well-prepared introductory cave divers, while cavern divers can visit the sea entrance.

The beach at Cala s'Algar; the seaward end of Cova dets Ases lies just beyond the headland

Access

No permission to dive is required for Cova dets Ases; however, permission is needed for some other locations.

Location

Mallorca is the largest of Spain's Balearic Islands and is situated in the western Mediterranean. Several local dive operators cover cavern diving activities, in particular in the north of the island. Puerto Pollensa is one of the better bases, as a number of undersea caverns are situated beneath the rugged cliffs of the Formentor peninsula and may be accessed by boat from this harbour. Plentiful caverns also exist around the eastern coast.

Cova dets Ases lies at Cala s'Algar, a small bay close to Porto Colom on Mallorca's south-eastern coast; a dirt road heads off to this beach from the corner of the north-eastern marina in the town. The cave has two entrances, one just underwater below a low sea cliff and another inland.

History

Local Mallorcan cavers documented the cave of Cova dets Ases in 1972 and reported that it terminated in a pair of sump pools. In 1989 British cave divers visited the site to continue the exploration. Ian Williams made the first foray into the left-hand pool, but it was Owen Clarke who subsequently passed Sump 1 after 30m; Ian then established a connection with the sea when he passed Sump 2.

Diving

The submarine caves on Mallorca are subject to seasonal variations: surface water temperatures range from 12°C to 24°C and visibility can reach

30m. However, while sea temperatures may fluctuate, the water deep inside the caves remains a constant 16°C year-round.

Cova dets Ases presents anyone of an adventurous disposition with a challenging and spectacular subterranean journey. Here, with adequate care and planning, it is possible to complete a traverse of around 400m through the cave. Most of the distance is above water, offering an interesting enough challenge in its own right and presenting no serious technical difficulty, while the remainder consists of diving through two easy and shallow sumps.

The entrances to Cova dets Ases may take time to locate. The submarine entrance is the easiest to find, lying beneath low, overhanging cliffs just beyond the headland to the north of the quiet bay at Cala s'Algar. From the beach car park, in calm conditions, a 25 minute swim of approximately 300m distance gains the spacious entrance, passing another short, blind cave on the way. The route into the cave is only 6m deep and a line will need to be laid. You will surface in an enormous cavern where the swell slops against the rocks; looking back, the distant glimmer of daylight is visible some 20m to 30m away.

It is impossible not to be extremely impressed by the immensity and splendour of the cavern that lies before you. Clearly, most

Cave formations in Cova dets Ases

visitors would be satisfied with this experience alone, but a short venture into the darkness will reveal much more. As you pick your way carefully through the cavern, tall pillars of pure glistening white suddenly appear. These extend from floor to ceiling as a profusion of columns with sword-like stalactites and stumpy, rounded stalagmites.

Finding Cova dets Ases

To locate the land-based entrance to Cova dets Ases start at the car park at Cala s'Algar, where you can park beside the sea. Take the small gate in the wall (39° 25' 45.66" N, 03° 16' 21.24" E) and follow the path left and northwards, parallel with the wall, passing a small stone shelter en route. After almost 300m the footpath leaves the wall and bends

Leave main path before the trees ▼

Cave lies beyond this tree ▼

The entrance

right (39° 25' 53.66" N, 03° 16' 16.88" E), then after another 100m it enters an area of trees and bears left (39° 25' 56.34" N, 03° 16' 19.32" E).

Here, take a slight path to the right, which may initially be obliterated by undergrowth but then becomes more obvious. Leave this path after about another 40m and strike eastwards towards the sea, heading for a prominent tree. The small entrance lies on the far side of the tree some 40m from the path (39° 25' 56.88" N, 03° 16' 22.14" E).

Coordinates

Dive site	Lat/Long
Cova dets Ases (sea)	39° 25' 50.40" N, 03° 16' 30.24" E
Cova dets Ases (land)	39° 25' 56.88" N, 03° 16' 22.14" E

Contacts and air supplies

Mallorca Diving: www.mallorcadiving.com
Isurus, Carrer de Magalhaes 8,
   07014 Palma de Mallorca, Islas Baleares
Tel: 971 73 09 43; www.isurussub.com

Emergencies

Emergency contacts: see Appendix A
Nearest hyperbaric centre: Palma de Mallorca
Nearest hospital: Hospital de Manacor, Carratera
   Manacor-Alcúdia s/n, 07500 Manacor,
   Islas Baleares; tel: 971 84 70 00
International telephone country code: +34

Further considerations

▶ A hood is required in all seasons, but gloves are not essential during the summer
▶ Wear suitable footwear such as boots or wellingtons for undertaking a traverse of the cave
▶ Take plenty of water: dehydration can be a problem, as the dry passages tend to be very warm and carrying heavy equipment is tiring
▶ Use a sturdy and comfortable rucksack to transport equipment to the cave and make two carries

Nature confronts her visitors with a very fine grotto where the utmost care must be exercised to avoid damage. Since 1989, when this section of cave was discovered from the inland entrance, several vulnerable pencil-like straw stalactites have been destroyed. One of these straws was the best part of 4m long – the longest known on the island – and our duty to conservation requires that we stay well clear of these fragile formations. Anyone intent on exploring further should pass the grotto by swimming through the short pool to the left, rather than risking unavoidable damage by attempting to stay out of the water. This is a magnificent sight, a veritable china shop of glistening crystal which transforms the darkness like some mysterious and dimly lit fantasy palace. It is a privilege to visit this unique cavern.

Some 100m of cave passage lie between the first and second sumps and, given the sharp and loose rocks that litter the cave, few people consider any further penetration is worthwhile. For the determined few, a bouldery section leads to two completely separate sump pools on either side of a steep, rocky slope. The pool to the right is the recommended route, being less than 30m long and no more than 3m deep; the other is 40m in length. Both dives reunite in another immense cavern. While the dives are relatively short, spacious and shallow, it is nonetheless imperative to consider what might go wrong and prepare for that contingency: these sumps are suited only to those with basic cave training and not for cavern divers.

A through-trip can be made by emerging at the dry inland exit some 300m further on, but unless the route has been checked on a prior reconnaissance, this is inadvisable. In any case, all diving equipment should be disassembled and suitably packaged for the journey. Entering and leaving the cave from the sea is far less arduous, even though you have to retrace your steps.

The land-based entrance is only around 500m from the beach car park, but it is secreted amid dense bushes and can be difficult to find. Making a recce of the dry cave will require a helmet, helmet-mounted lighting, sturdy footwear (*not* training shoes) and old clothes; placing a short rope as a handline and to help haul gear on the entrance climb will be a great help. The route inside the cave involves crawling, scrambling on short climbs and negotiating steep, slippery slopes, but navigation is relatively straightforward.

A number of Mallorca's other excellent inland sites comprise spacious tunnels with astounding, gin-clear visibility suited to fully trained divers (permission to access these can be negotiated by a local dive centre). Cova de sa Gleda, which lies around 1.5km from the south-east coast between Porto Cristo and Porto Colom, is the longest on the island and, indeed, is one of the longest underwater cave systems in Europe, having over 10.5km of passage. Although this is a wondrous site, it is a particularly complex and silty with limited access; divers are not generally allowed to visit it.

Menorca

Balearic Islands, Spain

Objective
A profusion of interesting cavern diving sites exists on Menorca with superb visibility and practically no silt but, disappointingly, the island has relatively little scope for more advanced cave dives. The maximum depth is 25m.

Access
No permission is required.

Location
Menorca is the most easterly of Spain's three main Balearic Islands, situated in the western Mediterranean, and is somewhat smaller than Mallorca, being only around 50km long and up to 20km wide. Most of the regularly visited locations lie around the southern coast of the island, but caverns exist throughout its coastline, the majority of which are accessed by boat.

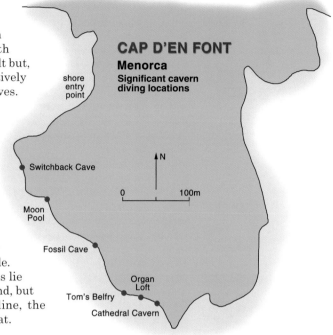

CAP D'EN FONT
Menorca
Significant cavern diving locations

shore entry point

Switchback Cave

Moon Pool

Fossil Cave

Organ Loft

Tom's Belfry

Cathedral Cavern

N

0   100m

Diving
Pont d'en Gil Cavern is a well-known and popular site found just west of Ciutadella at the western extremity of Menorca. Its name is derived from its close proximity to a headland joined to the island by a fine natural arch and it is one of the largest and longest caverns on Menorca, extending for 200m beneath the hillside. The water depth at the entrance is 17m, but within a short distance it then shallows to 11m. An airspace lies above and to the left-hand side of this magnificent canyon and visitors will quickly note the stalactite formations, discoloured by the sea and looking like some ochre-coloured candlewax which long ago dripped down the walls.

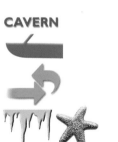

CAVERN

At the very back of the cavern it is possible to enter a section with clean, rippled banks of white sand and crystal-clear water. By this point the tunnel has narrowed considerably and, given the darkness, divers will acquire a feel for cave diving here, even though air lies but a few metres away. Divers often gain a different perspective of the cave on their exit by taking a closer look at the rich array of stalactites draped only metres above. It is also possible to climb out of the water onto a gentle slope part way back and explore a dry chamber – the Chamber of Columns.

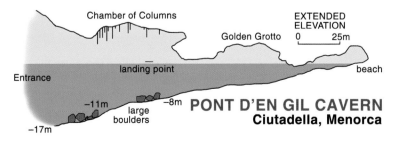

Chamber of Columns

Golden Grotto

EXTENDED ELEVATION
0   25m

landing point

beach

Entrance

−11m   −8m
large boulders

−17m

PONT D'EN GIL CAVERN
Ciutadella, Menorca

As a cavern diving destination Menorca is reassuringly good, in that if sea conditions deteriorate on one side of the island it is generally possible to dive at a protected location on some other part of the coastline, which is riddled with caverns and is something like a giant cheese full of holes. Indeed, one site just east of Punta Grossa on the north coast (16km north-north-west of Mahon) has been named **Swiss Cheese**. This is a hollow reef with a maximum depth of 23m which contains a maze of large chimneys and letter boxes to meander your way in and out of. Pierced by shafts of sunlight, it is a fine shore dive just 70m from the car park and is ideal if the weather is poor in the south.

In the east of the island an area that cannot be missed is the headland of **Cap d'en Font**, situated just south of the airport and south-south-west of the capital, Mahón (Maó in Catalan). This spectacular piece of rock is filled with tunnels and is home to other famous spots such as Tom's Belfry, the Organ Loft, Cathedral Cavern, Fossil Cave, the Moon Pool and Switchback Cave. Some sites may be visited via a shore entry point on the western side of the headland, although the most popular approach is by boat. The entrances generally lie in depths of around 15m.

At a depth of 18m lies the dual or split entrance to Tom's Belfry, the larger of which is about 10m high and over 10m wide, while the smaller is about one-third that size. About 15m inside the routes converge, where large and impressive pillars extend from the floor to the roof and you realise that the true width of the cavern is over 20m. At the back of the short, flooded cave – 50m from the entrance – the floor rises steeply to a depth of 3m and then reaches the surface to enable a view of the Belfry – a large, domed airspace, probably about 10m in diameter and 3m high with stalactite-coated walls. An underwater shelf at –3m is a good place to do a momentary 'lights out', instilling the real ambience of the setting. Given Menorca's excellent visibility and that the tunnel leading here comprises a classic 'cavern-light zone', when your eyes adjust, this is a striking scene.

The Organ Loft lies directly adjacent to and only a few metres to the east from Tom's Belfry and is named after the large organ-shaped formations inside. An easy, sand-floored tunnel allows a penetration of about half the length of Tom's Belfry.

Cathedral Cavern is the most southerly site on Cap d'en Font, just a few more metres east of the Organ Loft. This is the largest and deepest cavern on the headland with an entrance at 5m depth and a boulder-strewn floor about 20m below. The passage runs back for some 70m to 80m as a large tunnel for the entire distance, with a massive air surface for a substantial portion.

Several other caverns on the Cap d'en Font headland rise to air at points along their length, including Fossil Cave (with a maximum depth of 14m) and the Moon Pool (18m). After about 70m, the latter leads to a fine, circular 2m diameter shaft, above which divers may enter a cosy chamber that is just large enough to accommodate a group.

Using a boat to minimise swimming between the caverns and wearing a single 12 litre cylinder, it is possible to explore three of these caverns on one dive. However, while these sites are justifiably interesting and challenging, it is essential that divers are respectful of the environment and never let themselves succumb to complacency. The local dive centres will provide a

Further considerations

▶ All divers require a diving medical form and diving insurance

▶ The water temperature in the caverns is that of the open sea: between 13°C in March and 25°C in August

▶ Visibility can be up to 30m

▶ The local dive centres are well equipped for cavern diving activities

Contacts and air supplies

S'Algar Diving, Paseo Marítimo s/n, S'Algar, 07710 Sant Lluís, Islas Baleares
Tel: 971 15 06 01; www.salgardiving.com

Emergencies

Emergency contacts: see Appendix A
Nearest hyperbaric centre: Mahón
Nearest hospital: Hospital Mateu Orfila, Ronda de Malbuger 1, 07703 Mahón, Islas Baleares
Tel: 971 48 70 00
International telephone country code: +34

Pont d'en Gil Cavern

Coordinates

Dive site	Lat/Long
Cap d'en Font caves	39° 49' 36.82" N, 04° 12' 27.78" E
Pont d'en Gil Cavern	40° 00' 38.65" N, 03° 47' 39.56" E
Swiss Cheese	40° 01' 29.53" N, 04° 11' 40.14" E

knowledgeable briefing based upon experience and prevailing weather and sea conditions; divers should be extremely wary of activities beyond the scope of that advice.

Lanzarote

Canary Islands, Spain

Objective
Lanzarote contains several coastal caverns and swim-throughs that are suitable for all levels of ability. In addition, introductory cave diving skills may be practised at the inland lava tube of Cueva de los Lagos, for those more technically and physically inclined.

Access
No permission is required.

Location
Lanzarote is one of the smallest of the Canary Islands at 60km long by up to 20km wide, and lies in the Atlantic Ocean less than 130km from the north-west coast of Africa. The chain of islands owes its origin to volcanic activity and this land mass, lying at the north-eastern extremity of the group, is one of the youngest. Today, Lanzarote's cones and craters are dormant, but the landscape clearly indicates the dramatic events of the geological past. Views from the air are spectacular and, if you visit Timanfaya National Park, you will be awestruck by the scenery. Black molten lava lies twisted and contorted as though it were icing extruded on the face of some giant Christmas cake. Sulphur wafts in the air and the rocks are hot enough for demonstrations of grilling food. No vegetation is visible for an enormous distance – for all the world, it seems that the catastrophic outpouring took place last year. It kindles a vision of Mordor in J.R.R. Tolkein's *Lord of the Rings*, with a tragic history of communities consumed by lava, ash and darkness.

Peering into the shallow tunnel at Playa Chica

When the lava flowed and cooled, in places it allowed molten rock to continue to drain beneath the surface and eventually left behind tubes – cave systems that today may be flooded by seawater. Lava tubes are uncommon in comparison with limestone caves, but they are often of significant length and provide fascinating opportunities for diving. Formed in basalt rock, these tunnels vary in colour between dark grey and black, and this environment absorbs more light than most other caves. Apart from the general gloom, the tubes are frequently characterised by sharp rocks and many contain quantities of fine silt.

The tourist attraction within Jameos del Agua

Many cavern and cave diving sites are dotted along the eastern coast of Lanzarote, stretching from the holiday resort of Puerto del Carmen in the south to the northern tip of the island, including the area around Mala in the north-east, accessed at the small village of Charco del Palo. An interesting inland lava tube can be explored near the renowned tourist attraction at Jameos del Agua in the north.

History

The exploration of the caverns and caves on Lanzarote owes much to the curiosity of recreational open water divers, but one lava tube originating from the dormant volcano Monte Corona proved a major challenge. Where it descends to the coast at Jameos del Agua, the cave disappears beneath the ocean, producing an extended sump. The first dives in this massive passage, known as the Túnel de la Atlántida, were undertaken in the late 1970s by Antonio and José Manuel Guerra, who reached a point 370m from base.

In the 1980s some of the world's longest penetrations were achieved here by international teams, culminating in a world record by the Swiss diver Olivier Isler in 1986, when he reached a terminal blockage at 1,620m from base and a depth of 64m.

One of the caverns at Mala

Diving

The open water diving available on Lanzarote is undoubtedly some of the best in the northern hemisphere and, not surprisingly, it attracts a wide spectrum of divers, all keen to view the great variety of aquatic life including turtles, rays and possibly dolphins. Activities on the island are largely shore-based and, except during the most extreme conditions, this can be undertaken at sheltered spots year-round. The island can be very windy, but even when the white plumes of water seemingly rocket up the side of the low coastal cliffs, locations such as Playa Chica at Puerto del Carmen are wonderful. Vehicles can be parked mere metres from the beach, access to the water is easy and the sandy bottom continues down to whatever depth you feel comfortable with.

The gentle slope at Playa Chica comes to a sudden drop-off at around –20m; the wall is only 10m and below it the bottom descends into the ever-deepening grey gloom of the Atlantic. Secluded beneath the overhanging wall are the hull of a latter-day wreck and a couple of dark voids. Altar Cave is only a short recess, but just around the corner to the north lies an awesome sight, the mammoth opening to **The Cathedral**.

The Cathedral is located approximately 175m offshore; it is about 20m wide and over 10m high at its mouth. The vast tunnel

Contacts and air supplies

The Dive Shop, Centro Comercial Matagorda, Local 44, Avenida las Playas 103, Matagorda, 35510 Puerto del Carmen, Las Palmas
Tel: 928 51 28 65
www.thediveshoplanzarote.com

Emergencies

Emergency contacts: see Appendix A
Nearest hyperbaric centre: Arrecife; note the warning under Further Considerations
Nearest hospital: Arrecife General, Carretera San Bartolomé km 1.3, 35500 Arrecife, Las Palmas
Tel: 928 59 50 00
International telephone country code: +34

Further considerations

► A good 5mm semi-dry wetsuit is adequate, without a hood or gloves, to undertake an hour-long dive at any of the sites in winter

► In December the sea and cave water temperature is around 18°C

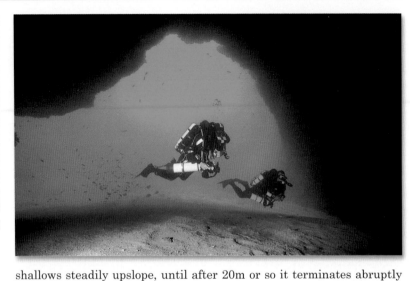

The Cathedral

CAVERN

CAVERN INTRO

Entering a tunnel at Mala

shallows steadily upslope, until after 20m or so it terminates abruptly at a blank wall. Starfish lie on the floor, eels peep from cracks, while an occasional large grouper quietly patrols its haunt. Marine life abounds, some of which is larger than even these normal residents: angel sharks and big rays are not uncommon. A visit to The Cathedral provides a good idea of the incredible natural lava tubes that can be found on the island.

Ascending from 30m back towards the sheltered water of Playa Chica, divers can make another subterranean foray into a short tunnel beneath the rock wall which forms the southerly limb of the natural harbour. Both the rocky walls which envelope Playa Chica are ancient flows of lava and, unknown to most visitors, below water level a void several metres wide and large enough to negotiate even with conventional equipment can be entered. At low water small air pockets may be found, but at high water the passage is completely water filled and scores of small golden cardinalfish, common in all the caverns of the Canaries, flit to and fro.

Many short swim-throughs and volcanically formed caverns can be enjoyed further north along the coast at **Mala**. Here, more distant from the large tourist centres such as Puerto del Carmen, the visibility is better and often in excess of 30m. The diving is well within a recreational sphere.

The most fascinating site on Lanzarote is the lava tube which dives beneath the sea at Jameos del Agua on the north-east coast. Amazing, intriguing, perhaps downright incredible, are all terms that can be applied to this renowned location. Jameos del Agua is, along with Timanfaya, a principal tourist attraction and hundreds, if not thousands, of people visit it daily to gain a splendid impression of the mysterious underground world and marvel at the way the accompanying environmental centre has been sympathetically developed. The tunnel is substantial – big enough to accommodate both a cafe and an auditorium capable of seating 600 visitors.

Volcanic activity, more precisely a huge, fast-flowing mass of lava, gave birth to the tube in a single short, sharp, bout of activity some 5,000 years ago. In one momentous event a flow of red hot lava drained to the sea like a giant river, leaving an immense tunnel in its wake – a passage generally well over 10m in diameter and frequently attaining a height of 15m or even 20m.

Perhaps the most amazing point to note is that, in common with most tubes, it lies but a few metres beneath the land surface. Other than at the occasional place where the roof has collapsed – known locally as a *jameo* – there is no indication above ground of where the tunnel runs. The tube has an overall length of over 7km, extending in roughly a straight line from the dormant Monte Corona to the sea, with the final 1.6km lying beneath the ocean and only accessed from a small tranquil pool in the Jameos del Agua showcave.

Sadly, the authorities no longer permit access to this most impressive of dive sites, which has been assigned special protection as it is the home of a multitude of small blind white crustaceans. Similar species are normally encountered in the deep ocean, so quite why these *Munidopsis polymorpha* cave dwellers exist here is not fully understood. While the creatures may appear conspicuously plentiful in the open water lake and are clearly thriving in the short section of cave accessible by the public, this species of crab is found nowhere else. Taking refreshments at the subterranean cafeteria, one can only wistfully imagine what this fantastic tunnel must be like to explore, but it is nevertheless worth a visit between dives elsewhere.

The grilled entrance to Cueva de los Lagos

An associated, upstream sector of the same tube can be entered at a neighbouring cave, **Cueva de los Lagos** (Cueva de los Siete Lagos: Seven Lakes Cave). Once open to all, in late 2012 the entrance was gated and permission and a key are required for access. Entry is via a fixed ladder where a 10m rope may aid in lowering gear. Sturdy footwear, overalls or old clothes and a headlight are also needed, as the underground journey from the entrance to the dive base is approximately 300m and the route is hot, dusty and involves scrambling over rough terrain (take a minimum of a litre of drinking water per person). This is not a trip to consider lightly and introductory cave diving experience is necessary: it is *not* a cavern dive.

INTRO

While it is possible to carry fairly bulky equipment through the approach passage, for safety, recce the route first and transport cylinders separately: a pair of 7 litre cylinders would form an optimum configuration. The

Cueva de los Lagos

Coordinates

Dive site	Lat/Long
The Cathedral	28° 55' 01.42" N, 13° 40' 03.52" W
Cueva de los Lagos	29° 09' 28.70" N, 13° 26' 19.46" W
Mala	29° 05' 01.25" N, 13° 26' 58.00" W

Los Lagos access

Cueva de los Lagos was gated to protect the endemic invertebrate fauna in this part of a national monument. The authorities suggest that 'tourist activities' will be permitted in the future, as long as conservation policies are adhered to and a permit is obtained. Make enquiries with the Ministry of Environment, the Consejería de Medio Ambiente of the Cabildo de Lanzarote at: Avenida Fred Olsen s/n, 35500 Arrecife, Las Palmas; tel: +34 928 810100 ext. 2280 (Spanish only); www.cabildodelanzarote .com).

time and effort in securing permission will be amply repaid; the diving here is absolutely superb with visibility in excess of 40m and, surprisingly, there is no silt.

The main Cueva de los Lagos tunnel extends to over 400m from dive base, a route subdivided into three or four separate sumps. An initial saltwater canal leads for about 75m to a dive of about 30m with a maximum depth of 4m, followed by a swim of about 70m to a short 10m sump. Another long swim gains the third sump of 40m, and a final long swim leads to the longest sump of something less than 200m. The maximum depth at the boulder-choked terminal point is 11.5m. Alcoves exist along the route, but no side passages.

Lines should be in place to the end of the cave, but take at least one reel in case they require attention: nylon lines of any thickness may be used. The end of the cave lies close to the Jameos del Agua showcave.

The Cueva de los Lagos dive base

Twin lines in Cueva de los Lagos

Tenerife

Canary Islands, Spain

Objective
Popular for open water diving and especially as a winter destination, the Spanish island of Tenerife is not renowned for cavern or cave diving, nevertheless it has a number of offshore lava tubes and swim-throughs that will add spice to any diving holiday. In particular, a rock arch at 40m depth provides a classic opportunity and, for fully trained and experienced cave divers *only*, the Cueva del Palm Mar is an interesting, though deceptively serious site.

Access
No permission is required, but dive qualifications must be carried.

Location
Roughly triangular in shape and around 80km long, Tenerife is the largest of the Canary Islands and is located in the Atlantic Ocean some 300km off the north-west coast of Africa. The Canaries were created by a series of volcanic eruptions and today Tenerife is dominated by the striking form of the volcano El Teide, which lies in the centre of the island and, at 3,718m, is the highest point in Spain. The cave diving sites of note both lie near the southernmost extremity, not far from the busy tourist resort of Playa de las Americas.

The cross outside Cueva del Palm Mar

History
Open water divers were the first to locate and explore these two sites.

Diving
All diving at the named sites is conducted by boat. The well-known wrecks of *El Condesito* and *El Meridian* lie off the southern coast of Tenerife; here too – 400m south of Las Galletas – is the **Coral Arch**, a classic rock swim-through at a depth of 40m which is superbly draped in an array of soft coral.

In the same area, 3km south-east of Playa de las Americas and 400m off Palm-Mar, lies **Cueva del Palm Mar**. Given that the seabed is flat and sandy here, and that the reef has an abundance of marine life, this has always been a popular venue with local dive operators. Sadly, the cave has seen five fatalities over the years and today two man-made structures close to the spot emphasise the fact that caves are dangerous places for the uninitiated. A heavily encrusted stone cross stands immediately outside the cave entrance, while a short distance away a statue of the Virgin del Carmen has been erected – both grim reminders of the past and hopefully a deterrent to the inexperienced.

Set beneath a solid rock face in 30m of water, the triangular-shaped entrance to Cueva del Palm Mar is 10m wide and about 2m high. The tunnel splits into two a few metres inside: one route veers to the right while straight ahead the passage continues, though somewhat smaller. After passing through a low section, spacious proportions are regained at

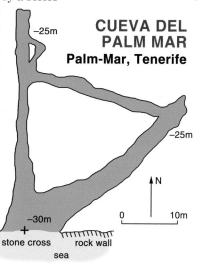

CUEVA DEL PALM MAR
Palm-Mar, Tenerife

−25m

−25m

N

0   10m

−30m

stone cross   rock wall

sea

FULL

Coordinates

Dive site	Lat/Long
Coral Arch	28° 00' 07.14" N, 16° 39' 17.40" W
Cueva del Palm Mar	28° 01' 38.76" N, 16° 42' 33.90" W

Further considerations

▶ Water temperatures in late December are typically 21°C or more
▶ Visibility is generally in excess of 20m
▶ A line reel is essential
▶ Cueva del Palm Mar contains few natural rock belays, so take drop-weights for belaying the line

Rising silt in Palm Mar and a pre-dive briefing

A cautionary tale

Without appropriate training, do not venture more than a few metres from the safety of open water at any location, cavern or cave. A rash, unplanned or ill-considered entry to a cave by the inexperienced can have dire consequences when a loss of visibility can lead to rapid disorientation, acute stress levels and an increased rate of breathing; without a line and only equipped with a single cylinder, divers will rapidly deplete their air supply.

Just such instances have tragically occurred at Cueva del Palm Mar, resulting in five fatalities. Perhaps ironically, the powerful lights that illuminated the divers' inward swim only lured them to their fate. If they had taken no lighting that day, they would have remained firmly within the daylight zone. If you are untrained in full cave diving, Cueva del Palm Mar is a site to avoid, where enthusiasm and curiosity are nothing more than a curse; dive operators normally advise their visitors to refrain from making any entry. A silt-out quickly destroys a buddy team and effectively means that each diver is diving solo – and the divers may not even be the cause of the loss in visibility. During one mapping project here a large ray, about 25m inside the cave, was as startled as the explorer and suddenly lifted off the floor to disappear into its self-induced cloud of silt.

Do *not* underestimate such deceptively innocent-looking sites – they must all be treated with caution.

30m from the entrance, where the visibility is excellent and is even better than in the open water outside. Here, another passage leads to the right and connects back to the previous junction.

Directly ahead again, the ongoing tunnel is now about 2m square and continues at 25m depth. Before it abruptly terminates about 40m from the entrance, two further openings are passed – these also join up with each other. Cueva del Palm Mar is therefore a short but complex site, with some 90m of tunnels and a maximum depth of 30m.

It is virtually impossible to avoid silting within the smaller passages – certainly so if two or more divers are operating together. In such an environment, a light is useless and you are totally dependent upon the line to navigate an exit. This site is *not* a place to undertake a cavern dive and divers with that level of training should not proceed. Beyond the 25m point Cueva del Palm Mar is only suitable for fully trained cave divers who are well experienced in line-laying techniques.

Contacts and air supplies

Aqua-Marina Oxygène Dive Centre, Centro Comercial Compostela Beach, Local 396A, Playa de las Americas, 38660 Arona, Santa Cruz de Tenerife
Tel: 922 79 79 44; www.aquamarinadivingtenerife.com

Emergencies

Emergency contacts: see Appendix A
Nearest hyperbaric centre: La Laguna
Nearest hospital: Hospital Universitario de Canarias, Carretera Ofra s/n La Cuesta, 38320 La Laguna, Santa Cruz de Tenerife; tel: 922 67 80 00
International telephone country code: +34

Costa Blanca

Alicante, Spain

Objective
The sea conditions on the Costa Blanca are generally less challenging than on the Costa Brava, further to the north, and the region holds attractive possibilities for both cavern and cave divers, with options for those at all levels of ability.

Access
No permission is required.

All sites are rich in marine life

Location
The Costa Blanca runs for around 200km along the central section of Spain's Mediterranean coast in the province of Alicante. A number of interesting caves and caverns are located in the coastal cliffs between Jávea at the northern end of the Costa Blanca and the well-known resort of Benidorm.

History
While the majority of sea caves owe their discovery to the curiosity of recreational scuba divers, Cueva del Moraig (pronounced Morach) has always been a site of interest. As early as 1000 BC the Phoenicians are reputed to have drawn water, a precious commodity in this area, from the mouth of the cave. In the early 1950s, in a continuing quest for greater water supplies, the major outflow at the cave came into sharper focus. The resurgence was first dived in 1974 by Eloy Parra, who began progressive salinity sampling as far as 200m from the entrance; the studies continued in 1982, when two explorers lost their lives diving here.

The coast looking north from Cabo Negro

In the mid-1980s a major mapping project was conceived, spearheaded by the German, Bernhard Pack. Cueva del Moraig was systematically explored into the early 1990s, involving ever longer penetrations to the furthest point at 1,160m and a total of over 2km of passages was studied. On 21 September 1992 Pack also lost his life in the cave.

British diver Rick Stanton continued the exploration of the main tunnel in 2000 and gained an airbell a short distance beyond his predecessor's limit. In the winter of 2005/6 another British diver, John Volanthen, made further progress in a divergent network of small and highly silted passages, but the hope of a major continuation seems to have been lost.

Diving
Around 7km south of Jávea, two caverns lie on the northern side of the prominent cliffs of **Cabo Negro**. The more southerly is a small but spacious 30m long cavern that is 5m high and 10m wide with a maximum depth of 14m, while a short distance to the north a more challenging, narrow 40m long swim-through may be tackled; the depth is 8m at the entrance. A boat is required for access.

CAVERN

Between Cabo Negro and Cabo la Nao, the next headland to the south, another interesting cavern swim-through is found beneath the small rocky

CAVERN

CAVERN

INTRO

island of **Escull**. The main entrance lies at 26m depth on the western side of the rock face, with a complex of twisting passageways leading 30m to an exit on the far side. The main passage is over 6m high and wide with a chamber roughly midway through; a boat is again required.

Further down the coast, due south of Jávea, a cavern and cave diving gem is situated near **Cumbre del Sol**. Park next to the entrance of a classic sea cave at the southern corner of the beach and follow a short flight of stone steps down into a beautiful, lofty cavern with a fine view across the bay to the north-east. Swell frequently breaks upon a dimly lit rocky platform here and it is this which determines how safe or practical it is to enter the underwater tunnels at the back of the cave. In low water a simple scramble over rocks gains the secret pool, but visitors must be wary that the terrain may be slippery or subject to the vagaries of the sea. If waves are breaking into the pool at the rear, the cavern dive may be impossible.

Underwater, a tunnel heads off at 4m to 5m depth – the dive is about 50m long and consistently wide before the open sea is encountered, but just past the midway point, the height of the passage reduces to about a metre. This section is straightforward to negotiate, but the ebbing and flowing current may become a significant factor: if a swell is running, visibility may reduce to a few metres.

More experienced introductory cave divers will continue on to visit the major cave system of **Cueva del Moraig**. To locate it, follow the submerged cliffs in a southerly direction for about 75m, round a corner and enter a small bay on the right. The water takes on a milky appearance here and the visibility deteriorates, the result of a substantial outflow of fresh water mixing with the salt water. Swimming to the large entrance, which stretches up above the surface, you enter a different world – this is a very remarkable spot, with water sloshing upon massive boulders. It is possible to scramble over the rocks on the right-hand side, but the easiest route into the cave lies against the left-hand wall where divers can swim between submerged boulders beneath the overhanging walls. Beyond, the surface is regained in shallow water and preparations can be made for the main dive.

Within a few metres the floor falls away to between 7m and 9m and a large submerged tunnel with rapidly clearing water leads onwards into the mountainside. No line is left *in situ*

Coordinates

Dive site	Lat/Long
Cabo Negro	38° 44' 43.92" N, 00° 13' 49.26" E
Cueva dels Colums	38° 37' 44.64" N, 00° 01' 12.55" E
Cumbre del Sol	38° 42' 29.04" N, 00° 09' 58.92" E
Cueva del Elefante	38° 33' 07.38" N, 00° 03' 31.18" W
Escull	38° 44' 33.42" N, 00° 14' 01.78" E
Cueva del Moraig	38° 42' 26.77" N, 00° 09' 58.04" E
Teddybears	38° 37' 37.60" N, 00° 01' 36.58" E

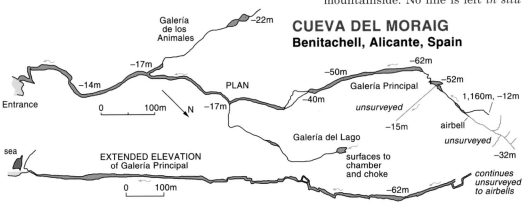

CUEVA DEL MORAIG
Benitachell, Alicante, Spain

The car park at Moraig, the entrance and dive base in the cave, and a gnome figurine installed inside

in this first 50m section of the cave, to deter the inexperienced, so divers must carry their own reel. Within 50m the water becomes crystal clear and then, against the right-hand wall, the permanent line begins where it is belayed to some sturdy metal poles left from a scientific research project.

The impressive, largely silt free passage meanders on with the depth gradually increasing; at around 200m from base the depth is 14m. Further in the complexities increase and a maximum depth of 62m is reached; penetrations of well over 1km have been undertaken in Cueva del Moraig and the cave's total length is now around 3km.

Moving on down the coast, at the south side of the Toix headland (twenty minutes by boat south from Calpe) lies a cavern known locally as the **Teddybears**, after a pair of small, stone teddy bear statues placed here (in Spanish it is called Cueva del Cabracho – which means Scorpionfish Cave). The entrance is at 7m depth, with a tunnel leading into the cave for about 10m to a small triangular hole on the right-hand side, which gains a chamber where divers can surface to view a set of beautiful white stalactites 10m or so overhead. A second smaller chamber is reached some 10m further on, where a flicker of daylight dimly permeates the darkness.

CAVERN

Laying line in Cueva del Moraig

CAVERN INTRO

From the Teddybears a second cave – **Cueva dels Colums** – is located approximately 600m further west along the wall towards the beach. This is a more challenging proposition where a large entrance at 18m depth leads to a gradually deepening tunnel. At between 50m and 60m from the entrance the depth reaches 23m, where you are confronted with the remains of a diver warning sign and some metal bars across the passage. Just beyond the bars the floor falls away sheer into blackness; this is not a place for cavern divers, but is suitable for experienced introductory cave divers. After heavy rainfall a flow of water may be emerging from the cave and suction has also been recorded: take care. Both caves lie close to the wreck of the *Galliana* at around 20m depth.

CAVERN

To the south of Calpe, roughly halfway between Altea and Benidorm, is the spectacular headland of Sierra Gelada. Its east side contains the well-known **Cueva del Elefante**, which takes its name from the conspicuous elephant-like rock feature in the cliff face above the entrance. After around a thirty-minute boat ride from Calpe, a group of divers can gather in a shallow, sheltered spot just outside the cavern before descending into the darkness at 12m depth. The large and colourful tunnel runs into the cliff for 20m, then makes an abrupt ascent to surface in a high level, about 10m square, that contains safe, breathable air.

▶ Fifty metres from dive base in Cueva del Moraig

Returning to the daylight, swim about 50m westwards along the cliff to another opening. This has a double entrance, one of which lies just below the water surface while the second is larger and can be entered at a depth of 9m. Both lead to a dry chamber with a large ongoing cave network that can be explored for a considerable distance on foot.

Further considerations

▶ Sea temperatures vary between 13°C and 27°C in winter and summer extremes
▶ A 5mm wetsuit is adequate in summer, but an additional vest or a drysuit might be preferable at other times
▶ A hood and gloves are unnecessary in summer, but are needed in other seasons
▶ Visibility can be 20m or more in good conditions, although storms may reduce this to a few metres
▶ The current is sometimes strong in the stretch of sea between Cumbre del Sol and Cueva del Moraig

Contacts and air supplies

Diving Jávea, Carretera Portitxol 135, Toscamar, 03730 Jávea, Alicante
Tel: 966 47 27 82; www.divingjavea.com

Les Basetes Dive Centre, Carretera Calpe a Moraira km 2, 03720 Benissa, Alicante
Tel: 965 83 54 28; www.buceobasetes.com

Emergencies

Emergency contacts: see Appendix A
Nearest hyperbaric centre: Alicante
Nearest hospitals: Hospital de Dénia, Partida Beniadlà s/n, 03700 Dénia, Alicante; tel: 966 42 90 00
Hospital de la Marina Baixa, Avenida Alcalde en Jaume Botella Major 7, 03570 Villajoyosa, Alicante; tel: 966 85 98 00
International telephone country code: +34

Costa Brava

Catalonia, Spain

Objective

The Costa Brava is a superb venue and has considerable scope for cavern and introductory cave diving activities, taking participants to a maximum depth of 25m.

Access

Given their rich and varied ecology, the Medes Islands were granted special protection by the Catalan government in 1983. This was extended in 1990 when the islands were made a marine reserve, since which the sea life has massively regenerated in the area. The numbers of visitors is closely controlled and a permit is required for diving, with a charge made per dive. No permission is required for the mainland sites.

Location

The Costa Brava coastline lies on the Mediterranean in Catalonia in north-east Spain. L'Estartit is the focus of activities and is the ideal place for joining a cavern tour of the Medes Islands, 1.5km distant. Numerous undersea caves can also be found along the 8km stretch of the Montgrí coast to the north, between L'Estartit and L'Escala, where the impressive limestone cliffs have heights of over 170m.

Diving

All sites

CAVERN

Diving in this region is boat-based with some ten operators to choose from in L'Estartit. However, as the name Costa Brava – 'Wild Coast' – suggests, sea conditions can be highly variable. Winds from the east, known locally as the *levant*, present the greatest problems and divers are generally advised not to venture out under these conditions.

Another factor influencing diving is poor visibility which, due to particles in suspension, can be as low as 3m. However, it is these very particles that supply nutrients for the rich flora and fauna in the area, so the marine life simply would not exist without the cloudiness. Apart from the usual species of starfish, octopus and moray and conger eels, barracuda, eagle rays, sunfish, wrasse, sea bass, red mullet, bream, tuna and some exceptionally large groupers can be seen. Some of this last species are said to be over 25 years old. Perhaps the most colourful sighting will be the displays of red coral and the multicoloured gorgonians, not forgetting the phenomenally beautiful, if small, nudibranchs.

The finest view of the Montgrí coast is from the summit of Rocamaura at an altitude of 225m, directly overlooking L'Estartit harbour and the Medes Islands

The water temperature varies considerably according to season and depth: in August it may reach 23°C on the surface, but by –35m it is only 17°C, while in January the surface water may be 13°C.

Much of the cavern diving involves entering spacious tunnels at depths of between 15m and 25m. Sites along the mainland coast to the north of L'Estartit include the popular and pleasant through-dives such as the **Pedrosa Tunnel** and the **Ferriola Tunnel**, approximately half an hour distant by boat. Both consist of a very large passage and pass beneath small islands, the former a 50m swim-through from a landward entrance at 12m to emerge at 24m

Coordinates

Dive site	Lat/Long
Dolphin Tunnel (north entrance)	42° 02' 39.42" N, 03° 13' 34.05" E
Dolphin Tunnel (south entrance)	42° 02' 38.28" N, 03° 13' 34.89" E
Ferriola Tunnel	42° 05' 04.03" N, 03° 11' 50.60" E
Pedrosa Tunnel	42° 04' 26.31" N, 03° 12' 18.03" E
Cueva de la Vaca (north entrance)	42° 02' 52.31" N, 03° 13' 35.83" E
Cueva de la Vaca (south entrance)	42° 02' 50.84" N, 03° 13' 35.35" E

depth, while the latter is approximately half the length at a similar depth.

These are suitable introductory venues for most divers, while others – such as Cova de les Vetes, which lies about 600m north of Ferriola island – demand great respect. A triple fatality occurred in this cave in the mid-1990s, occasioned by a silt-out and the lack of a dive line; the site does not feature on the main dive centre itineraries.

The Medes Islands – approximately 20 minutes from L'Estartit by boat – provide a wonderful setting for activities, with a large number of interesting caves to explore, including **Cueva de la Vaca** on the east side of Meda Gran. Its lofty, 10m high main tunnel runs north to south through a promontory for a distance of 40m at depths of 11m to 25m. Another north–south traverse, around 60m away at the neck of the same promontory, is suitable for more experienced divers of introductory cave certification or above. Several other spacious caves lie nearby, all being colourful with a profusion of marine life.

Perhaps the most renowned cave is the **Dolphin Tunnel**, which runs through Meda Xica on the south-east side of the Medes Islands. The most popular dive is a 45m traverse between the two entrances which

Poor visibility in the Pedrosa Tunnel

are frequently visited by recreational divers. A statue of a dolphin has been installed at the south entrance, although sightings of dolphins are very rare. This site involves a large tunnel at a maximum depth of less than 15m. Divers need to be aware that the Dolphin Tunnel is part of a more extensive network and leading off the east wall of the traverse is another passage over 80m long which links to two other entrances. This connecting tunnel is suitable for more experienced divers of introductory cave level. The depth in this easterly part of the complex is between 15m and 25m. This is clearly a committing dive with very little light reaching the inner reaches and is normally undertaken without the use of a line.

While the caverns of the Costa Brava offer magnificent diving under optimum conditions, consulting local dive operators is essential with regard to the weather, sea conditions and site accessibility.

A diver in the North Entrance to Cueva de la Vaca, and Pedrosa Island; the start of the tunnel is on the right-hand end

Contacts and air supplies

Calypso Diving Estartit, Carrer de la Cala Pedrosa 1, PO Box 148, 17258 L'Estartit, Girona
Tel: 972 75 14 88; www.grn.es/calypso

Unisub Estartit, Passeig Marítim 10, 17258 L'Estartit, Girona
Tel: 972 75 17 68; www.unisub.es

Diving permits for the Medes Islands:
Parc Natural del Montgrí, les Illes Medes i el Baix Ter, Passeig del Port s/n, Espigó de Llevant, 17258 L'Estartit, Girona
Tel: 972 75 17 01; www.gencat.cat/parcs/illes_medes

Emergencies

Emergency contacts: see Appendix A
Nearest hyperbaric centre: Palamós
Nearest hospital: Hospital de Palamós, Calle Hospital 36, 17230 Palamós, Girona; tel: 972 60 01 60
International telephone country code: +34

Further considerations

▶ The specific licence required for diving in the Medes Islands has strict rules, including boat use and mooring, with certain documentation required for those using their own boat
▶ A hood is recommended in all seasons, but gloves are not essential during the summer
▶ These sites are very popular with open water divers, which may cause a reduction in visibility to a few metres
▶ Conditions on the surface can be distinctly choppy and any approach should be made with care

Murcia

South-east Spain

Objective
The Murcia limestone area presents fine opportunities for diving at all levels of ability, from cavern diver through to fully certified cave diver, with a maximum depth of less than 30m.

Access
No permission is required.

Location
The small village of La Azohía (pronounced 'Lathoya') lies 15km south-west of the historically important city of Cartagena on the south-central section of Spain's Mediterranean coast, west of the Costa Blanca. A number of superb submarine entrances exist between La Azohía and Cartagena, the majority being approached by boat, whereas Cueva del Agua is an inland site near Isla Plana, around 5km west of La Azohía.

History
The first dive took place in Cueva del Agua in the early 1970s when the first underwater chamber was explored by divers from Exploraciones Subterráneas de la Diputación Provincial de Murcia. In the mid-1980s there followed dives by José Luis Llamusí and Andrés Ros of the Centro de Excursionista de Cartagena group. The overall length of the cave was extended to 200m and the furthest point was 100m from the dive base. As a result of work during the rescue operation of a dual fatality in the cave in 1996, the length increased to 800m, with the distance from dive base now at 200m.

The entrance to Cueva del Agua and the view across La Azohía bay

In 1998 José and Andrés began a concerted long-term campaign of systematic exploration and study (Project 2000) and in June 2001 José, Alberto Achica and Vicente García found the continuation of the main passage at around 200m from base. This was wide, but it had substantial quantities of loose sediment on the roof, making further exploration very difficult and slow. By the end of 2003 the advance had taken the team to 750m from dive base and the total length of the system had risen to over 2.1km.

Diving
Cueva de la Ovaza (III) and Cueva de la Virgen are the very spice of diving life. **Cueva de la Ovaza (III)** is a short sea cave in the cliffs of Cabo Tiñoso, having multiple underwater entrances at a depth of 10m. With bright orange cardinalfish flitting to and fro in the shadows and sufficient space for a diver to manoeuvre, entering Ovaza is an exciting experience for any newcomer to the world of cavern diving. A smattering of sand and odd pieces of seaweed detritus have to be contended with, but in essence this is a relatively silt-free site. After perhaps 20m of horizontal passageway you can rise to the surface inside the cave and savour that remote, isolated feeling that such places engender. Pitch black it may be, but it has more than ample space to wait a while and enjoy that first encounter as water sloshes gently around the walls.

CAVERN

A clean-washed tube in Ovaza (III)

The entrance to Cueva CT-12

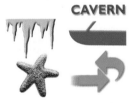

CAVERN

Cueva de la Virgen occupies a discreet location nearer to the city of Cartagena. Named after a natural rock feature at the entrance, this is a very large and spectacular passage at 15m depth that acts as a portal to an even more splendid cavern beyond. Diving along the immense black tunnel for 40m, you ascend a gradual incline through a wispy halocline to find fresh water, underwater stalagmites and then a fine, air-filled cathedral-like room illuminated by daylight from an opening high above. Off to the side is a short flooded passage with further underwater flowstone draperies.

Neither Ovaza nor Virgen has an extensive network; both are suitable for divers at all levels of ability with relatively little chance of becoming lost or disorientated.

CAVERN

Cueva CT-12 (sometimes known as Cartagena Cave no. 12 or Cueva de la Herradura) also lies in the sea cliffs of Cabo Tiñoso, around 800m west of Ovaza, and is a little more challenging. The cave is special – it is the prime training cave in the area and possesses two entrances with over 100m of passageway trending back inland. The lower entrance lies at 23m depth, giving access to a spacious tunnel that rises steeply to a depth of about 12m. Here it levels off at a junction, presenting a possible quick return to open water, less than 20m distant, via a wonderful rounded tunnel. The

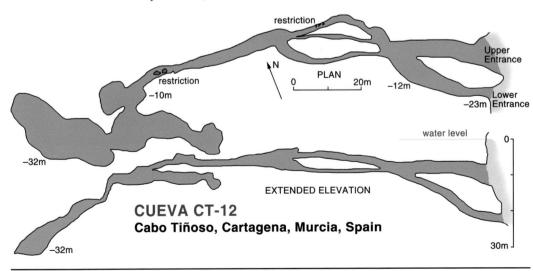

CUEVA CT-12
Cabo Tiñoso, Cartagena, Murcia, Spain

distance from entrance to entrance is in the order of 50m and this forms a good and interesting short circuit for most divers.

Given the mixed terrain and a couple of slight restrictions beyond the junction, the innermost passages in CT-12 are only suitable for divers with (or who are undertaking) cave diving training. This section contains significant chambers and arrays of darkened flowstone formations and the temperature remains constant at 18°C year-round.

For more experienced divers of introductory and full cave certification, the finest site in the region is **Cueva del Agua**, an inconspicuous hole in the ground to the north of and directly adjacent to the E-22 road between La Azohía and Mazarrón.

The entrance lies only 10m from the road and access to the water, at the bottom of a rocky but short descent of some 10m from the entrance, is straightforward. Here, the floor levels off to provide a perfect kitting-up area with room for an entire group to prepare at the same time; the place is indeed spacious. There is sufficient daylight in which to work and, with the inviting prospect of clear, calm water, newcomers to the site could easily be deceived by the benign setting. The sea lies barely

Floats used to support the permanent line in Cueva del Agua

INTRO

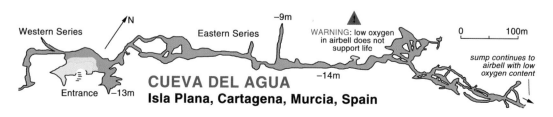

Western Series

N

Eastern Series

−9m

WARNING: low oxygen in airbell does not support life

0   100m

sump continues to airbell with low oxygen content

CUEVA DEL AGUA
Isla Plana, Cartagena, Murcia, Spain

Entrance ▽−13m

−14m

No place for the unwary

At Cueva del Agua, inexperienced divers require protection against their lack of awareness. In 1996 a line ran from the entrance area into the further reaches of what was then a partially explored section of the cave. Some 70m inside the flooded tunnel, a passage dipped to the right and the line appeared to be buried beneath silt. In crystal-clear water, two divers continued onwards, presumably thinking that they would shortly see the line reappear beyond the mudbank – they must also have thought that making an exit would present few difficulties.

It is uncertain what happened next, other than that the divers did not resurface. Recovery teams quickly discovered that the line hadn't been pulled into a silt bank, but that it was buried by a fallen slab of rock from the roof. By this stage the visibility in the tunnel was very bad and many days during the following month were spent searching the system. When eventually the bodies were located, they were separated: one was relatively close to but beyond the point where the line had been buried, while the second lay against the roof about 200m from dive base. The latter's bottle, which was removed from the body during its recovery, still lies in a cleft in the floor.

While the two divers may have been experienced scuba divers, operating with familiar equipment, they were ill prepared for an underground environment. From the moment they lost sight of the fixed line, they broke more than one of the now accepted rules of cave diving. The visibility in the low point of the tunnel would have reduced to a few centimetres in a matter of seconds; without a line reel or the all-important training for such eventualities, their disorientation would have been rapid. The outcome in these circumstances was inevitable.

a stone's throw away and in April, when the Mediterranean has yet to warm up and it is a chilly 15°C offshore, inside the cave the surface pool beckons at a balmy 21°C.

But there is more ... at about 10m depth divers will find a thermocline where the temperature increases to 29°C: the cave has fresh water at the surface, salt water below and, due to some abnormal quirk of nature – deep geothermal heating – the entire water mass is warmed well above anything that might be anticipated. The Romans, among others, took advantage of this resource and constructed a bathing place nearby. Diving in such conditions seems a very attractive proposition.

Now for the downside. Despite the evident large tunnels and the blissfully warm water, this is not a place for the inexperienced and basic cave training should be undertaken before commencing any underwater activity here. The cave contains a lot of silt and thick, clay-like ooze carpets every surface from the floor to the roof. The geological setting is such that the very nature of the rock gives cause for consideration as, while the place may be inherently stable, the ceiling appears to be somewhat friable. Underwater, exhalations result in significant silt-fall (percolation) from above. When you are diving along the main line this effect is not

A line junction with line arrows in Cueva del Agua

immediately apparent nowadays as, after years of diver traffic, much of the loose silt has been displaced, but if you move away from the line by only a few metres you will be confronted with a different and disturbing situation.

Directly outside the cave entrance a plaque set high on the wall attests to the incident in 1996, when two enthusiastic police officers lost the line only a short distance inside. This is a chilling reminder that there is no room for complacency in cave diving anywhere, no matter how innocuous the surroundings may appear. Today, therefore, the initial sector of the cave has no *in situ* line, a deliberate measure to deter any casual scuba diver from entering.

Further inside, divers visiting this cave will be amazed at how thoroughly the permanent lines have been laid. All the fixed lines are sturdy and belayed well clear of the silt, some with the novel method of using floats to hold a section of 11mm diameter rope off the floor. Local practitioners have done all they can to ensure safe lining – but they cannot remove the silt.

Cueva del Agua is a complex cave system and has been explored for over 2km, with work still ongoing; the maximum depth is 21m. The diving is fascinating, as long as divers have the appropriate training and experience. The history of cave diving throughout the world records many tragic incidents that have arisen due to silting and we should all take heed of such events. Inside a cave, mine or wreck a continuous well-laid guideline is essential and everything possible must be done to avoid disturbing silt at any location.

Further considerations

▶ Sea temperatures are 15°C in early April, warming to 24°C in the autumn
▶ Visibility is normally excellent in the sea caves and may be 20m or more
▶ A 5mm wetsuit is adequate in summer, but an additional vest or a drysuit might be preferable earlier in the year
▶ A hood and gloves are not necessary in summer
▶ A 3mm nylon line is the preferred choice in the sea caves

Contacts and air supplies

Rivemar Diving, Carretera a La Azohía 151, 30868 La Azohía, Murcia
Tel: 968 15 00 63; www.rivemar.com

Emergencies

Emergency contacts: see Appendix A
Nearest hyperbaric centre: Cartagena (two)
Nearest hospital: Hospital Santa María del Rosell, Paseo de Alfonso XIII 61, 30203 Cartagena, Murcia; tel: 968 32 50 00
International telephone country code: +34

Websites

Project 2000: www.cuevadelagua.net

Coordinates

Dive site	Lat/Long
Cueva del Agua	37° 34' 34.96" N, 01° 13' 11.71" W
Cueva CT-12	37° 32' 17.10" N, 01° 07' 49.00" W
Cueva de la Ovaza (III)	37° 32' 13.43" N, 01° 07' 11.78" W
Cueva de la Virgen	37° 34' 05.60" N, 01° 06' 15.30" W

Ancient stalagmites in Cueva de la Virgen

Pozo Azul

Burgos, Spain

CAVERN
INTRO
FULL

Objective

The Pozo Azul resurgence is one of the world's finest cave diving sites with opportunities for divers of all levels of ability. The beautiful entrance area of the first sump may be tackled as a cavern dive, while serious technical divers may plan to pass the spectacular Sump 1 to surface after 700m, taking in a maximum depth of around 20m.

Access

No permission is required to dive in Pozo Azul but, given its remote location and to avoid a lengthy journey to no avail, aspiring visitors should contact local sources to ensure that the access conditions have not changed.

Location

Pozo Azul is situated in northern Spain just outside the small village of Covanera, which lies on the N-623 main road 80km south of Santander and 50km from Burgos. The resurgence is located 780m above sea level, high in the headwaters of the Ebro valley. To reach it, turn off the highway directly alongside the Bar Muñecas in Covanera and, having crossed a small stream, turn immediately left. Some 200m further park on the left side of the road. The final 250m approach is on foot and the path to the cave is signposted.

The setting for Pozo Azul

History

Pozo Azul was first dived in 1964 by Joaquín and Pedro Plana from Burgos, who made a 120m penetration; then in 1966 Joaquín extended the dive to 200m. It was some years before a further advance was achieved, when in 1978 Carlos Medina, José 'Pepe' Medina and Carlos Ruiz of the Asociación Deportivo Cultural STD reached 570m. The following year a very strong team comprising Pepe with Fernando de Fuentes,

Rick Stanton with a scooter, leaving the surface

Alejandro Granda, Carmen Portilla and Fernando Santamaría set their mark on the cave. Pepe and Fernando Santamaría reached thirds around 700m into the sump at a depth of only 3m, having been to a maximum depth of 20m. They turned back incredibly close to the sump's end and it was passed a short while later by Carmen and Fernando de Fuentes, making Pozo Azul the longest cave dive in Spain at that time.

The onslaught began on Sump 2 in the early 1980s and its length was slowly increased by various cave divers from Madrid-based clubs until Alfredo Ruiz and Francisco Seguro reached 780m and −39m in 1991. In 2001 British cave diver Jason Mallinson was introduced to the area and he, over the next few years, quietly extended the line distance; by 2007 he had reached a point 3,530m into the sump and attained a depth of 70m. Then in 2008 a team from the European Karst Plain Project progressed a further 490m to 4,020m.

British divers mounted a major expedition in 2009 and on the first push John Volanthen and Dutchman René Houben extended the line to 4,395m at 30m depth. Three days later Jason reached 5,020m, before a third penetration was made by Rick Stanton, who surfaced beyond Sump 2 at 5,160m from the dive base and, after a 70m section of dry cave, explored Sump 3 for 160m. Rick was underground for nineteen

The surface pool: a calm, sunlit place belies the extent of the underground tunnels, entered here by John Volanthen

Leaving the surface with
the aid of a scooter

POZO AZUL
Covanera, Burgos, Spain

Entrance
Sump 1 −24m
Based on compilation survey by Jason Mallinson
0   1km
Sump 2   EXTENDED ELEVATION
−50m
−70m   −70m

Tipperary
−30m   −8m
Sump 3
Sump 3 continues for 3,275m to the dry, 180m long Razor Passage and Sump 4

hours on this outstanding mission. With a total diving penetration of 6,020m, Pozo Azul was established as the longest cave diving penetration in Europe and Sump 2 itself is arguably the longest sump to be passed in the world.

In 2010, again with strong support from Spanish divers, the same team progressed the exploration to a point 2,965m into Sump 3, making the cave's total length 9,195m. With a total diving penetration of 8,825m, Pozo Azul was established as the longest cave diving penetration in the world.

The hard work continued in 2011 and Sump 3 was subsequently passed after a total of 3,275m

to a short 180m section of dry passage leading to the inevitable Sump 4, which was left undived. At the time of writing Pozo Azul stands at 9,685m long, with 9,135m of diving required to reach the end.

The Sump 2 dive base

Diving

The water flow from the resurgence varies in volume, but the temperature is constant at 12°C. The visibility is generally crystal clear, unless divers have recently been active beyond Sump 1.

The sump entry is easy, as a gravel-floored bank and a rocky slope lead gradually downwards into the hillside. At 10m depth a substantial pillar of rock creates a slight restriction, but a few metres later divers enter a spacious chamber over 3m wide and about 5m high. The dive line is attached to the right-hand wall, from which point a meandering route high in the tunnel leads on at depths of less than 13m. Unlike the majority of cave systems, the line has been installed at ceiling level in Pozo Azul to minimise gas consumption, as the floor is perhaps 10m deeper. The well-belayed line follows the right-hand wall consistently and, given its position, visibility remains excellent at all times.

At 700m from base the sump surfaces and a winding deep-water canal continues for approximately 200m. Eventually, the walls narrow and the stream emerges from a fast-flowing narrow fissure. To avoid loss, scooters and other diving equipment may be attached to ropes here. A short swim and a climb over a low cascade lead to a stretch of some 80m of impressive walking-sized boulder-strewn passage to a gravel beach at Sump 2.

Further considerations

▶ Fixed 3mm lines are present throughout Sump 1
▶ A sturdy rucksack will assist in carrying equipment, but a sack truck fitted with pneumatic tyres is invaluable for heavy loads
▶ During the summer, early morning starts are highly desirable to mitigate the effects of the intense heat
▶ A decompression incident at Pozo Azul would have severe consequences; plan your dive carefully and ensure a good supply of oxygen is available. Keep your insurance card, passport and European medical card handy in case an incident occurs

Long penetrations at Pozo Azul require high-tech equipment, as shown by Jason Mallinson (*top*) and René Houben

Passing the narrow section near the entrance in Sump 1

▶ The spacious Sump 1 and (*inset*) passing beneath the habitats in Sump 2

Contacts and air supplies

Divers must make their own provision for air fills in this area. Please respect local residents and do not endanger the goodwill of the people in the village: do not make noise in their vicinity and, if using a compressor is essential, do not operate it anywhere nearby.

Emergencies

Emergency contacts: see Appendix A
Nearest hyperbaric centre: Santander; see the note under
    Further Considerations
Nearest hospital: Hospital General Yagüe,
    Avenida del Cid 96, 09005 Burgos; tel: 947 28 18 00
International telephone country code: +34

Websites

Pozo Azul: www.pozoazul-cavediving.org

Sump 2, as one of the longest dives in the world, is a very serious undertaking – especially because the depth quickly exceeds 40m and then runs at over 60m depth (with a maximum of –70m) for perhaps 2km. Beyond 4km from the dive base the route shallows to less than 30m depth, then very gradually ascends until the end of the sump is reached at 5,160m. Any penetration into Sump 2 should be as a result of an extremely well-planned operation.

Coordinates

Dive site	Lat/Long
Pozo Azul	42° 44' 08.84" N, 03° 47' 45.78" W

The Caves of Fethiye and Ölüdeniz

Muğla, Turkey

CAVERN

All sites except Cathedral Cavern

Cathedral Cavern

Objective

The south-west coast of Turkey is a superb diving holiday destination in an area of outstanding natural beauty, where pine-clad mountains plummet into the turquoise Mediterranean Sea. It is home to some fine caverns that provide a suitable mixture of difficulty at all levels of experience with a maximum depth of 30m.

Access

No permission is required to dive at any site, but diving certification should be carried.

Location

The diving centres of Fethiye and Ölüdeniz are situated in Turkey's Muğla province, around 500km due south of Istanbul and not far from the Greek island of Rhodes. Fethiye is a fair-sized town with lots going on while Ölüdeniz, some half-hour distant, is much smaller, though it seems that its famous Blue Lagoon features on almost every advert for Turkey.

History

The cavern sites in the Fethiye and Ölüdeniz area were discovered during the early 1990s by a group of divers including Yilmaz Abi, Alf and Steve Chappell and Haldun Kayarlar. Haldun subsequently created detailed maps of the sites, which are still in use today for briefings by dive guides.

Diving

▶ Entering Mexican Hat and some of the rich marine life to be found: corals and fan worms on the cave walls

A briefing on board a dive boat

All the sites are reached by boat, with typical times in excess of half an hour. Aladin's Cavern and the adjoining Turkish Bath and Mexican Hat, together with Three Tunnels, are best approached from Fethiye, while Grouper Lair and Cathedral Cave are best accessed from Ölüdeniz. Even though they are physically closer to Ölüdeniz, the Secret Garden and Chambers Cavern are often reached from Fethiye.

The marine life is varied and plentiful, with some of the finest diving in the eastern Mediterranean. In spring, water temperatures are cool at 15°C, rising to 24°C in October. The visibility is well in excess of 20m in all seasons.

The best known cave in the Fethiye area is **Mexican Hat**, where two sites are separated by a 180m swim. The first is a cavern some 25m deep and a spacious 6m to 7m high which runs into the rock face for 10m. A narrow opening in the roof gives access to a further, smaller room normally festooned with shrimps.

The second cave unquestionably offers a fine and memorable dive that consists of following a very straightforward single tunnel for about 40m at less than 12m depth. Daylight reaches the back of the cave and, because the floor is composed of gravel and coarse sand, there is little risk of any significant deterioration in visibility. A weak halocline occurs about 30m in and a small air pocket may be found at the furthermost point. Ascending into this means you are venturing into a zone of total darkness and, in addition, divers should always be aware of the possibility of a tainted air content in such small enclosed pockets, though this one has enough room for several people to surface and chat prior to their outward swim.

Nearer to Fethiye, on the same stretch of coast, lies **Three Tunnels**, where some very short (less than 20m in length), shallow caverns may be dived at a depth of around 10m, together with some easy swim-throughs.

Approached by heading south from Ölüdeniz, around 1.5km north of the local landmark of Butterfly Valley lies **Grouper Lair**, a 20m long recess in a sheer wall that is entered at 24m depth. The interest value of this site is not so much its distance or depth of penetration, it is the sheer luxuriance of the marine life adorning the walls. In the twilight world of the daylight zone the colours are not immediately apparent, but a light will dramatically transform the scene: the cave is a veritable oasis of colour with purples, reds, yellows and oranges, not to mention the delicate white lace coral.

Further south along the coast is **Cathedral Cave**, which is deeper than anything else in the area and presents an interesting and very spacious 40m long swim-through at a depth of 36m; be warned that this is deeper than a normal cavern diving site. About one-third of the way through, a short side passage on the right is renowned for its chamber full of shrimps.

The finest cavern site accessible from Ölüdeniz is the **Secret Garden**, a half-hour boat ride to the west. Sheer limestone cliffs overhang the sea here and when you drop off the boat the water is a very deep cobalt blue with depths clearly in

Further considerations

▶ A 5mm wetsuit is adequate from June onwards, though earlier in the season a vest, hood and gloves will be appreciated

▶ The diving season closes at the end of October

The entrance to the Turkish Bath

◀ A narrow crack in Aladin's Cavern

excess of 30m. As you descend to 10m on the cliff face, the wall suddenly recedes into blackness, disappearing as a level roof. Then you stop to take stock and your eyes adjust to the lower light levels – it will become apparent that you are floating in an absolutely huge, cavernous void. Before you an immense tunnel over 20m wide is revealed that runs back beneath the land, with the floor just about visible at a depth of around 30m and where impressively large tube fan worms cling to the outer walls. These submarine worms are quite fascinating. When first sighted they present a beautiful 360° fan-like display waving gently in the current. However, if you go too close, like the flick of a conjuror's wand, the delicate structure retracts and instantly disappears. You are left looking at a very ordinary stubby little tube, its magical flourish now secreted somewhere inside.

Coordinates

A line through the Dardanelles and the Bosphorus straits in northern Turkey is commonly accepted as the border between Europe and Asia so, technically, Fethiye and Ölüdeniz lie in Asia, not Europe. However, as they are close to and commonly associated with Europe and are widely used by European divers, they have been included in this book.

Dive site	Lat/Long
Aladin's Cavern	36° 34′ 51.93″ N, 29° 01′ 30.99″ E
Cathedral Cave	36° 27′ 45.31″ N, 29° 06′ 51.63″ E
Chambers Cavern	36° 32′ 23.67″ N, 29° 02′ 20.15″ E
Grouper Lair	36° 30′ 49.05″ N, 29° 07′ 19.92″ E
Mexican Hat (cavern 1)	36° 34′ 45.10″ N, 29° 01′ 53.49″ E
Mexican Hat (cavern 2)	36° 34′ 43.66″ N, 29° 02′ 00.49″ E
Secret Garden	36° 32′ 22.57″ N, 29° 02′ 22.27″ E
Three Tunnels	36° 35′ 50.03″ N, 29° 01′ 40.97″ E
Turkish Bath	36° 34′ 53.62″ N, 29° 01′ 34.97″ E

Further in, the tunnel narrows and shallows slightly until at 30m from the entrance a distinctly murky halocline is encountered. An ascent through its brackish haze will gain crystal-clear fresh water and a substantial air surface with, to one side, a narrow ledge where it is possible to stand and chat beneath stark, creamy-grey walls. This is a wonderful recreational dive; the darkness of the huge cavern is alleviated by the reassuring blue glow of the open sea some 30m or so away: it is a spectacular site.

▶ Blue and gold: the sublime entrance to Aladin's Cavern, and well-deserved relaxation after a day's diving

Chambers Cavern is located at the back of a rocky gully at 24m depth, 75m or so west from the Secret Garden, though it is much less striking. The cave is significantly smaller and has the potential for silt disturbance, so a line must be laid or followed. Immediately inside the entrance is a choice of two tunnels, but neither apparently extends for more than 20m.

Aladin's Cavern is situated over 550m west of Mexican Hat and consists of a tall, vertical fissure dropping directly to the seabed at 30m. Seeing divers high overhead in the clear water, framed between the black walls, is a memorable experience for anyone. Several narrow cracks and short recessed areas at about −26m provide sanctuary for marine life – a profusion of lace corals and significantly large quantities of shrimps can be observed. Natural light is very good in this cavern, but a handheld light will bring the colours to life.

Contacts and air supplies

European Diving Centre, 2 Karagözler, Fevzi Çakmak Cad. No. 133, 48300 Fethiye
Tel: 252 614 9771; www.europeandivingcentre.com

LykiaWorld, Kıdrak Mevkii, 48300 Ölüdeniz-Fethiye
Tel: 252 617 0200; www.lykiaworld.com

Emergencies

Emergency contacts: see Appendix A
Nearest hyperbaric centre: Marmaris
Nearest hospital: Fethiye Devlet Hastanesi (Fethiye State Hospital), Akarca Mah. Çalış, 48300 Fethiye; tel: 252 613 3546; Tourism Health Department: 252 613 7242
International telephone country code: +90
(within Turkey add a zero before the telephone number when dialling direct between cities)

After enjoying perhaps five or ten minutes here, ascend to between 18m and 15m and begin a 120m swim along the coast in a north-easterly direction to the second part of the dive, the **Turkish Bath**. The entrance to this short cavern, with airspace above, is via a swim-through at between 5m and 6m where a safety stop is normally carried out. Two windows allow plenty of natural light into this area, which is otherwise totally enclosed.

Appendix A
Incidents and Emergencies

I N the UK the rescue services are alerted via a 999 or 112 call to the police or, in the case of coastal or offshore sites, to the coastguard. Once the police have been contacted following an incident at an inland site, the police should notify cave rescue services and that team will coordinate all operations, including diving underground. It is essential to communicate the precise location of the incident and that of the caller, full details of what has occurred and the number of people involved.

In Europe the primary emergency telephone number is 112. This number can be used to contact the emergency services in any country in the European Union from a fixed or mobile phone free of charge; a translator should be available for some languages. In Turkey, 112 was originally specifically for calling the ambulance service, though the use of 112 for all emergencies is being phased in and this is the number you should dial. This first point of contact will mobilise local rescue teams and, if necessary, arrange for helicopter extraction and hospitalisation. It is extremely important to have your insurance card, passport and European medical card available when dealing with these professional teams.

Rescues may involve falls, lacerations and trauma or basic human frailties such as a heart attack or stroke, including after diving has concluded. For cave diving activities, especially in Europe, of major concern is decompression illness (DCI). Sudden pain or impairment following a dive should always alert a diver or first responder to the possibility of DCI and, to minimise the extreme danger this may present, it is essential that professional advice is taken at the outset. Ideally, a doctor with diving experience should attend as a matter of urgency.

For convenience, contact details appear below for hospitals and hyperbaric centres that are local to dive areas. However, in the first instance contact a national centre for specific advice; these centres will have information concerning the status and availability of chambers, for example.

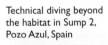
Technical diving beyond the habitat in Sump 2, Pozo Azul, Spain

The nearest hyperbaric chamber is not always the best suited to treat a particular type of DCI. Certain chambers may only be able to treat relatively minor and stable cases of decompression illness; more complex cases will require additional diving medical expertise, emergency medical assistance and additional equipment. Many hyperbaric chambers do not provide a 24 hour service and assembling a hyperbaric team will take time.

Remember that telephone numbers and physical locations may change – it is dangerous to rely on

Murky conditions in the Doux de Coly, France

A diving light penetrates the gloom at the entrance to the Émergence du Ressel, France

potentially outdated information in an emergency, so use a national number for the correct support information and prior to a dive always ensure that the printed details given here are still current.

Such factors should be part of every dive preparation.

Specialist advice

National Hyperbaric Information
Urgent specialist advice is available by contacting the Duty Diving Medical Officer as appropriate:

ENGLAND, WALES AND NORTHERN IRELAND
British Hyperbaric Association: 07831 151523 (24 hours)
www.hyperbaric.org.uk

Diving Diseases Research Centre: 01752 209999 (24 hours)
www.ddrc.org

SCOTLAND
Ask for the emergency hyperbaric doctor at Aberdeen Royal Infirmary:
0845 408 6008 (24 hours); www.hyperchamber.com

EUROPE, INCLUDING REPUBLIC OF IRELAND
Divers Alert Network, main Europe office: +39 085 8930333

DAN 24 hour emergency hotline: +39 06 4211 8685; www.daneurope.org

In Europe it is imperative that divers are thoroughly prepared for unforeseen eventualities. Adequate insurance is essential and joining an organisation such as the Divers Alert Network (DAN) provides the all-important cover. Given the changes that take place over time, DAN does not provide a direct contact number for recompression chambers. Instead, this leading organisation coordinates the process, not only involving the evacuation of an injured diver, but also assisting with the assessment and management of the injured diver prior to evacuation to a recompression chamber.

Clear water in Dinas Silica Mine, South Wales

Divers visiting European destinations are strongly advised to take out membership of DAN, which will provide a 24 hour hotline for injured divers and all relevant information on recompression facilities and emergency services. The organisation will also offer assistance, advice or medical direction, as required. All divers should carry specific insurance for the type of activity they plan to undertake.

DAN assistance can:

▶ Dispatch emergency services
▶ Notify the receiving medical facility of the injured diver's condition and time of arrival
▶ Assist health care professionals to arrange for recompression

DAN assistance

If the injured diver is not a DAN member, call the same emergency number – advice will still be supplied, however, DAN will be unable to initiate services and a cost element will be involved, such as transport to a hyperbaric centre, repatriation or medical expenses.

If the diver's condition is stable, transport should be arranged to the nearest 24 hour casualty centre. If the diver's condition is unstable, they should not be moved. Life support should be continued while awaiting the arrival of the emergency services.

Guidelines for Managing Injured Divers

Any emergency and or life-threatening problem should be managed in order of priority and urgency. This is exemplified in the ABC – Airway, Breathing, Circulation – of basic life support. Management decisions will vary according to factors such as transport times, methods, distances and the severity of an injured diver's condition.

▶ Follow the ABC of basic life support: Airway, Breathing, Circulation
▶ Keep an injured diver in a horizontal position. Provide assisted ventilation or cardiopulmonary resuscitation (CPR) if required
▶ Administer 100% oxygen, ensuring that the patient is breathing adequately. If not, provide mouth-to-mouth, mouth-to-pocket-mask or assisted ventilation
▶ Provide oral fluids only if the victim is fully conscious and able to drink unaided
▶ Keep the patient comfortably cool

Corals on the cave wall in Grotta Azzurra, Capo Palinuro, Italy

Hyperbaric centres: UK and Ireland

UK

International telephone
country code: +44
*Drop the preceding zero from
the local number*

*The hyperbaric centres in this
section of Appendix A are those
relevant to the cave and mine
diving sites described in this
guidebook. They provide services
for divers and have 24 hour
emergency cover.*

**From any
country:**

**Emergency
services: 112**

**DAN: +39 06
4211 8685**

Aberdeen, North-east Scotland

Hyperbaric Medicine Unit
Aberdeen Royal Infirmary, Foresterhill, Aberdeen AB25 2ZN
Tel (day): 01224 553264
Emergency tel: 0845 408 6008
www.hyperchamber.com

Fort William, North-west Scotland

The Underwater Centre
Marine Walk, Carmichael Way, Fort William PH33 6FF
Tel (day): 01397 703786
Emergency tel: 01631 563729 (Oban Coastguard)
www.theunderwatercentre.co.uk

Gosport, Southern England

Hyperbaric Medicine Unit
Royal Hospital Haslar, Haslar Road, Gosport PO12 2AA
Tel (day): 023 9276 2970
Emergency tel (mobile): 07831 151523
Hospital tel: 023 9258 4255

Plymouth, South-west England

Hyperbaric Medical Centre (DDRC Plymouth)
Research Way, Tamar Science Park, Derriford, Plymouth PL6 8BU
Tel (24 hour): 01752 209999
Hospital tel: 01752 777111
www.ddrc.org

Poole, Southern England

The Diver Clinic
7 Parkstone Road, Poole BH15 2NN
Tel (day): 01202 678278
Emergency tel (mobile): 07770 4 23637 or 07770 4 BENDS
www.thediverclinic.com

Rugby, Central England

Midlands Diving Chamber
Hospital of St Cross, Barby Road, Rugby, CV22 5PX
Tel (day): 01788 579555
Emergency tel (mobile): 07940 353816 (24 hour)
www.midlandsdivingchamber.co.uk

Wirral, North-west England

North West Emergency Recompression Unit
Murrayfield Hospital, Holmwood Drive, Thingwall CH61 1AU
Tel (day): 0151 648 8000
Emergency tel: 0151 648 8000
Hospital tel: 0151 648 7000

IRELAND

International telephone country
code (Northern Ireland): +44
*Drop the preceding zero from the local
number. When calling Northern Ireland
from the Republic of Ireland replace
the dialling code 028 with 048*

Portadown, Northern Ireland

Regional Recompression Chamber Unit for Northern Ireland
Craigavon Area Hospital, 68 Lurgan Road, Portadown BT63 5QQ
Tel (day): 028 3833 4444
Emergency tel: 028 3833 6711

FINLAND

Helsinki

Medioxygen
Museokatu 26, FI-00100 Helsinki
Tel: 09 454 0544 (24 hours)
www.medioxygen.fi

International telephone
country code: +358
*Drop the preceding zero from
the local number*

FRANCE

Avignon

Polyclinique Urbain V (private)
Service de Médecine Hyperbare, Chemin du Pont des Deux Eaux, 84000 Avignon
Tel: 04.90.81.33.00

International telephone
country code: +33
*Drop the preceding zero from
the local number*

Marseille

Clinique Cardio-Vasculaire de Valmante
100 traverse de la Gouffonne, 13009 Marseille
Tel: 04.91.17.18.65

Montpellier

Hôpital Lapeyronie
555 route des Ganges, 34295 Montpellier CEDEX 5
Tel: 04.67.33.82.69 or 04.67.33.82.70

Toulouse

Unité de Soins Hyperbare
Place du Dr Baylac, 31059 Toulouse
Tel (day): 05.61.77.22.95; (night): 05.61.77.22.84

GREECE

Athens

Naval Hospital of Athens
70 Dinokratous, 115 21 Athens
Tel: 21 07216166; DAN office in Athens: 21 03462898

International telephone
country code: +30

ITALY

La Maddalena (Sardinia)

Ospedale Civile Paolo Merlo
via Ammiraglio Magnaghi, 07024 La Maddalena OT
Tel: 0789 791200

International telephone
country code: +39
*Do not drop the preceding zero
from the local number*

Pisa

Ospedale Santa Chiara
via Roma 67, 56100 Pisa PI
Tel: 050 992111 or 050 993111

Salerno

AOU San Giovanni di Dio e Ruggi d'Aragona
via San Leonardo, 84131 Salerno SA
Tel: 089 672078 or 089 672663 or 089 672756
(AOU is Azienda Ospedaliera Universitaria or University Hospital)

Sorso (Sardinia)

AMI, Strada Litoranea,
Marina di Sorso, 07037 Sorso SS
Tel: 079 359008

MALTA

International telephone
country code: +356

Victoria (Gozo)

Gozo General Hospital
Victoria, Gozo
Tel: 2156 1600

Msida (Malta)

Mater Dei Hospital
Msida, MSD 2090, Malta
Tel: 2545 5205

SPAIN

International telephone
country code: +34

Alicante (Costa Blanca)

Medibarox
Hospital Perpetuo Socorro, Plaza del Dr Gómez Ulla 15, 03013 Alicante
Tel: 965 21 14 09; www.medibarox.com

Arrecife (Lanzarote)

Medicina Hiperbárica de Lanzarote
Hospital Insular de Lanzarote, Calle Juan de Quesada s/n, 35500 Arrecife, Las Palmas
Tel (mobile): 629 18 39 21; www.hiperbaricalanzarote.com

Cartagena (Murcia)

Servicio de Medicina Hiperbárica
Fundación Hospital de la Caridad, Calle Navarra s/n, 30210 Cartagena, Murcia
Tel: 968 51 03 00

La Laguna (Tenerife)

Unidad de Medicina Hiperbárica
Hospital Universitario de Canarias, Carretera Ofra s/n La Cuesta, 38320 La Laguna,
     Santa Cruz de Tenerife
Tel (hospital): 922 67 80 00; *tel (chamber):* 922 67 84 63

Mahón/Maó (Menorca)

Consell Insular de Menorca
Parque de Bomberos n° 1, Mahón, Islas Baleares
Tel: 971 35 10 11

Palamós (Costa Brava)

Unitat de Medicina Hiperbarica
Hospital de Palamós, Calle Hospital 36, 17230 Palamós, Girona
Tel: 972 60 01 60

Palma de Mallorca (Mallorca)

MEDISUB Hyperbaric Research Institute
Clínica Juaneda, Calle Company 30, 07014 Palma de Mallorca, Islas Baleares
Tel: 908 83 99 99
Emergency tel (mobile): 666 444 999; www.medisub.org

Santander (Pozo Azul)

Unidad de Terapia Hiperbárica Valdecilla
Hospital Universitario Marqués de Valdecilla, Avenida Valdecilla s/n, 39008 Santander,
     Cantabria
Tel: 942 20 25 20

**From any
country:**

**Emergency
services: 112**

**DAN: +39 06
4211 8685**

TURKEY

International telephone
country code: +90
*Within Turkey add a zero before the
telephone number when dialling direct
between cities*

Aksaz Navy Base
Marmaris
Tel: 252 421 0202 or 252 421 0161 (ext 2653)

Appendix B
Sites to Aspire to

THE majority of the caves and mines covered by this book are classic sites that divers with suitable training and experience may visit with relatively little preparation. However, many other sites have not been included because, apart from the physical or technical difficulties in most of these, access is more strictly controlled. For example, due to environmental or safety concerns, some caves or mines are gated and locked, with only qualified members of specific organisations permitted access. Other sites may require personal negotiations with the landowner and those admitted must hold appropriate insurance cover.

The three sites listed in Appendix B are suitable only for fully experienced cave divers. They are included here as they are well known and documented, being readily highlighted by any search of cave- and mine-diving sites; although not accessible to all divers, they are sites to aspire to.

It is obvious that thousands of cave diving sites can be found throughout the UK and Europe, and many of these offer some excellent diving, possess a fascinating history and are places to aspire to visit. Thorough research must be undertaken to establish the precise access protocol for these and within the UK the Cave Diving Group is a good first point of contact. The organisation has four subsections based on geographical regions and divers wishing to gain further experience are welcome to attend meetings, see how the group functions and perhaps consider membership.

Historically important caves in the UK are represented here by Keld Head and Wookey Hole, while Ojamo in Finland is an important and classic site to aspire to, with equally stringent requirements for access.

UK

Keld Head
a historically significant site

North Yorkshire
NGR: SD 6958 7658
Lat/Long: 54° 11′ 02.81″ N, 02° 28′ 03.67″ W
Permission is required

The major resurgence of Keld Head lies in the north-west bank of Kingsdale Beck, just over 3km north of the village of Ingleton in North Yorkshire. It is the longest submerged system in the British Isles with about 8km of tunnels.

Keld Head resurges in Kingsdale in the Yorkshire Dales; the surface pool is central in this picture, just below the road

The pioneer of British cave diving, Graham Balcombe, made history at Keld Head in 1945 when, using a rebreather, he undertook the first dive at the site. A serious penetration had to wait until 1970, when Mike Wooding began a project that eventually reached 338m from the entrance. Then, five years later, Oliver Statham and Geoff Yeadon started a progressive exploration that ultimately saw a connection with Kingsdale Master Cave, located up-valley, and in the process established a world record traverse of 1,829m at a maximum depth of 18m in 1979. Later still, Yeadon and Geoff Crossley made a further connection with King Pot on the other side of the valley and on a momentous dive in 1991 they realised a world record traverse of some 3,100m, descending to a maximum of 30m.

Exploration continues, but access is *not* freely open and it is imperative that interested divers contact a local member of the Cave Diving Group to ascertain the current situation: do *not* attempt a dive without permission.

Those who do undertake a dive will find it very challenging because of the cave's complexity and its variable flow and visibility. The water clears only after a long dry spell and the visibility is often as poor as 1m in temperatures that are normally around 6°C year-round. Side-mounted configurations are recommended but, again, this is a highly complex cave appropriate only for experienced, fully trained cave divers used to the vagaries of UK sumps.

Wookey Hole
a historically significant site

Contacts

**Cave Diving Group of
Great Britain**
www.cavedivinggroup
.org.uk

Somerset
NGR: ST 5319 4802
Lat/Long: 51° 13' 45.15" N, 02° 40' 18.04" W
Restricted access

Wookey Hole is a renowned showcave on the southern edge of the Mendip Hills in Somerset. Here, 2.5km from the town of Wells, the water from caves located high on the Mendip plateau such as Swildon's Hole, St Cuthbert's Swallet and Eastwater Cavern rises to form the River Axe.

Without question this is the most famous British cave diving site and arguably the most historic one in the world. Wookey – the cradle of UK cave diving – has witnessed the progression from brass-helmet standard equipment diving in 1935, through a variety of rebreather operations up until 1961, to momentous open-circuit and mixed gas diving in the years that followed. In 2005 pioneers Rick Stanton and John Volanthen, using compact, custom-built, side- and stomach-mounted rebreathers, took the furthermost limit to a depth of 90m some 300m beyond

The resurging river at Wookey Hole, and following the line in Chamber 15

the last airspace in Chamber 25. Their operation was accomplished by a large team effort and must be regarded as one of the most serious cave diving undertakings in the world.

This is a magnificent location for cave diving and, in the vicinity of the showcave, is suitable for introductory and fully certified cave divers, provided that they are equipped with a side-mounted configuration. Access is restricted to members of the Cave Diving Group; the group makes arrangements with the showcave prior to each visit. Experienced cave divers will feel more than privileged when they

Chamber 20 in Wookey Hole

view the spectacular dry gallery in Chamber 24, which involves passing four sumps totalling 400m of diving at a maximum depth of 21m. With its diverse terrain and rich history, Wookey Hole presents a pinnacle of diving achievement.

Finland

Ojamo Limestone Mine
a site to aspire to

Lat/Long: 60° 14′ 20.47″ N, 24° 2′ 11.10″ E
Restricted access

Ojamo Limestone Mine lies 1.75km south-west of the small town of Lohja in Finland, some 50km west of the capital, Helsinki. Though once worked at depth, today the mine is flooded and all that is visible is a 250m long by 60m wide stretch of placid water.

The mine has only limited opportunities for cavern diving, but for introductory and fully certified cave divers it is an exceptionally challenging and fascinating place. Dives may only be undertaken by prior arrangement with the Ojamo Mine Divers Organisation; however, even given the restrictions on access, the quality of diving attainable makes this somewhere to aspire to.

Minerals are in short supply in Finland and limestone has always been a valuable resource. Small-scale extraction began at Ojamo in the

1500s, although it was not until 1925 that production increased. The limestone deposits were limited, so the geology dictated that the mine was extended ever deeper to win the rock as cheaply as possible. Levels were driven at 28m depth, 40m, 58m, 88m and 138m until, by the end of the mine's life, the miners were chasing the reserves at a depth of 238m.

The work was hard under conditions of poor air quality. Much of the mine advanced beneath a local lake and at one point the mining was accidentally and critically directed upwards to such a height that the roof was only a few metres

below the lake bed. It was a miracle that the thin section of rock took the strain; a breach would have cost the lives of perhaps 200 men and ruined the mine. A huge concrete wall was promptly erected to redress the situation – and the work continued on downwards.

Cutting a hole in the ice at Ojamo, and preparing to dive in the flooded mine

Nowadays, many kilometres of tunnel stretch out from beneath the flooded mine entrance. In winter the water temperature ranges from

Mining remains at Ojamo

freezing at the surface to 4°C below 6m depth (the year-round norm). Finnish divers are hardy enthusiasts who have eagerly embraced all aspects of technical diving and have penetrated to –150m. Clearly, deep dives have to take place during the summer months when surface water temperatures might reach 20°C, an essential boon to help combat the rigours of the long periods of decompression.

Also, the hours of darkness are long in winter: January only holds nine hours of daylight, when the air temperature may be as low as –20°C and a small cabin at the edge of the lake serves as the divers' 'warmhouse'. During the winter the huge lake is frozen and entry can only be achieved by using a special set of ice-cutting tools.

All diving equipment – open circuit and rebreather alike – is prone to freezing in these temperatures and care is required prior to and immediately following entry to the water. Visibility improves significantly during the winter months, when the lake is covered in snow and ice and the algal bloom, which develops in sunlight, dies away. In summer, the warmer surface water becomes distinctly murky, with a visibility of perhaps only 1.5m, and it diffuses naturally for a limited distance into the mine.

Further considerations at Ojamo

▶ All diving equipment is prone to freezing
▶ Thermal considerations are crucial in dive planning and extra clothing layers will inevitably require greater weighting
▶ Good 5mm wetsuit gloves may be adequate, depending upon their quality; however, the locals all wear dry gloves
▶ Given the depths, using mixed gas or trimix and a small bottle of argon for suit inflation is extremely desirable; this may be available through the Ojamo Mine Divers Organisation

In clear conditions the mine is spectacular. The most frequented tunnel is that at 28m, a level which has a string of large chambers set at regular intervals which are known as the Pearls and are numbered from 1 to 13. The maximum possible penetration here is 750m.

Deeper dives require greater and even more thorough preparations. The next deepest level at 40m is closer to the water entry point than the 28m passage, but the descent is steep in a huge quarry-like expanse. At 40m depth the tunnel turns momentarily through a much smaller roofed section, then heads immediately out and over a vast chasm. In the misty, algal-bloom water the

Cold, clear water at Ojamo

structural features and the passage proportions are difficult, if not impossible, to make out. Yes, a line follows close to the right-hand wall, but beyond that lies an empty void in all directions. For the next 50m or so it is only the dive briefing – the memory bank of information – which can make sense of the mine. The roof soars somewhere, 20m or more, overhead and a floor of sorts lurks down below at a depth of 78m: buoyancy problems are not a permissible option in a setting such as this. The major concern is that of a torn drysuit, as the onset of hypothermia would be rapid.

Shortly, reassuring rocky walls, roof and floor appear as you progress into crystal-clear water and return to your comfort zone. How far any diver is able to penetrate this labyrinth depends upon many factors, but one thing is certain – it will leave a memorable impression.

As no global uniformity has been established for mine diving standards, the Finns have set up their own system to preserve an exemplary safety record. While scuba divers can be accommodated in the huge expanse of open water (when it's not frozen!), more rigorous standards are necessary beneath ice and deep within the mine tunnels. Divers are required to undertake some 25 dives in the shallowest tunnel at –28m before being allowed to progress into the 40m level.

Diving at Ojamo demands great respect and it is without question one of the most challenging and extreme underwater locations on earth. Many artefacts can still be found in the tunnels and one wonders what the Russian prisoners of war in the 1940s and other enforced Finnish convict labour in the years to follow would now think of the fact that, since its closure in 1965, the mine has become the premier recreational diving attraction in Finland. Complete records, photographs and surveys of the network still exist and, in the annals of mining history, Ojamo is of international importance, a fantastic dive to aspire to.

Contacts

Ojamo Mine Divers Organisation
www.minedivers.com

Emergencies

See Appendix A: Finland for emergency contact details, including the Medioxygen clinic in Helsinki, which is also the Divers Alert Network's primary treatment site in the country

At a depth of 40m in Ojamo

Glossary

Additional terms appear in the companion volume *Diving in Darkness*

Laying line in Chambers Cavern, Turkey

adit: A horizontal mine tunnel driven from the surface (see *level*)

aven: A vertical opening in a cave roof

bedding or bedding plane: A typically horizontal layer in rock, along which a low and wide passage may develop

choke (boulder choke): A localised collapse blocking a passage; a route through or past the choke may or may not exist

DAN: Divers Alert Network

DCI: Decompression Illness, which describes a collection of decompression symptoms in the body and encompasses DCS (Decompression Sickness)

dip: The angle of a rock layer with respect to the horizontal: up-dip and down-dip refer to the direction of travel along an inclined passage

duck: A water-filled passage with limited airspace

fault: A tear or displacement in the rock strata

fossil cave: A dry cave abandoned by its original watercourse

halocline: A layer of water with significantly impaired visibility at the boundary where fresh water and underlying salt water meet and mix

helictite: A small, irregular formation formed from calcite or aragonite crystals, sometimes referred to as an eccentric

joint: A vertical crack or fissure in rock

lava tube: A cave formed by the flow of molten lava, which crusts at the surface to leave a void below

level: A horizontal mine tunnel driven from a shaft or *adit*

percolation: The downward movement of silt displaced from a passage roof by a diver's exhaust bubbles, reducing visibility

phreatic: Any part of a cave which formed below the water table

restriction: A constricted section of passage which restricts easy diving progress

resurgence: The point where an underground stream or river leaves a cave and reaches the surface

rift: A vertical fissure in a cave (sometimes also applied to a mine)

showcave: A cave used as a tourist attraction

sink or sinkhole: The point where a surface stream or river disappears underground

speleothem: A cave formation such as a stalactite, stalagmite, straw or *helictite*

thermocline: A water layer where a distinct temperature change occurs, which may be encountered during a descent or ascent

Index

Cave and mine names are colour coded for the minimum level of training required:
CAVERN INTRO FULL
NB: Not all areas of each site may be suited to that level of training

Source de Landenouse

An old boiler house in the flooded Cambrian Slate Mine, North Wales